Knight with a Briefcase

Knight with a Briefcase

The Life of Knight of Bahá'u'lláh Ezzat Zahrai

by

Judith Kaye Logsdon-Dubois

George Ronald
Oxford

George Ronald, *Publisher*
Oxford
www.grbooks.com

*A catalogue record for this book is available
from the British Library*

ISBN 978-0-85398-565-5

Cover design: Steiner Graphics

Contents

Illustrations

In memory of my parents

Erma and Kline Logsdon

Acknowledgements

Over 20 years have passed since I first began working on this book, collecting the information, interviewing Mr Zahrai and his friends and family, researching the background and putting all the bits and pieces into a coherent narrative. Over the years I was helped by many people and my greatest fear now is that I will forget someone who was kind when I asked for their aid. I can only hope they will be as generous with their forgiveness as they were with their assistance when I needed it.

Of course, Annette and Ezzat Zahrai helped me most by opening their hearts and their lovely home to my curiosity. Ezzat put at my disposal his time, his memories, his journals, his notes and countless documents. Few biographers worked in more pleasant surroundings than I did, sitting on the terrace of La Blanche, sipping Earl Grey tea.

When I was actually writing the first version of the book, I was greatly helped by my daughter Joëlle. Still in her teens, she took over almost all the household tasks, cooking and cleaning and keeping the peace with her younger sisters so that I could concentrate on the task at hand. I doubt that I told her how much I appreciated it at the time, but I've never forgotten the way she seemed to grow up before my eyes.

Kae Parker, Cynthia Hewitt and Hannah Robins are dear friends who read the manuscript and gave me their opinions, helping me to improve the text. Their feedback was invaluable. A very special thanks to Kae, who read several versions over the years and never seemed to tire of it. Her friendship has been one of the great blessings of my life.

And lastly I wish to thank Wendi Momen who has been a kind, competent, understanding and very patient editor.

Introduction

My alma mater, a small, private liberal arts college, frequently awarded honorary degrees to businessmen whose sole exploit in life seemed to have been the writing of a generous last Will and Testament. I remember one of my teachers asking why I had not attended a talk given by the most recent honouree and I replied, with what I now realize was considerable arrogance, that since a businessman's only goal in life was to make as much money as possible, he could have nothing to say that would interest me. Yet many years later I found myself sitting on a terrace in southwest France, listening to the former division president of a multinational company speak of spirituality, of visions, of ideals, of mystic experiences, of hardships, prison and persecution, of truth, of destiny, of God. His professional success had not prevented him from being faithful to his spiritual ideals in circumstances far more difficult than any I had known.

The glowing western sky cast the shadow of an enormous cedar across the terrace of the old French manor. The long-steeped heat of a summer day gave way to the cool night air. The man sitting on the terrace spoke quietly, sometimes in French and sometimes in English, with a slight accent in both languages. He had the smile, the grey hair and the gentle blue eyes of a mystic but in his daily life he wore a suit and tie, drove an air-conditioned Honda and carried a briefcase.

He and his family spent their holidays in the old manor near a little village perched among the hills of southern France; the rest of the year they lived in a comfortable home in Paris. He had an attractive wife and three children who had worked hard at school, passed their exams and found respectable jobs. As a retired businessman, he seemed to represent the kind of material success that I had been so disdainful of.

Listening to his story, I gradually realized that he did not consider his 'worldly success' as a deserved reward but rather, with a certain wry humour, as something unexpected and rather amusing. Here was a man who cared very little about the status of wealth, who had no taste for luxury, who would have unhesitatingly sacrificed his life for the Faith he believed in. He had set out in life dedicated to a mission, a knight whose every decision was dictated by service and obedience to an ideal.

His Faith had its martyrs, some of them people he had known, relatives he had played with as a child, but the brave, gallant gesture in the face of death had not been allotted him. To him had fallen a role that may be far more difficult in our modern society, that of the businessman with a conscience. He was neither wistful nor ungrateful; status and money were tools that he used to serve his Cause efficiently. Wearing his suit and tie, reading financial reports and dictating letters to secretaries, he had gone forth into a strange new world, the western world of high finance and modern management,

dedicated to fighting ignorance, indifference and prejudice, a knight with a briefcase. I asked him to tell me
about the beginning, how he had first come to take up
his mission.

Judith Logsdon-Dubois
'Tremisat'
47130 Port Sainte Marie
France

Part I

Persia

1

Childhood

*If . . . the child be trained to be both learned and good, the
result is light upon light.*[1]

'Abdu'l-Bahá

My parents named me Ezzatu'llah and called me Ezzat.
They were Persian Bahá'ís, a religious community used
as scapegoats under the Shah, and even more ferociously
persecuted today as heretics.

Persia is a land of contrasts and paradoxes. Its arid
deserts and lush, tropical beaches, its high mountains
and harsh wastelands are the home of a culture that is
very old. Situated at the crossroads between Europe and
Asia, India and Africa, it has preserved its most ancient
traditions while watching Cyrus, Alexander the Great,
Trajan, Abu Bakr, Genghis Khan and Tamerlane sweep
across its plains like ocean waves beating against an age-
less rock. Since biblical times the Persians have been
known as artists and warriors, law-givers and scholars,
poets and merchants. Throughout the ages they have
produced both philosophers and fierce fanatics, gifted
artists and blood-thirsty tyrants, the gentle Sufis and the
Assassin order, craftsmen skilled in the creation of intricate designs and diplomats skilled in intrigue.

In 1926, when I was born, Iran was considered a

backward and primitive land by the upstart Europeans. Its Pahlavi sovereign, Reza Sháh, was determined to drag his country into the 20th century. A former Cossack army private who had fought his way through the ranks to become the Shah of Shahs, he intended to abolish superstition and fanaticism by edicts. His picture adorned all the schools and public buildings. Statues of him stood in the parks and public squares of his land. He was a big, stern man, more feared than loved, who stopped at nothing in his efforts to westernize his country.

The country he renamed Iran could fit into the southwest corner of the United States, covering the states of California, New Mexico, Arizona and Texas. The heart of the land is a high plateau which contains two sterile deserts – Dasht-i-Kavir and Dasht-i-Lut – and salt marshes, the remains of prehistoric lakes, where even snakes and lizards cannot live. These are said to form the largest wasteland in the world. Mountains encircle the plateau, protecting the fertile coast lands in the north and the south from the harsh desert winds. Because of the geographic diversity, my people say, 'Persia has seven climates'.

It is also a country of many different languages, ethnic stocks and religions. In 1926 almost a quarter of the population still lived as nomads, following their herds of sheep, goats and camels from one grazing land to another. Most Iranians, descendants of the original Indo-Europeans, speak Farsi, which has its roots in ancient Persian. The people of Persia were Zoroastrians until their land was conquered by Arab tribesmen from the desert in the 7th century who adopted their refined culture and carried it to all the lands of the Muslim conquests, eventually influencing the European Renaissance, much as the Romans spread Greek culture throughout the Mediterranean lands. There are still a few Zoroastrians but most modern Iranians are Shi'i Muslims and a small minority belong to the Sunni branch of Islam.

Jewish colonies in Iran date from biblical times and small communities of Armenians and Assyrians have maintained their religious and cultural identities. The western mountains are populated by the nomadic Kurds and semi-nomadic tribes that speak Persian dialects. Almost one fourth of the population speaks Turkic dialects. There are small clusters of Arabs living along the Persian Gulf.

The largest minority group in Iran, numbering over 300,000, is the Bahá'í community. Its members are drawn from all the different ethnic and religious groups, reflecting the diversity of Iranian society. The Bahá'í Faith, with its roots in Shi'ism, much as Christianity has its roots in Judaism, is considered by fundamentalist Muslims as a heretical sect. Teaching religious tolerance, favouring the education of both boys and girls, and recognizing the essential oneness of the human race, Bahá'ís easily accepted the westernization the Shah was trying to introduce. Yet, whenever the tensions between the government and the reactionary Muslim mullahs grew too severe, Reza Sháh found it convenient to blame the Bahá'ís for the evils of modernization and hand them over to fanatic mobs, using the same tactics Hitler used with the Jews.

The 1906 constitution granted minority rights to the Jewish, Christian and Zoroastrian communities, but the country's largest minority had no such rights because its existence went unrecognized. The same situation continues today. During periods of persecution Bahá'í women were gaoled as prostitutes because their marriages could not be registered. At other times, when there was no political need to appease the mullahs, the Bahá'ís were allowed to live invisibly on the edge of Persian society. During such lulls, their belief in the importance of education, their law-abiding principles and their work ethic often brought them prosperity, subsequently making them convenient targets for the jealousy of their enemies.

In 1926 Iranian cities had separate quarters for Muslims, Armenian Christians, Jews and Zoroastrians, but the Bahá'ís were scattered throughout the different sections of towns. At best their Muslim neighbours tolerated or ignored them. At worst they were the easy victims of mob violence. As a result, the Bahá'í community was closely knit, looking to each other for support and fellowship. As much as possible they tried to be self-sufficient. One of the most obvious differences between the Bahá'ís and their neighbours, and in the eyes of the mullahs one of the most unforgivable, was their treatment of women. From the very beginning of their existence, Bahá'ís denounced polygamy and proclaimed women's equality as one of the basic tenets of their faith.

My parents were from Qazvin, a city of north central Iran, in a fertile plain on the southern side of the Elburz mountains. The roads from Baghdad, Turkey and the

Caspian Sea come together at Qazvin, a major crossroads situated only 125 miles from Tehran. During the 16th century it was the capital of Persia and several mosques and palaces testify to its former glory. Qazvin was also famous for its grapes and dried fruit. Seen from afar, it was a beautiful city, with turquoise domes and graceful minarets. Its streets were lined with graceful old trees. When doors opened you could glimpse courtyards and gardens and terraced homes. There were cool bazaars under arcades, public gardens and trees planted everywhere. We Persians love trees, the symbols of man's victory over the desert. We say, 'When man dies, the tree dies.'

My mother, Razieh, was the daughter of a goldsmith of the Samadani family. Their clan originally came from Lahijan, a tea-growing area with an almost tropical climate on the Caspian Sea. Violent persecutions against the Bahá'ís had forced them to flee but they were able to sell their properties and buy land around Qazvin where the Bahá'í community was stronger. Although in Iran at that time it was quite rare for Muslim women, even among the wealthiest families, Razieh had learned to read and write at home. Anticipating the women's rights movements by over a century, the Bahá'ís taught that if a family could not afford to educate both son and daughter, the daughter should be given the priority because of the importance of the mother's role as educator. One of the 18 original followers of the Báb had been Ṭáhirih, a well-known woman poet and scholar. She had caused a scandal by taking off her veil in public and became one of the early martyrs of the Cause, along with other brave Bahá'í women who fought and died for their beliefs.

Yet we Bahá'ís did not deliberately seek to provoke or shock the society we lived in. In Muslim countries where it was the custom, Bahá'í women wore veils in public, and men and women met separately to avoid scandalizing their neighbours. As a result, there were few opportunities for boys and girls to meet, to get to know each other and choose their lifetime partner. So our Bahá'í families, like their Muslim neighbours, often had to count on female relatives to arrange marriages. My mother may have seen my father, a handsome widower with a teen-age daughter from his first marriage, for the first time on their wedding day. Her brother also married into the Zahrai family, thus uniting the two clans. Yet, although I believe it was an arranged marriage, my mother seems to have fallen in love with her husband and remembered her wedding as a lovely day. She described it to me as 'right out of a fairy tale'.

Our family was respected in the Bahá'í community but we were not numerous nor particularly prosperous. We had lost our family lands; no one remembers exactly how. My paternal grandfather had been a musician and an army officer, the director of the military orchestra. I saw a picture of his home with three armed sentinels standing guard. My father, Massih (Masíhu'lláh) Zahrai, attended the *mektab*, the Quranic school, the only public form of education then available, and on graduating entered the new postal service that Reza Sháh was creating in Iran. His first post was in Sirdan, where I was born.

I remember the village as a cluster of small buildings made of adobe bricks. The roofs were flat terraces where whole families slept during the hot dry season. There was a small market, a police station, a dispensary and a mosque, but the village had no school. Because only the larger towns and cities had schools, Iranian villagers were often illiterate. When I was seven years old my parents gave me a grey wool uniform with short pants and sent me to classes in nearby Qazvin. During the school session my two older brothers and I lived with our paternal grandmother. She was kind but quite strict with us, and like mother-in-laws everywhere, she found fault with her daughter-in-law. When one of us boys displeased her she would sigh with exasperation, 'What can one expect? The seeds are good but such ground is fit only for growing weeds.'

In Qazvin I often visited my mother's relatives. The Samadani's large, rambling house built around a courtyard lodged several generations of the clan and there were plenty of cousins to chase in the big garden. Whenever space was lacking to house the constantly growing Samadani clan, a few more rooms were added on. My grandfather, a goldsmith, lived in large rooms with stained-glass windows and a terrace that overlooked the courtyard garden, shaded by tall trees under which I played with my cousins during the hot summer days. Fruit trees and flowers grew beside the walks. Persians love flowers and our poets have always described paradise as a garden.

One of my maternal uncles was a doctor and another

was a pharmacist. They had studied modern medicine as well as traditional herbal medicine. Out of respect for his western learning, my uncle the pharmacist was called 'Monsieur'. The doctor's patients would often puzzle over his prescriptions for foreign medicines written in Persian script, but the pharmacist understood his brother's transcriptions. They both had shops in Sepah Avenue, the main street of Qazvin. The doctor's office was almost opposite the 'Álí Qápú, a striking example of Safavid architecture dating from the 16th century. Like any other shopkeeper, every morning the doctor would unlock his shop, put out his sign and wait for customers. In the evening he would put the sign inside and lock up the shop.

I remember my uncle coming to see me when I was sick as a child. He did his rounds on foot, for in those days there were no cars and only a few *droshkies*, horse-drawn carriages, for hire on special occasions. Uncle Doctor always began by chatting for a little while with my grandmother, as if it were merely a social visit. Then he would smile at me and say, '*Khúb*, all right, let's say a prayer.' He had a deep, melodious voice and was often asked to chant the prayers at the 19 Day Feasts, the Bahá'í community gatherings. After the prayer for healing, he would examine me, give a treatment and write out a prescription. The visit might last over half an hour; I usually felt better as soon as I saw the doctor's kindly face.

Although the Samadani clan counted merchants and craftsmen as well as a doctor and a pharmacist among their number, a good part of its revenues came from the vineyards which the family owned outside of the city. I eagerly looked forward to the grape harvests; all the clan members would ride donkeys out to the vineyards early in the morning while it was still cool and pick grapes until the heat grew too intense.

The harvesters carried picnics and lowered pails containing grapes and watermelons into the deep wells to cool. When they stopped for the midday meal the fruit hauled out of the well was cold and delicious. While the adults lay in the shade and talked, my cousins and I ran through the rows of vines shouting and playing, while a few couples sat in secluded corners and had long serious conversations about nothing they could ever remember afterwards. Parents smiled and pretended not to see, but kept a watchful eye on them. Late in the evening we would all return home, the donkeys laden with grapes. The clan would share some of the grapes, which the women used to make syrup for sweetening yoghurt and jam. The rest of the harvest was sold on the market to be dried as raisins. Only the Armenians and the Jews made wine from grapes.

Although I was a good student, especially in composition and mathematics, I did not enjoy school. The teachers enforced their strict discipline with corporal punishment. When the boys did not know their lessons they were whipped with willow switches. For more serious infringements, we could be given a bastinado, like common criminals. The culprits were forced to lie down on the floor and their ankles were tied to a wooden plank. Then they were whipped on the soles of their feet with thin switches that cut into the flesh. After a severe bastinado some pupils were unable to walk for a while.

Once I had my palms switched for having made a joking remark which offended a Muslim student. The other boy lied to the teacher, saying I had used an obscene expression. That was years and years ago but I still remember the injustice. We Bahá'í children learned early to avoid taking liberties with non-Bahá'í students, which reinforced our isolation.

All students, whatever their religion, had to attend a Quranic class. I had a Quranic teacher who seemed to tolerate the fact that I was a Bahá'í. One day the teacher jokingly twisted my ear and said, 'I told you not to become a Bahá'í, but you didn't listen to me.' Unfortunately, other Muslims were far less open-minded.

On Fridays, the Muslim day of rest, my brothers and I went to the Bahá'í Centre, a simple building that served as a meeting place for the Bahá'í community. There volunteer teachers taught us the fundamental principles of the Bahá'í Faith in co-educational 'character classes'. Even when Bahá'ís were being severely and violently persecuted in Iran, they found ways to organize these classes for their children so that they would not be deprived of spiritual training. In villages where there were no schools these children's classes were not limited to religious training. Since the founders of the Bahá'í Faith had said that both boys and girls should be given an education, the Bahá'í community asked for volunteers to teach reading, writing and arithmetic. Classes were held either in a home or in the Bahá'í Centre, if the community had one.

We learned that the first Bahá'í school had opened in Russian Turkmenistan in 1897, and within a single generation illiteracy had been wiped out in the local Bahá'í population. In Iran, the Bahá'í schools, such as the well-known Tarbíyat schools in Tehran, stressed the importance of educating girls. They were open to all creeds and were recognized, and even highly rated, by the government. During the first quarter of the 20th century almost half of their students were from the families of liberal Muslims, Jews and Zoroastrians. Throughout the time I lived in Iran it was not uncommon to hear non-Bahá'í Iranians boast that they had been educated at Tarbíyat.

For my brothers and me, our 'character class' was the big event of the week. We learned about the Báb, the forerunner who in 1844 had announced the coming of a new divine Messenger and who died as a martyr in 1850, executed by the mullahs. We studied the writings of Bahá'u'lláh, the founder of the Bahá'í Faith who had been exiled by the Shah, then imprisoned by the Sultan of the Ottoman Empire. We especially liked the lessons about 'Abdu'l-Bahá, the son of Bahá'u'lláh, who had carried the Bahá'í message from a prison in Palestine to the major cities of the western world. You have heard of Kahlil Gibran? He met 'Abdu'l-Bahá and drew His portrait. Many believe 'Abdu'l-Bahá inspired him to write The Prophet. Woodrow Wilson's daughter was also familiar with His teachings concerning a world in which disputes between nations could be solved by arbitration, and many find several familiar ideas in Wilson's Fourteen Points. In our 'character class' we also learned about

'Abdu'l-Bahá's grandson, Shoghi Effendi, the Guardian of the Faith, who lived in Haifa, Palestine. Pilgrims returning from the Holy Land often stopped in Qazvin to tell about meeting him and to share his messages of encouragement and compassion.

In our 'character classes' the Bahá'í children, both boys and girls, also talked about being polite, honest and industrious. 'Abdu'l-Bahá had said, 'A child that is cleanly, agreeable, of good character, well-behaved – even though he be ignorant – is preferable to a child that is rude, unwashed, ill-natured, and yet becoming deeply versed in all the sciences and arts.'[2]

'Abdu'l-Bahá also said, '. . . cleanliness will conduce to spirituality . . . although bodily cleanliness is a physical thing, it hath, nevertheless, a powerful influence on the life of the spirit.'[3]

So we washed, cleaned our nails, brushed our teeth and combed our hair before we left for the class.

I looked forward to the classes, to meeting my friends, singing and playing games and learning about the heroes of Bahá'í history. One of the stories was about a little boy like me. One Friday on his way to a character class, the boy had been stopped by a stranger who wanted to know where he was going all dressed up when the schools were closed. The boy took the stranger to his teacher. The man learned about the Faith and eventually became a Bahá'í. Every Friday when I dressed and combed my hair, secretly I hoped that along the way I'd be stopped by a stranger and questioned. I too wanted to bring people to the Cause.

In 1934, when I was eight years old, the Iranian ministry of education gave in to complaints from the Muslim clergy and shut down the Bahá'í schools, on the grounds that they were illegally closed on Bahá'í religious holy days. To provide modern schools for the non-Bahá'ís who had formerly attended the Bahá'í schools, the government was forced to invest in education, opening new government schools in the largest cities. I was later able to attend the new secondary school which opened in Qazvin.

During the school holidays my brothers and I returned to the little village of Sirdan, free to spend our time as we liked. I used to call my father Áqá Ján, and I loved to follow him around the village. His pockets were always full of nuts, raisins and other treats for little boys. The mail in such a small village was soon sorted and distributed, so my father had a lot of leisure time which he spent conversing with the chief of police, the tax officer and the local doctor.

Dr Irani was a tall man with a gruff sense of humour. Once someone asked him where he had studied and he replied, 'At the University of Nothing-at-all.' The adults nodded and did not pursue the matter, but I spoke up and asked where Nothing-at-all was. My father liked to tease his friend about that.

Like many people in the middle and upper classes of Iran, some of my father's friends smoked opium. In those days there were no restrictions on selling the drug and it was Mashmehdi, the mailman who worked for the post office, who supplied the village with opium. Sometimes my brothers and I heard people knocking on the post office door early in the morning, calling out in the local Turkish dialect, 'Mashmehdi, *tiryák*, opium!'

The drug came in boxes and looked like dark, yellowish candlesticks. The opium smokers would sit around a brazier with their long pipes. They put a lump of opium in the bowl of the pipe and held it over the charcoal fire until it began to melt and steam. Then they would inhale the smoke and pass the pipe on to their neighbour. Bahá'u'lláh forbade the use of opium, so Bahá'ís did not smoke it. They did, however, sit with opium smokers as they talked together.

When the older men sat and talked, I remember being fascinated by the different ways they occupied their hands. My father smoked cigarettes, another man kept a ball of beeswax in his pocket that he took out frequently to knead. He said it made his fingers strong. Another carried a small string of beads that he flipped back and forth incessantly as they talked. The clicking of his beads punctuated the long, lazy stories the men told to pass the time.

Scorpions lived on the edge of the dry lands bordering the southern desert. One day I was sitting, listening to my father's friends chat when I saw a scorpion crawling towards me. I cried out and grabbed my father's arm but the older men burst out laughing. One of them picked up the scorpion, which was not a scorpion at all, but a cockroach. As a joke they had made a scorpion shell out of beeswax and put it on the cockroach.

An important participant in the games my brothers

and I played was Fandog, our little brown poodle. We pampered him and let him sleep in the house, to the horror of our neighbours who considered dogs unclean. The Muslims kept dogs to guard their herds and their houses but they rarely petted them or allowed them indoors.

One morning when I was seven, Fandog disappeared. My brothers and I looked for our dog all day but no one had seen him. Later in the evening our father told us that Fandog had gone into the hills and been killed by wolves. I cried and cried. It felt like I had lost my best friend. Finally Áqá Ján went out and brought me another puppy. I loved him but I still missed Fandog.

That year the rains began early and the country around Sirdan was flooded. The river turned brown and menacing, and when my brothers and I went down to the river, we saw houses, furniture, dead animals, huge trees and boards being carried away by the current. Some of the adobe houses in the village melted under the heavy rain and turned into piles of mud. As soon as the rain stopped the villagers began building new homes on top of the ruins of the old ones.

Eventually my father was transferred to Rasht, close to the Caspian Sea. While the climate in Sirdan had been hot and dry, the lands around Rasht were green with luxuriant vegetation, almost tropical. Mother delighted in serving us fresh fish and rice, considered luxuries in other parts of Iran. It was while they were living there that Reza Sháh published a decree saying that Iranian women should no longer wear the chador, the long black veil that covered a woman from head to foot. Although the chador had originally been imposed by Muslims, Bahá'í women were so accustomed to wearing it that when Reza S̲h̲áh's decree came out, my mother was intimidated by the idea of appearing in public in European clothes. It made her feel undressed. Although her religion did not require her to wear a veil in public, the society in which she lived did.

Since my father was a civil servant, his wife was expected to set an example for others. A date was set, some six months away, and the women were told that they would be required to appear unveiled at an official reception on that day. Reza S̲h̲áh ordered thousands of women's hats from Europe and had them distributed to the wives of civil servants as substitutes for the chador.

Even with her imported finery, my mother was terrified. Áqá Ján was understanding and came up with a solution. Long before the reception he began taking her for walks late at night when the streets were dark and no one could see her. Each evening they would start out a little earlier and gradually my mother got used to going out wearing European clothes. When the day of the reception came she scarcely blushed.

My father was transferred once again, this time to Qazvin, and we boys were delighted to be living near our cousins again. We moved into the Zahrai family home with our paternal grandmother, Ábájí. Highly respected by the community, she was a proud woman who insisted on her independence, preferring to prepare her own meals and eat by herself. She had a hookah and would sometimes sit on her terrace smoking it, looking quite aristocratic. I thought that she enjoyed smoking the hookah partly for the impression it made on others.

In Qazvin we boys enjoyed pretending to have a post office in the family garden. My two older brothers, Aziz and Ehsan, were the postmasters and I, of course, was the postman who took their orders, carrying the mail from one office to another in a handmade wagon that I pulled with a string. We spent hours drawing stamps for our letters, using our mother's needles to make holes for the serrated edges. When our cousin Shahab joined us, I was given a promotion and assigned my own post office in another corner of the garden. Shahab replaced me as the postman.

Shahab was the only son of our father's sister, a widow who lived nearby, raising her four children by working as a seamstress. Since his mother shared a small house with a non-Bahá'í family, Shahab did not have free use of the garden and spent most of his playtime with us.

Although my mother hoped that I would become a musician like my paternal grandfather, I showed early signs of commercial aptitude by deciding to open my own grocery shop. I begged some tea, sugar, dried raisins and nuts from my mother and set them out in small quantities to sell to the other children.

One day mother came home with a big surprise for us. With her savings she had bought a violin so we could learn to play. She told us that 'Abdu'l-Bahá had said, 'music, sung or played, is spiritual food for soul and heart'.[4] But I think it was her own love of music that had prompted her. We boys dutifully took lessons and I learned well enough to teach other children to play, but none of my brothers took up a musical career. My own early dream was to be a sailor and travel around the world visiting all the strange lands whose names I saw on the bright-coloured stamps in my father's post office.

It was in Qazvin that we saw our first moving pictures. A Zoroastrian businessman had bought a projector and he showed movies in the town's only hotel, the Grand. My brothers and I laughed at the antics of Charlie Chaplin and were thrilled by the wonderful, hair-raising adventures of Richard Talmudge. Like the rest of the audience, we took dried watermelon seeds to the movies to crack, suck and spit while we watched. Since most of the movies were silent, you could hear watermelon seeds being cracked all over the hall.

In Sirdan my mother had had a cook and a washing woman but in Qazvin she did all the housework herself. She sometimes had more than she could handle. When she wanted some peace and quiet she could not call a friend and ask her to watch her youngest, because there were no telephones. So she would ask me to go to my aunt's and fetch a box she needed.

'Which box do you want?' I would ask.

'The box called "*Bigír Binishán*".'

Glad to be of service, I would run to my aunt's house and deliver the message, never wondering why a box was called 'take-him-and-keep-him'. My aunt would smile and say, 'I'm busy now. Play a while with your cousins. I'll look for that box when I have time.'

A couple of hours later, my aunt would give me a mysteriously wrapped box to take home to my mother. I would run all the way home, proud of having completed my mission. A few days later I was not surprised to see my little cousin show up saying that her mother needed the box back. What was amazing was that it always took the mothers two or three hours to find the box.

We boys helped our mother with the chores. Several times a day we drew water for drinking and washing from the *abanbar*, a reservoir in a brick vault under the street in front of our house. To reach the reservoir we went down a long narrow stairway which was always dark and cool. In winter we had to be careful not to slip on the icy steps. The reservoir was filled once a year. The whole family stayed up that night, eating cakes and sweets and waiting for the man we called the *Míráb*, the Emir of the Water. When the channels were opened and the water came rushing in, we watched to be sure there were no leaks or loss, that the water went through the right openings and filled our reservoir. For days afterwards, until the sediment settled, the water was too muddy to use.

Another task was to air and clean the Persian carpets that covered all our floors. We boys would take them outside and beat all the dust out of them. In those days Persians had no social security system or savings accounts, and insurance policies were unknown, but they had their carpets. When they were prosperous they invested their extra money in beautiful handwoven carpets. When hardship struck they sold a carpet. I often heard people say, 'Poor so-and so. He's been very ill;

they've had to sell a carpet to pay for the medicine.'

The best carpets were laid out in the largest room in the house, which was reserved for receiving guests. To keep the carpets clean, everyone took off their shoes before walking on them. There were chairs lined up against the walls but most of our guests preferred to sit on the thickly carpeted floor. On one wall was a framed verse from the Qur'án in Persian calligraphy that had been given to my father by his *maktab* teacher. Although they are not Muslims, the Bahá'ís respect Islam and consider both the Bible and the Qur'án as sacred texts. My father kept in a special cabinet a few books of great value and the family treasure of which he was very proud: a book containing Tablets of Bahá'u'lláh which had been handwritten in beautiful calligraphy on silk paper.

Winters can be very cold on the high plateau of Iran and at that time central heating was unknown. A few wealthy families had portable oil burners, but most people used wood stoves or a *kursí*, a low table set in the middle of the room over a brazier of glowing coals and charcoal. In our household the *kursí* was not set up in the reception room but in a smaller room where we gathered together and had our meals. The table was covered with a large, heavy quilt. The whole family would sit on mattresses around the table and stretch their legs under the table. The quilt covered our laps and kept in the warmth coming from the brazier. During the cold weather our family ate and slept around our *kursí*.

But my childhood was not always pleasant. At times the Muslims' prejudice and discrimination against the

Bahá'ís became violent. I can remember people outside our house shouting and cursing and throwing stones that broke the windows. I remember adults speaking in hushed voices of terrible things that had happened. When the Bahá'ís gathered in one of their homes, as they did every 19 days, they were careful to arrive alone or in pairs so as not to attract the attention of the neighbours. When the 19 Day Feast was over, an elderly person in the host family would sit outside to watch the street. When the way was clear he would signal for a small group to leave the house. The sentinel would wait until they were out of sight before he signalled that another group could come out. It would be a long time before the last guests left. At a very young age I realized that most of the people I knew and loved were Bahá'ís and that in Iran there were people who hated them. I could not understand why.

Having no land, we had to make do with my father's salary alone, whereas the members of the Samadani clan had additional income from their vineyards and pistachio plantations. Since Áqá Ján gave his widowed mother an allowance, it was often difficult to make ends meet with what remained of his salary. I remember needing a new winter coat when there wasn't enough money to have one made. The family decided to consult about the matter, using the Bahá'í method. We invited my half-sister's husband to attend the consultation because he had the reputation of being a good businessman. The family sat around the *kursí* and discussed what could be done. Everyone gave their opinion, even the children. They discussed whether or not my old coat could be turned or lengthened somehow, or whether I could make it last another six months. The son-in-law knew a wholesale dealer who could sell them enough material for a coat. Shahab's mother was a seamstress; perhaps she could make the coat. In the end I had a winter coat that served me many years and I had learned firsthand how decisions are made and problems handled in a Bahá'í family.

So the years went by and I grew taller. I finished elementary school and entered the public high school to prepare for the university entrance exams. Although it was a government school, there were books to be bought and other expenses. With three boys in school, our family had to live on a strict budget.

2

Youth

The Bahá'í community of Qazvin traced its origins back to the early days of the Faith. It was quite large and had its own Centre with facilities for meetings and putting up guests. When I was 15, the Local Spiritual Assembly, the community's elected governing council of nine members, was worried that as a result of repression, persecution and ostracism the young people would become estranged from their religion. They requested the National Spiritual Assembly in Tehran to find teachers to work with the youth and help adults to deepen their faith. Shortly afterwards a remarkable young couple, Mr Abu'l-Qásim Faizi and his wife Gloria, came to Qazvin to work with the Bahá'í youth.

They had both graduated from the American University of Beirut and had taught in a Bahá'í school in a village near Isfahan until the government closed it. Mr Faizi was a tall, handsome, athletic man. We youngsters decided that he resembled the movie actor Victor Mature. To our joy, one of the first things he did was to organize a volleyball court and gymnastic facilities in a garden belonging to one of the Bahá'ís. After character classes he took us there to play. We all loved him, for he had the gift of bringing out the best in each of us. Mr Faizi seemed to know what each of his students did best, whether it was reading poetry or playing an instrument or gymnastics, and managed to give us all an opportunity to shine before the others. He won our respect without having to rely on willow switches. He organized theatre groups and songfests. He and his wife worked to give the Bahá'í youth a sense of fellowship and unity, helping them to maintain their identity in a hostile environment.

Mr Faizi also shared with us his love of literature and encouraged us to read widely. Fluent in French, English, Arabic and Persian, he told us about books written in English by Shoghi Effendi which had not yet been translated into Persian. He frequently quoted from classical poetry to prove a point. He had a soft, gentle voice and was often asked to speak in Bahá'í meetings, for he was as popular with the adults as he was with the children. Mrs Gloria Faizi was small and dressed with style. The whole community was in love with the attractive young couple.

On holidays Mr Faizi took the children on picnics and outings in some of the outlying villages. In those days, partly because of the difficulties of transportation, there was a wide social gulf between villagers and townspeople. In the villages, without electricity or modern conveniences, life went on very much as it had for centuries and many villagers still wore the traditional costume seen less and less often in the westernized towns. In some villages the Bahá'ís were numerous and received the young people from the town as honoured guests. While the community leaders discussed their problems with Mr Faizi and he gave them messages from other communities, we children were treated to bread and yoghurt with grape syrup. Then we sat and listened to tales of martyrs and heroes of the Cause. Often the stories were about people we knew or whose names we had heard before.

Perhaps the most important thing that we learned on these outings was to respect the villagers, who were often devout and kindly without the sophistication of western educations. Mr Faizi told us a story about how one of the greatest scholars of the Bahá'í Faith, one of the first to carry the message of the new religion to the United States, Mírzá Abu'l-Faḍl, had learned about the Faith from a simple village blacksmith. To this day I remember that story:

Once Mírzá Abu'l-Faḍl was travelling by donkey to a sacred shrine with a group of other mullahs. Mr Faizi made us laugh by imitating the mullahs who, riding on their donkeys, continually held out their hands as they ambled along for passers-by to kiss. Mírzá Abu'l-Faḍl's donkey lost a shoe and the mullah stopped in a small village to have it shod. The blacksmith was a Bábí, as the Bahá'ís were called in those early days.

He said, 'Sir, I don't really have much love for mullahs, but you seem to be quite different. So I'm going to ask you a question.'

Mírzá Abu'l-Faḍl thought a village blacksmith could not be expected to have courtly manners.

'What is your question?'

The villager screwed up his face, looking very puzzled and bewildered.

'Is it true the sacred commentaries say that by the grace of God each raindrop is brought by an angel, and once that drop of rain is delivered to the earth, the angel returns to the kingdom of God? Is this true?'

Mírzá Abu'l-Faḍl smiled at the man's perplexity.

'Yes, this is true. Rain is a benediction from God brought by angels.'

The blacksmith nodded, bent over the shoe and pounded in a nail. A moment later he looked up again.

'There's another thing I wanted to ask you. Since dogs are supposed to be unclean, like pigs, I've been told that angels don't go where there are dogs. Is that true?'

Mírzá Abu'l-Faḍl said, 'Yes, it is quite true.'

The blacksmith went on pounding the nail. Then he looked up once more.

'Does that mean that in places where there are dogs, it doesn't rain?'

The learned scholar was shocked to find that he had no answer that would put the impertinent blacksmith in his place. The mullah asked, 'Who are these Bábís? What is it that makes them willing to die for their faith and allows blacksmiths to match wits with scholars?'

The longer I attended Mr Faizi's classes, the more I admired him. Like many others, I was inspired to follow his example and dedicate my own life to the Bahá'í Cause. I wanted to learn more about the history of my Faith, so I began to get up early in the morning to study the sacred texts and meditate. I also read *The Dawn-breakers*, an account of the early Bábís.

My parents did not object to me spending time on studies that were not related to my schoolwork. They also rose early in the morning for their prayers and daily meditation. They found it natural that I followed their example as I grew older. Occasionally my father would copy my lesson notes for me so I didn't lose too much sleep and still had time for my morning studies. Within my heart I felt a growing certainty that my personal destiny was linked with that of the Cause.

Just as they had in the early days of the Faith, Persian pilgrims on their way back from the international headquarters of the Bahá'í Faith in Haifa often stopped in Qazvin and gave the Local Assembly messages and news of how the religion was spreading around the world. In 1940 they brought a message urging young Iranian Bahá'ís to study English and Arabic.

At that time English was not the international language it has since become. Up until the Second World War most schools in Iran offered only French and occasionally German as a second language. I wanted to follow the instructions from Haifa but there were no English classes available in the government school I attended. Then Mrs Faizi, who had studied English in Beirut, announced that she would teach a course if there were enough students interested. I immediately signed up for the class. A Bahá'í family loaned us a room, a blackboard was found and the classes began. I enjoyed them tremendously and turned out to be a good student.

Mrs Faizi asked a small fee for the classes. I had enough saved out of my pocket money to pay for the first month but my family's very restricted budget did not allow me to continue. When I had no more money for the classes, I went on studying English on my own. I used a self-help book which illustrated the adventures of a fictional character, a debonair young Englishman called 'Mr Priestly'. His lifestyle could not have been more different from mine if he had come from Mars. I memorized the vocabulary and taught myself phrases and sentences that I repeated over and over and wrote down in a notebook. It may not have been the easiest method but I eventually learned enough to be able to hold a simple conversation. The results in the government school were not much better. One of my French teachers taught us boys to conjugate *fenêtre*, a noun meaning window. 'I window, thou windowest, he windows. We window, you window, they window!'

By then the western world was in the throes of World War II. Germany invaded Russia and the Soviets asked Iran to honour an ancient agreement giving the Russians and their allies the right to occupy Iran if Russia was in danger. At that time Nazi Germany appeared to be winning the war and it seemed a good opportunity for Iran to assert its independence. Reza S̲h̲áh refused to allow Russian soldiers and their allies on Iranian soil. Almost immediately the country was invaded by the Russians in the north and by their British and American allies from the Persian Gulf.

One day on my way to school, I heard a loud, droning roar coming from the sky. I looked up and saw a dozen fat, dark grey airplanes flying low over the city. Then I heard the spitting crack of machine guns. I dashed into a nearby doorway and found myself huddling with an Armenian family in the stairwell leading to their water reservoir. The planes seemed to have flown over and I started to stand up when there was another series of loud explosions.

The Armenians and I waited for a long time, expecting one of the blasts to bring the roof down on our heads. When the bombs and planes could no longer be heard, people rushed into the streets, shouting and calling to each other. The air was filled with thick dark clouds of grime and smoke. I choked and coughed at the acrid stench of burning crude oil. The Russians had bombed the oil tanks outside Qazvin.

Most Iranians, tired of being the puppet of the world powers, had favoured the Shah's declaration of independence. It had not occurred to them that the costly Iranian army was incapable of defending their national territory. After the bombings, the entire population of Qazvin panicked and there was a mass exodus. Since there were no cars available and the few horse-drawn cabs had been taken over by the military authorities, my father arranged for our family to leave with a camel caravan.

To be honest, I was more excited at the idea of riding a camel than frightened by the bombs. Late at night my family and I left Qazvin under a full moon shining in the clear, star-filled sky. The sandy road gleamed in the moonlight like dull silver, streaked with the grey shadows of fig and pistachio trees. As the camel gently rocked along I could hear the soft tinkling of harness bells and an occasional child whimpering in its sleep. We travelled all night and I was soon tired of the rocking motion and the stench of the camel. Finally we reached

Ghadim-abad, a village in the county of Zahra that was said to have belonged to my family in the old days and where there were many Bahá'í families. My family name, Zahrai, means the people of Zahra.

A mud wall around the village protected it from the wind. The headman's house was in the centre of a cluster of smaller homes made of adobe, most of which consisted of one room and an attached kitchen. They had no windows, only doors. When the weather was hot the villagers slept on the roof or outside in the courtyard. They had no furniture but sat, ate and slept on brightly coloured carpets that covered the ground. The small village was surrounded by green irrigated fields. Beyond lay the dry, grassy plains.

My stay there was like an unexpected school holiday. My brothers and I enjoyed the fresh yoghurt and grapes, watermelons and peaches while we helped our cousins work in the fields. We were tanned and muscular by the time word came from our father that the war was over and we could return to Qazvin. After three days of fighting, Reza Sháh had given a cease-fire order and surrendered. He was forced to abdicate in favour of his son, Muhammad Reza.

I found Qazvin greatly changed. Because of its situation it had become a vital link permitting the Allies to maintain supply lines to Russia during the German attack on Stalingrad. British, American and Russian troops occupied Iran and monopolized transport in order to keep food and weapons flowing into Russia. At first the local population was frightened by the strange-looking

Left to right: Colonel Ali Morad Khan, Haji Muhammad Ismail Khahli, Haji Colonel Khan (Ezzat's paternal grandfather), Colonel Nurollah Khan, Haji Mirza Ibrahi Davaforoch

Left to right: Dr Mehdi Samandari, Knight of Bahá'u'lláh Soheil Samandari, Hand of the Cause Tarazu'lláh Samandari, Mr Samadani (Ezzat's maternal grandfather), unknown

Ezzat with his father,
Massih Zahrai

Ezzat as a young boy

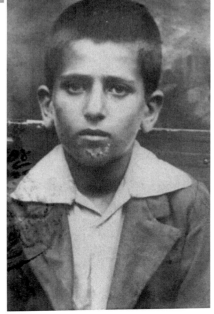

Front row, left to right: Ezzat's father, Massih Zahrai; Ezzat; Ezzat's
mother, Razieh Samadani;
Back row, left to right: Ezzat's brothers, Ehsan and Aziz; third person
unknown

Sunday school theatre in Qazvin

Some Sunday school students with their teachers

Youth committee, Qazvin.
Ezzat, *standing far right*

Some of the students in Ezzat's English class in Qazvin, together with some other local Baháʼís. *Ezzat, standing far left*

Ezzat's mother, Razieh Samadani, *circa* 1950-1

foreign soldiers, the black Americans and the Indian Sikhs. The Russian, American and British troops built three camps near Qazvin. The Grand Hotel became the headquarters of the medical services of the American army. The Allies were buying all the meat, vegetables and fresh fruit that could be found and they had taken over the country's entire transportation system. Crops were rotting in the fields because the peasants had no means of getting them to market. As a result very little could be found in the markets and food prices soared.

Because of the war, imported goods were no longer reaching Iran; shortages became chronic. With her ration coupons all my mother could buy was dark, gritty bread, but we suffered most from the lack of sugar, which normally came from Russia. The bazaar shops, which used to sell tall white cones of sugar that housewives broke into lumps with small hammers, were closed. In our home Razieh had one small dish of precious sugar lumps which she saved for guests and 19 Day Feasts. We had to get used to taking our morning tea without sugar.

My brother Aziz was drafted. My cousin Shahab and my brother Ehsan could have found work in Qazvin but Mr Faizi's influence had touched an entire generation of young Bahá'ís. Shahab and Ehsan volunteered to serve the Cause by teaching Bahá'í children in small villages where there were no schools. Ehsan went to a poor village that could furnish him with only a tiny, cheerless room. He had to draw his drinking water from the village well and walk several miles to the nearest public bath. Unable to afford a new coat, for over a year he wore an old one with patches on the elbows. I was full of admiration for him.

In Qazvin everyone who could was building houses for the occupiers. Rumours in the bazaar said that there was work for anyone who wanted it and the foreigners paid well. With the high price of food, it was more difficult than ever to stretch my father's meagre salary far enough to feed the family, and neither Aziz nor Ehsan were making money to help out. There seemed no way to continue paying for my school expenses. I realized that since I spoke English, I might be able to find a job with the Allied forces. A friend of mine had been hired by the British as a civilian translator. I told my parents that I wanted to stop my studies for the time being and look for work. They worried about my not having finished my university preparation, but eventually they accepted my decision. I was convinced that the sooner I started working, the sooner I could start to serve the Cause.

I went to the Allied headquarters and said I spoke English and was looking for work. They sent me to see a certain Mr Hannibal, who was at the head of the United Kingdom Commercial Corporation, a company created by the British to transport supplies for the occupying forces throughout Iran. Mr Hannibal gave me a simple test and seemed to find my English adequate, for he gave me the job. Of course, at that time in Qazvin there were not many people who spoke English at all.

Ali Hannibal was a rather mysterious foreigner who had married a Persian woman. No one knew if that was his real name or even what nationality he was. He spoke an archaic, literary form of Persian, and frequently quoted from classical Persian poetry. He claimed to speak 13 languages and it may have been true. Besides me, the company had only two other employees, a driver and a junior clerk. The UKCC office lay on the northern outskirts of Qazvin, with nothing but wastelands beyond. It consisted of a few small offices and an enormous parking lot where trucks were constantly being dismantled and repaired. The office's prestige was considerably enhanced by a field telephone that the British installed. At that time the only telephones to be found in Qazvin were in government offices and one public booth in the post office. Private lines were unheard of.

The Russians occupied the country north of Qazvin and the British and American allies occupied the south. At Qazvin the supplies coming from abroad were handed over to the Russians through the UKCC office run by Mr Hannibal. The quantities were vast and the goods were often stored outside. There were acres and acres of sugar, cheese, flour and oil, but also arms and ammunitions staked out and covered with green tarpaulins. Some truckloads of goods were diverted to the Russian sector without being unloaded.

The office had no typewriters; all the accounts and correspondence were handwritten. I saw the Americans doing their calculations on small machines that worked with a crank, and, sitting next to them, the Russians who did their accounts just as quickly on an abacus. I met a lot of British and American officers and the Americans in particular were quite friendly. With practice my English improved and became more serviceable. Besides learning American slang, I picked up a little Russian, enough to make myself understood when necessary. Twice a week I went to see one of the Samandari brothers, Mr Kazemoff, who had lived in Baku. With him I studied Russian grammar.

When pay day came, I was making more money than my father did as a civil servant. Up until then I had never had more than five Rials pocket money in my possession. I was proud to take my first month's salary, 1000 Rials, home to my parents, but my father insisted that I keep it.

'It is your money. You earned it; you do as you wish with it.'

This did not prevent me from helping with the family expenses, but it taught me to be responsible for my money, deciding what bills I should pay and how much I could spare for my own pleasures. My evenings after work were busy. More and more young people wanted to learn English but Mrs Faizi and her husband had left Qazvin on another teaching mission. The Bahá'í youth committee decided to organize afternoon English classes and asked me to teach four classes a week, two for the beginners and two for advanced students. The Local Assembly bought blackboards and benches and converted part of the Bahá'í Centre into a classroom. My students were motivated and rarely missed classes. They worked hard at their lessons. In the following years many of them were to volunteer as Bahá'í teachers in distant countries around the world. Years later, in Haifa, I met one of my former students, a daughter of the Samandari family. She had become a member of the International Teaching Centre.

One day the mystery concerning Mr Hannibal's nationality was solved. Something had happened to make him furious and he suddenly began cursing in what I recognized as fluent Russian. To this day I believe that my first employer was an agent of the KGB. When the occupying forces left Iran at the end of the war, Mr Hannibal and the UKCC disappeared. And I was out of a job.

3

Tehran and Tabriz

If my parents had insisted, I might have continued my studies, but after two years of bringing home a good salary, I was reluctant to return to being a student and sitting in school all day. Aziz had opened a small clothes shop in Qazvin. Ehsan had finished his year of voluntary service and was going to work in Tehran with a construction company belonging to a wealthy Bahá'í. I decided to go to live with him and look for work in Tehran.

The capital had many modern buildings, though the tallest were not more than four or five storeys high. To the north Mount Damavand raised its snow-capped peak. Its green lower slopes stretched to the outskirts of Tehran. To the east lay a range of dry, arid hills. The climate was cold and snowy in winter, green and wet in the spring, hot and dry during the summer. The bright sun and the cool breezes from the north made autumn a pleasant season to stroll through the many parks and gardens. At prayer time the city rang with the minaret cries of 'Alláh-u-Akbar!'

I went for an interview at the Imperial Bank of Iran and was hired as a translator-clerk and assistant account-ant, thanks to my now fluent English. The pay was even better than what I had been making with the UKCC. The bank was British owned and had branches in all the major cities of Iran. In order to improve my chances of promotion, I signed up for evening courses in management training and finance, organized by the Ministry of Finance.

My brother Ehsan and I rented a room in the house of an Armenian woman. It didn't take us long to realize that neither of us knew how to cook. We could not afford to eat in restaurants or bazaar shops every day and eventually, after some trial and error, resigned ourselves to a monotonous diet of fried eggplants and tomatoes, the only dish we knew how to make. It was not long before we both fell ill.

Marhamat, our half-sister, was then living in another part of Tehran. When she came to care for us, the landlady told her, 'I was expecting this. For months and months they have eaten nothing but tomatoes and fried eggplant.'

Marhamat scolded us for not taking better care of ourselves. Then she went out and bought us a couple of the copper pails in which workmen carried their meals. The ingenious pails had several tiers so that vegetables, meat sauces and other dishes could be carried separately. She told us that she would cook for us and we could carry the meals home in the copper pails and reheat them later. We thanked her from the bottom of our hearts. She saved our lives. Many years later she moved to Toronto to be near her children. I visited her there in 2002 and reminded her that we would never have survived our own cooking. The food that she prepared was certainly healthy, for she lived to be over a hundred years old.

There was an active group of young Bahá'ís living

in Tehran at that time. They organized a youth club and someone came up with the project of publishing a monthly magazine for Baháʼís. I had dreamed of being a writer and enthusiastically plunged into the venture. They named their magazine *Áhang-i-Badíʼ, The New Melody*. The staff was half a dozen young people who were barely in their twenties. With a friend I was responsible for finding material, preparing the texts and editing. Then we typed the text onto stencils. I spent hours on the layout, measuring lines and calculating how much of each article would fit on the page. Ehsan was on the production committee; they mimeographed the stencils, stapled the pages together and distributed the magazine. They had more fun than us editors, for the production team often stayed up until three o'clock in the morning, drinking tea and eating sandwiches, while they cranked the mimeograph machine and stapled pages.

The New Melody was immediately popular for there was a real need for expression in the Baháʼí community and the number of subscribers grew and grew. However, in spite of our success, we could not have it printed by a professional printer because Iranian law forbade the publication of Baháʼí materials. Everything the Baháʼís produced had to be either copied by hand or mimeographed. The few printed books we Baháʼís possessed were imported from Egypt, a British protectorate that had religious freedom. But the Baháʼís were ingenious in finding alternative methods of reproduction and there was a Baháʼí bookbinder, Mehregui, who made books by binding mimeographed sheets within hard covers. The result looked like a printed book, except for the mimeographed text. I still have one of Mehregui's books.

In spite of the restrictions, *The New Melody* flourished and we were delighted. The experience taught me to be optimistic. I had learned that with faith and perseverance wild dreams could become reality.

During the years following the war Tehran was growing into a modern metropolis. Many people were coming from the provinces looking for jobs and new opportunities. To cope with the growing numbers, the post office was forced to expand and my father learned that there was an opening in Tehran for him. Aziz's clothes shop in Qazvin was not doing well; he thought he might find work in the capital. My mother missed her two youngest sons. Our paternal grandmother had recently died. We gathered for a consultation and made the important decision to sell our home in Qazvin and move to Tehran. There we bought a house and began considering ourselves Tehrani, people of Tehran.

At about the same time my cousin Shahab decided to go to the Persian Gulf as a pioneer. We Bahá'ís call people who volunteer to move into territories where they can serve the Faith 'pioneers'. They are simple laymen who receive no salary from the Bahá'í community and have to work for their living, for Bahá'ís have neither clergy nor missionaries. Our communities are governed by elected bodies. Pioneers, like all Bahá'ís, are not allowed to proselytize, merely to represent the Faith and reply to the questions of those who seek to learn more about it. We Bahá'ís believe that if we live our Faith fully and adhere to its principles, those who live around us and have open minds will become curious and ask questions. Bahá'í pioneers often remain in a post for years before seeing any tangible results of their presence. Yet their methods, which may seem too discreet to be effective, have allowed our Faith to spread from a handful of Persian exiles to more than five million believers around the world.

My cousin Shahab was still the grinning boy who had played being a postman with my brothers and me in our garden. His widowed mother had no other child and had worked hard to raise him. He knew that she would not want him to go so far away. Fearing a tearful parting, he told her that he was going south to Shiraz, the Báb's birthplace, on pilgrimage. From there he wrote her a letter telling her his true intentions and asking her to forgive him. My aunt accepted the news far more calmly than anyone had expected.

'I thought as much,' she said. 'I saw him selling his things and I thought that it wasn't necessary for a short absence. If this is God's Will, he must do it and I can accept it.'

I too wanted to do something for my Faith. The general exodus to Tehran represented a danger to the smaller Bahá'í communities in Iran. In general, those who moved were the younger, more dynamic members. If the exodus continued, the local Bahá'í Assemblies would be too weak to keep up the task of educating the youth. The Iranian National Spiritual Assembly decided to counteract the tendency by sending enthusiastic young volunteers from Tehran to the smaller towns where the Local Assemblies needed to be strengthened. As a result the Bahá'í National

Spiritual Assembly approved a 45-month plan to develop and deepen knowledge of the Faith throughout Iran and asked for volunteers. When I saw the list of towns that were targeted, I realized that the Imperial Bank had branches in many of them and I thought it would not be difficult to be transferred.

I went to Mr Faizi who was then working in Tehran and told him that I was interested in going to a pioneer post. Mr Faizi was pleased.

'Take Tabriz,' he said. 'The Bahá'ís there need some new blood. The local Bahá'í population is old and perhaps a bit conservative. They are afraid their young people are growing away from the Faith. They need some young animators with new ideas.'

'_Khúb_,' I said. 'Okay, I'll do that.'

I immediately obtained an appointment with the bank's personnel manager, Mr Cull, and asked for a transfer. He was a middle-aged Englishman and my request puzzled him. Posts in Tehran were in high demand and it was unusual for an ambitious young employee to request a transfer to a provincial town. He questioned me, and when I said that I had no family living in Tabriz, my desire to go there seemed even more suspicious. He warned me that I would have to accept a ten per cent salary cut. Obviously it was not a wise move for my future career. When I told him that I accepted the lower salary, Mr Cull decided that the only reason for such a sacrifice must be an unhappy love affair and he approved my transfer to the branch agency in Tabriz.

Tabriz, situated in a narrow valley in the mountains of

northwest Iran, close to the Russian border, is an important shrine for Bahá'ís. In 1848 the Shah sent a special prisoner to Tabriz. He was the Báb, the first prophet of the Bahá'í religion. Christians might compare Him to John the Baptist. He preached against the corruption so prevalent in Persian society and urged a spiritual renewal based on love and compassion. His movement was spreading throughout Persia and had thousands of converts. Although the Muslim clergy did not hesitate to use violence to repress its progress, the Bábí movement, as it was then called, seemed to spread all the faster, to every corner of the Shah's empire and beyond. The clergy's persecutions merely fulfilled the prophecies concerning the return of the twelfth Imam, the promised messianic figure of Shi'i Islam. Fearing to make a martyr of the Báb, the mullahs initially allowed Him to live but sent the prophet to a remote fortress in the Azerbaijan mountains, in hopes His followers would forget about Him. Later an ecclesiastical court, similar to those that were restored by the Islamic revolution in Iran in 1979, tried Him for heresy and condemned Him to a bastinado. A European physician was called in to see Him. Dr William Cormick, an Irishman, was the only westerner ever to meet the Báb. He left a description of his patient.

> . . . a very mild and delicate-looking man, rather small in stature and very fair for a Persian, with a melodious soft voice, which struck me much . . . In fact his whole look and deportment went far to dispose one in his favour.[1]

In 1848 Muhammad S͟háh died and three different factions struggled to take over the imperial throne. A new strong man, Mírzá Taqí K͟hán, installed his puppet, the 16-year-old crown prince, Náṣiri'd-Dín S͟háh, on the throne and had himself appointed prime minister. In order to establish his control more firmly, Mírzá Taqí K͟hán encouraged the persecution of the Bábís.

European observers were horrified at the violence and cruelty of the persecution. Bábí men, women and children were tortured, raped, mutilated and massacred. According to conservative estimates, 20,000 were killed at that time. One group defended themselves in a fort at Ṭabarsí, holding off an army for seven months. In the end, the besieging commander offered the Bábís their freedom if they would leave the fort. When the surviving Bábís surrendered their arms, their enemies set upon them and massacred them.

The Bábí movement was reaching all levels of society. Increasing numbers of merchants, tradesmen, artists and members of the aristocracy came to accept the Báb. In Tehran seven well-known and respected personalities – merchants and scholars – were executed for refusing to recant their belief in the young prophet. In spite of, or perhaps because of, the Seven Martyrs of Tehran, large numbers continued to adopt the Bábí religion. Appalled by the Báb's growing popularity, Mírzá Taqí K͟hán finally decided to have Him publicly executed, in hopes the movement would die with its founder. He gave orders to the governor of Azerbaijan for His execution, but the governor, a shrewd man, failed to obey the prime minister's orders, finding excuses to delay acting on them. He may have acted thus out of respect for the Báb, or he may have thought that in the long run the Bábís would win. In the end, Mírzá Taqí Khán sent his own brother to supervise the Báb's execution.

A Muslim ecclesiastical court made no difficulties about signing a death warrant and on 9 July 1850 a crowd was assembled in a public square of Tabriz to watch the Báb's execution. Several non-Bahá'í eyewitness accounts have come down to us, transmitted by western commentators then living in Iran. The Báb and a young companion who refused to leave his master were tied in front of a firing squad of 750 muzzle-loading rifles. After the first volley, when the thick cloud of gun smoke finally cleared away, the Báb was nowhere to be seen and His companion was standing free, unscathed. The bullets had cut away their ropes without harming them. After a frantic search, the Báb was found in His cell, dictating to a scribe. When He had finished His correspondence He calmly turned to His executioners and told them that now that He had finished, they should carry out their duty.[2]

The local soldiers were Armenian Christians. They refused to fire a second time. A new firing squad had to be assembled and this time the two martyrs were riddled with bullets. Their corpses were thrown into a moat on the edge of the city for dogs to feed on, but during the night they disappeared, taken by faithful Bábís. For many years the bodies were kept in secret hiding places. They were brought to Palestine in 1899 and, after the Young

Turk Revolution, were buried on Mount Carmel in 1909. Today one of the first things visitors to Haifa see is the golden dome of the Báb's tomb overlooking the city.

When I went to Tabriz in 1947, it had an important carpet industry and commercial ties to Russia and Turkey. A lot of rebuilding was being done after the war, streets were being widened and public gardens were being laid out with fountains and pools. There were still very few modern buildings, and these were built on the outskirts of the town, far from the bazaar where most of the business was carried on. American missionaries had built a large mission and a hospital. There was a British consulate. Transportation facilities in the city were almost non-existent; the streets and alleys of the bazaar were too narrow for cars. Everyone went on foot, except for those who travelled by the few horse-drawn *dorosheke*. Although Farsi is the official language of Iran, in Tabriz most of the population spoke Azeri, a Turkish dialect. The Azeri were a proud people with a long and ancient history. There was also a large Armenian population, many of whom were able craftsmen.

I had picked up a little Azeri while I was living in Qazvin. In order to be better able to communicate and to speak in Bahá'í meetings, I studied Azeri. I was soon able to converse fairly easily and the bank's clients appreciated that someone coming from Tehran had made the effort to learn their dialect.

The main bazaar of Tabriz, like bazaars throughout the Middle East, was an organic growth allergic to straight lines and any form of street planning. Designed for pedestrians, the narrow little streets wandered up and down stairs, right and left, with no logic whatsoever. Arcades over the booths and shops protected their goods from sun and rain, creating a cool, dark haven. I spent hours strolling in the bazaar, admiring the craftsmen and their goods. There were carpets with rich designs that were passed on from one generation to the next, goldsmiths like my grandfather, silversmiths and copper-smiths pounding their intricate patterns into the metal, the bright colours of silks from Asia, lovely porcelain dishes and calligraphy artists who could turn a text from the Qur'án into a delicate drawing. The air carried whiffs of rich spices, mint and saffron. At intervals a narrow opening between two shops led into a large courtyard. These courtyards, called *serais*, were surrounded by brick buildings containing *ḥujrihs*, the offices of wealthy merchants. Often a *serai* specialized in a particular kind of trade. One housed textile importers, another was occupied by cotton and hide exporters.

The Imperial Bank was located just off the main bazaar. All of the important merchants of Tabriz were just a short walk away. At that time a businessman's stock and trade was his word of honour, for almost all of the business of the bazaar was carried on verbally, without written contracts. I often saw a broker walk into a *serai* and shout out the goods and prices he had to offer. Buyers would stick their heads out of the windows of their *ḥujrihs* and place their orders without so much as a handshake. The broker would note everything down and leave, never doubting that he would be paid. A few days later he would return, bringing his customers their profits. There were surprisingly few conflicts, for merchants were fiercely proud of their reputation for honesty.

Every day on my way to the bank I walked past the Ark, the old fortress, in ruins. A brick and stone stairway led to the upper floors of the fort where the Báb had been held prisoner before being executed. Of course there was no monument, but the local Baháʼís pointed out to me the exact location of His cell. When Baháʼí visitors came to Tabriz, I took them to the spot and they would say a few discreet prayers. We had to be careful not to attract the attention of passers-by and the Muslim authorities. One of the visitors I took to the Ark was Robert Gulick, a nice young man from America who stayed in my apartment. He must have found our living conditions rather rustic. When he left he gave me a tie that I kept as a souvenir for many years.

In 1947 Iran was still a country in which most people spent their entire lives in the town they were born in. Anyone coming from another province was considered a foreigner. Since people traditionally lived with their families, it was hard for a young bachelor to find lodgings. I finally found a room in the Armenian district. It was unfurnished and had no heating system, not even a *kursí*. I bought a 'Primus', a small kerosene burner, for cooking and for heat. When it got very cold I had to scrape the ice off the windows with a wooden spatula to see through them. In winter I would say my early morning prayers sitting under several layers of blankets, wearing as many sweaters and overcoats as I owned. In *Nabíl's Narrative* there is a passage which tells how the Báb, during His imprisonment in Tabriz, saw the water freeze on His hands while doing His ablutions before His morning prayers. But I was only 21 and following in the footsteps of the early believers. I thought all my hardships were a marvellous adventure.

After I had been in Tabriz for three months, two other young pioneers came from Tehran. Bijan worked for the oil company and had obtained a transfer to Tabriz in much the same way I had. The other young pioneer, Dr Amín Lámi', taught in the university that had just opened. He came from an Azeri family that had formerly lived in Tabriz and they owned a house there. He invited Bijan and me to move into his family home with him. I agreed immediately. Not only would I save money on rent, but I would have company too. The house was in poor condition, having been empty a long time, and was in a rather dilapidated part of town called Qara-dam-dash, but I was so busy with my job and my Bahá'í activities that I paid little attention to the strange women I sometimes encountered around our new lodgings.

Shortly afterwards, I had a skin disease that became so severe that I had to be hospitalized in the American hospital for almost a week. Dr Lamb, the American doctor, quickly cured me with penicillin, but my fellow employees at the bank knew where I lived and jumped to the conclusion that I had caught a venereal disease.

At work I could order *chellokebab* – a dish of buttered rice with eggs and roasted lamb – and *dúgh*, a kind of diluted yoghurt, from a bazaar shop and eat my lunch at the bank in a room set aside for the employees' use. Tea came from a teashop, for there were no cooking facilities, just a few tables and benches. One day the bank cashier, a very kind elderly gentleman, came and sat beside me while he was having his lunch. He started telling me that he understood how difficult it must be for young bachelors to live in a foreign town, far from their families.

'Why are you talking to me about all this?' I asked.

'I know it's difficult to be a bachelor, but you can catch venereal diseases in the places where you go.'

'What do you mean? I've never been to such a place.'

'We often see you coming out of Qara-dam-dash. We talked it over and thought we should tell you and warn you. It would be terrible if you caught something.'

'But that is where I live.'

My elderly friend was horrified. 'Why on earth did you choose that place? Couldn't you find anywhere else?'

We did eventually decide that we could afford better quarters. We rented a house together, a recently built two-storey building on the outskirts in the new part of Tabriz. There were no real conveniences, no heat or running water, but the address was respectable and by then I had bought some secondhand furniture, a bed and a rug, and the new house seemed far more cheery than my first lodgings. We shared the cost of hiring a servant who made our life more comfortable and saved all of us from my cooking.

Our servant's name was Balaja, which in Turkish means 'the little one'. He came from a nearby village, Saysán, where more than half the population were

Bahá'ís. He told us stories about life in the village and the Bahá'í community there. He had a great admiration for Mr Furútan, a well-known Bahá'í, a member of the Bahá'í National Spiritual Assembly. A young honours graduate from the University of Moscow, he had returned to Iran and turned down a job with the Ministry of Education in order to teach in Saysán, where there was no school.

Balaja kept the apartment clean, kept the wood stove in the dining room burning and cooked meals in our rather rudimentary kitchen which had neither table nor cupboards. The pots and pans were set on the floor around the 'Primus'. On working days Balaja would prepare lunch for us and carry it to me at the bank, so I didn't have to order *chellokebabs* every day.

At work I met a young Muslim businessman, Ali Akbar, who ran an import agency. He represented foreign manufacturers of textiles and carpet dyes, earning a commission on the sales he made to local traders. He was young and ambitious and he wanted to develop his business. We got along well, and when Ali received business correspondence from abroad in English he frequently brought it to the bank and asked me to translate his letters. Occasionally he invited me to dinner in his home with other business relations. He was a pleasant host and I enjoyed his company, not to mention the good meals.

One evening I walked through the bazaar on my way to Ali's home. I left the bazaar and entered the main street of Tabriz, then turned into a small winding passage that twisted right and left, then went up and down a few narrow steps. Finally I came to a big, thick, wooden door reinforced with metal studs. I knocked and a veiled woman servant opened the door, greeting me respect-fully. I followed her into a courtyard where small trees and flowers were planted around a pool. The ground floor was occupied by servants' quarters and the kitchen. A stairway led to a large room on the first floor overlook-ing the garden. Ali Akbar was waiting for me there. He greeted me warmly and invited me to sit down. There were a few ornamental chairs, but Ali and I sat on the floor covered with several thick Persian carpets. A couch ran around the edge of the room. The women and chil-dren of the family were out of sight in another part of the house. To my surprise, that evening I was the only guest.

After chatting about the weather and business in gen-eral, Ali Akbar led me into the dining room, furnished much like the sitting room. There was no table but a white cloth had been spread on the floor in the middle of the room and a large variety of dishes had been set out for us. Plates and silverware were stacked at the edge of the cloth. We filled our plates and ate. I found the dishes exquisite, even better than usual.

I suspected that my friend wanted to propose some-thing, and wondered what he had on his mind. I went on eating and asked no questions. After dinner we returned to the sitting room and drank fragrant hot tea in *istikán*, small glasses in silver holders. Ali Akbar talked about some interesting offers he had recently received and it grew quite late before he got around to the real purpose of his invitation.

'Look, my friend. We have known each other for quite

some time now. Through the translation work you've done for me, you know that I have made some very interesting arrangements for importing Mexican cotton piece goods. Once this starts my business will develop very fast and I will not be able to cope with all the work. I speak no foreign language and know very little about banking and international trade. Why not leave the bank and come to work with me? I will make you a junior partner to start with.

I didn't want to offend my friend by laughing at his proposition. But what man sane of mind would leave a prestigious international bank with a guaranteed salary and a pension plan for a one-man operation, however prosperous and promising? I told Ali Akbar politely but firmly that I had no intention of leaving the Imperial Bank. Then I said goodbye and took a horse-drawn cab home. There were still only one or two private motor cars in Tabriz.

Ali Akbar did not let the matter drop. Every time he saw me in the bank he urged me to reconsider, asking me to set my own conditions and promising to meet all of them. Finally, in order to settle the matter once and for all, I decided to set conditions Ali could not possibly meet. In addition to a percentage of the profits, I asked Ali Akbar to double the salary I was then getting at the bank, to pay me a year's salary in advance and to grant me the nine Bahá'í holy days. Ali Akbar came from a very religious family; I thought that even if he were mad enough to grant the financial conditions, he would never accept to recognize Bahá'í holy days. To my surprise, however, Ali Akbar immediately promised to meet all of my requirements, including the religious holidays. Later I learned that Ali Akbar had had to borrow money to be able to pay my year's salary in advance in cash. I felt humbled when I realized that he thought of me so highly that he was willing to meet all my demanding conditions. Now it was up to me to make sure that his business prospered.

I resigned from the bank and began working with Ali Akbar. Our partnership quickly developed into a lucrative business. Cotton piece goods were manufactured according to our customers' specifications in Mexican mills and shipped through Vera Cruz to the Iranian port of Khorramshahr. From there they came by road to Tabriz. Ali Akbar delivered the goods to wholesalers who paid him a commission and then sold the goods to merchants all over Iran. I helped Ali Akbar modernize his business methods. We always gave samples of our goods to buyers and wrote out contracts which we asked customers to sign to avoid misunderstandings that could lead to conflicts.

Although Ali Akbar was a Muslim and I was a Bahá'í, we respected each other and worked together for several years, getting along quite well. Ali Akbar kept his promise to let me off for Bahá'í holy days and respected my fasting period. Yet he never once asked me anything about the Bahá'í religion or its principles.

Still a young man, I found myself with a comfortably growing bank account. I didn't change my style of life and I had no family to provide for, so I was able to put most of the money I earned into a savings account. Within five years, it had developed into a small capital.

My two roommates and I were very active in the local Bahá'í community. We were able to organize large gatherings and classes for children. We worked with the teenagers, teaching them the religious history of all the major religions and deepening their understanding of our own Bahá'í Faith. We encouraged them to question us and to investigate the claims of other religions. Our creed forbids coercing children to accept our Faith; Bahá'ís have to be 15 before they can consider themselves Bahá'ís. I like to think that our efforts helped the young generation to understand and remain loyal to the Faith of their fathers in spite of the government's efforts to stifle it.

The older members of the community might have resented our innovations, but instead they appreciated our work so much that two of us were elected to the Local Spiritual Assembly. This was particularly remarkable in the light of the Bahá'í method of election.

Critics of the Bahá'í Faith often fail to understand the democratic principles which underlie its administrative structure. At its birth Bahá'u'lláh outlined the principle of consultative decision-making which was shaped by 'Abdu'l-Bahá and further developed by Shoghi Effendi. Every community chooses by secret ballot nine of its members to administer the community for a year; it also selects a delegate to a national convention where the members of a National Spiritual Assembly are elected. Authority is not held by individuals but by the elected Assemblies as a group. The electoral process itself is unique. All forms of electioneering as the western world knows it, including nominating candidates and campaigning, are forbidden. The members of the community, men and women, are asked to avoid discussing possible candidates and to pray and vote by secret ballot for the nine persons that they personally consider best qualified. We do not consider membership on an Assembly as a source of power or prestige but as a responsibility to be accepted and a service to be rendered. The system gives 'maximum freedom of choice to each elector' and avoids the 'power-seeking behaviour inherent in many other forms of election'.[3] It is interesting to note that in case of ties, the advantage is given to the member of a minority.

The Assembly of Tabriz was also responsible for Local Assemblies in the rest of the province of Azerbaijan. There were many villages with large Bahá'í populations, such as Saysán, and Bahá'ís among the Kurds and the Persian-speaking semi-nomads who set up their black tents in the valleys during the winter and high on the mountains during the summer. If fanatical local authorities began persecuting the Bahá'ís, the Assembly in Tabriz was sometimes able to convince the provincial authorities to put pressure on their representatives to stop the persecutions.

One day I received a telegram from Tehran saying that my father was seriously ill. An airline had just opened a route between Tabriz and the capital, allowing me to take one of its first flights and reach Tehran the day after I received the telegram. My father had cancer of the oesophagus and was suffering intensely. For years he had been a heavy smoker of strong Turkish cigarettes. At first I blamed my brothers for not having let me know earlier. Actually, Áqá Ján had not told anyone that he was ill and even now kept talking about things that he intended to do when he got better. He was in a modern hospital that had been built and financed by the Bahá'í community. I talked to a specialist, assuring him that I was ready to pay any expense to save my father. Even when the doctor told me there was nothing that could be done, I insisted, wanting to send Áqá Ján to Europe for treatment.

The doctor sighed and shook his head.

'I'm sorry, Mr Zahrai. No matter how much money you spend, there is no one, here or in Europe, who can save your father. All we can do is alleviate his pain.'

The days that followed were a nightmare. Everyone but my father knew that there was no hope. Áqá Ján insisted on telling us that he would soon be better and faced death with the same gentle patience he had shown throughout his life. One morning very early Razieh came into my room to tell me that Áqá Ján had died in his sleep during the night.

My father, Massi'hullah Zahrai, was buried in the Bahá'í cemetery of Tehran. (Today the cemetery has been destroyed by Muslim fanatics.) Friends and family gathered around the grave and read a prayer together. The Bahá'í religion has only two rites of passage, both very simple, a marriage ceremony and a burial ceremony. My brothers and I ordered an appropriate tombstone. Our mother was inconsolable. The man that she had seen for the first time on the day of her wedding had been a true friend throughout their life together. She kept saying, 'I have lost everything.'

I flew back to Tabriz knowing that I had lost not only my father but also my best advisor, my best friend. Now there would be no one to turn to in times of difficulty. I would have to make my own decisions and solve my own problems. Little did I suspect the momentous decision I would soon have to make.

In 1951 some shipments of goods from Mexico did not meet the specifications that we had set. Our customers complained and refused to pay the price which had been agreed on. After a series of letters and telephone calls, it became obvious that someone would have to go to Mexico to settle the problem about the specifications with our supplier. Ali Akbar wanted me to go, since I was the one who spoke English well enough to negotiate with Teodoro Krauthamer, the president of Belmartex, the Mexican company. It was a wonderful opportunity for me, for at that time few Iranians could afford to travel abroad.

The problem was that Shoghi Effendi, the Guardian of the Faith, had asked Persian Bahá'ís not to go to the United States at that time. To reach Mexico City I would have to transit through a US airport. Since I was a boy, I had always dreamed of travelling to foreign lands and I did not want to cancel the trip.

I wrote to the National Spiritual Assembly in Tehran to request permission to make a few hours' stopover in the United States on my way to Mexico. I was convinced that I was making a reasonable request that would be granted without any problems. The National Assembly relayed my request to Shoghi Effendi in Haifa. Early in 1952 I received a letter signed by Mr Furútan, secretary of the National Assembly, which was to change the course of my life.

I kept that letter for many years, until it was taken away from me by the police when I was in prison in Laurenço Marques. That was almost 60 years ago but I had read and reread it so often that I still know it by heart. The short letter said simply,

> In reference to your letter to Shoghi Effendi, the Beloved Guardian, we have received the following from Dr Ḥakím, his secretary:
>
> I referred your letter to the Beloved Guardian and he said to write that Ezzatu'llah Zahrai was not allowed to go to Mexico. Instead Shoghi Effendi urges him to go to Africa for teaching work and he will pray for his success.

Mr Furútan had signed the letter without any further comment or explanation.

The matter was clear. There was no ambiguity. The request concerning a simple business matter had been made for purely material reasons. The Guardian's answer was of a spiritual nature. Now the decision was mine and no one else's.

Part II

Africa

4

Departure

. . . hesitate not, though it be for less than a moment, in the
service of His Cause.[1]

Bahá'u'lláh

Mr Furútan's letter surprised and disappointed me. I had
trouble explaining to Ali Akbar why I could not go to
Mexico, for he knew how excited I had been about the trip.

'Why can't you just go anyway?' he asked me. 'We can
say you are going to Europe. Who will know? What can
they do?'

'They would do nothing,' I told him. 'I would know,
but no one would do anything. It's not a question of punishment. The only thing that prevents me from going is
that Shoghi Effendi has asked me not to. When I chose
to become a Bahá'í, I chose to obey him. Voluntary obedience is one of the covenants of my Faith. It is difficult
to understand perhaps, but my religion is not based on
being punished for sins. It is based on striving to draw
nearer to God. Wrong actions draw us away from God. It
is a very individual thing. No other Bahá'í has the right to
judge my actions. In my own conscience I have considered the matter and decided I will obey the message from
Shoghi Effendi. What I'm trying to say is that someone
else must go with you to Mexico.'

Ali Akbar was unhappy but by this time he knew me well enough to know that where my Faith was involved, I would not budge.

'So be it,' he said. 'Nobari can go with me. Make the arrangements and brief him, though I'm afraid his English is not as good as yours.'

With a sad heart I contacted the airline agency and made all the arrangements for the wonderful trip I wouldn't be making. And I began thinking about the second part of the message from Haifa. Shoghi Effendi wanted me to go to Africa 'for teaching work'.

I discussed the matter with several older Bahá'ís. They assured me that there was no urgency. I could leave for Africa later, when I was married and when I had a bit more money. It seemed unwise to give up my position with Ali Akbar when the business was doing so well. They pointed out that I was already serving the Cause in a pioneering post. They encouraged me with the rather convenient idea that there would be plenty of time later to go pioneering in Africa.

On a short business trip to Tehran I stopped by to see my mother. When I explained to her why I wasn't going on the trip to Mexico, she said nothing. I took her to see a movie, one of the Hollywood musicals that she enjoyed so much. Back home she prepared a special meal for me with my favourite dishes.

'This is lovely, <u>Kh</u>ánum, my dear lady,' I said. 'I feel like a honoured guest.'

She nodded.

'I wish to honour my son who has been given a mission

Members of the National Spiritual Assembly of Iran with members of the Local Spiritual Assembly of Tabriz and local Bahá'ís on the occasion of the centenary of the Martyrdom of the Báb, Tabriz, 1950

Members of the National Spiritual Assembly of Iran and of the Local Spiritual Assembly of Tabriz, *circa* 1951. *Standing, left to right*: Colonel Mogharrabi, Mr Ghavami, Mr Nikbeen, Mr Kohldooz (business name), Mr Balazadeh, Mr Djalili, Mr Assadu'llah Zadeh (martyred during the Islamic revolution); *seated, left to right*, Dr Farhangui (martyred during the Islamic revolution), Mr Zikrullah Khadem (appointed Hand of the Cause in 1952), Mr Fatheazam (father of Hushmand), Mr Ali Akbar Furútan (appointed Hand of the Cause in 1951), Mr Ali Nakhjavani (elected to the Universal House of Justice 1963 to 2003), Mr Valiyu'llah Varqa (appointed Hand of the Cause in 1951), General Shu'a'u'llah `Ala'i (appointed Hand of the Cause in 1952); *sitting on the floor*: Dr Amn Lameh, Ezzat Zahrai

Youth group in Tabriz, *circa* 1950-1. *Far right*, Masrour Dakhili

The photograph used in Ezzat's first passport, 1951

Ezzat, *second from left*, departs from Tehran airport for Karachi and Bombay, en route to Africa, November 1952

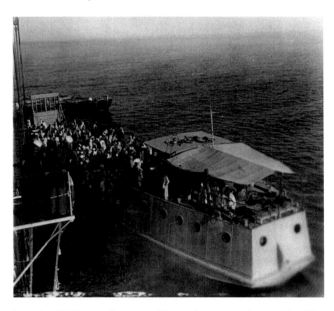

Boarding the SS *Kampala* on 11 November 1952, bound for Zanzibar, Dar-es-Salaam and Durban

Ezzat and a travelling companion aboard the SS *Kampala*

Nair Patel, *centre*, who befriended Ezzat on the SS *Kampala*

Aziz Yazdi

Violette and Ali
Nakhjavani

Hand of the Cause
Enoch Olinga

Hand of the Cause
Musa Banani

Bahá'ís in Nairobi, including Richard St Barbe Baker, *second from left*; Soraya Yazdi, *third from left*; Aziz Yazdi, *seventh from left*; and Ezzat, *far right*

by Shoghi Effendi.'

I stared at her. Her hair was still dark and thick, her eyes, carefully drawn in kohl, still lovely. Her beauty had aged but she was well groomed and dressed attractively.

'The Guardian wants you to go to Africa.'

My brothers and I had often teased our mother about her faith. She believed so wholeheartedly that she considered everything associated with the Bahá'í Faith to possess holy virtues, even the sugar lumps left over after a 19 Day Feast. For weeks I had been mulling over the strange message which had come from Haifa, trying to understand what was wanted, consulting with older, wiser men, trying to interpret it in a way that was convenient for my career. My mother was the only one who saw through my personal wishes and disappointed ambition to the heart of the matter.

'Khánum, do you really want me to go Africa? Who knows when I might return.'

She lay down her teacup and sighed.

'I will be sad to see my youngest son go so far away. And very proud to know that he is serving the Cause. As proud as Shahab's mother. Your father would have been proud. Do you remember what the Báb told his great-great-grandfather?'

There was a legend in our family that one of our Zahrai ancestors, a rather hot-headed young man, had learned that the Báb was being taken under armed guard to Tabriz and had gathered a group of determined young Bábís to rescue Him. He was able to obtain a secret interview with the prisoner at Siyáh-Dahán, a small village near Qazvin. The Báb thanked His would-be rescuers but told them not to attempt anything, saying, 'We should not do anything against the Will of God, because the Will of God will take place anyway.'

'If Shoghi Effendi wants you to go to Africa,' my mother said, 'it will surely happen.'

I thought over her words and became convinced that she was right. My partnership with Ali Akbar, which had seemed so important to me, may simply have been God's way of providing me with the means of going to Africa to teach. Shoghi Effendi's message was a reminder that my main goal in life had always been to serve the Faith.

'Thank you, <u>Kh</u>ánum. You are right. This is what I must do. I didn't go to Tabriz to seek my fortune but as a pioneer for the Cause.'

Now that my mother had looked at the matter with her clear vision, it all seemed so obvious. I remembered how reluctantly I had accepted Ali Akbar's proposition, holding out for terms I was sure he would never accept. Now I found myself with enough money to travel abroad and live for some time until I could find work. If I had remained with the bank I would never have been able to save so much money.

My mother smiled.

'Yes. This is God's Will.'

She raised her head, closed her eyes and began chanting a hymn of praise.

All praise, O my God, be to Thee Who art the Source of all glory and majesty, of greatness and honour, of

sovereignty and dominion, of loftiness and grace, of
awe and power.[2]

I joined in, vowing to remember that it had taken her
simple faith to solve the riddle of Shoghi Effendi's message.

The very next day found me was standing in Ferdowsi
Avenue outside a showroom. The sign over the door said
Tufenkjian and Company. I knew the company because it
had been a subcontractor of UKCC. I went in and asked
to see the manager, Mr Aziz Yazdi, who was a member
of the newly-formed Africa Committee which was coordinating the efforts of Persian pioneers wanting to go to
Africa. A tall, slender man with thick, dark hair greeted
me with a big smile and a warm handshake.

Aziz Yazdi was a remarkable man. His parents had
been sent to Egypt as pioneers by Bahá'u'lláh. When
he was a child they lived in Haifa and he remembered
seeing 'Abdu'l-Bahá there. He spoke Farsi with a slight
accent but his English, Arabic and French were fluent.
He had studied in England and had an engineering
degree. I learned that some years before he had been a
pioneer in Tabriz and I discovered that we had many
mutual friends.

'You want to go to Africa? That's wonderful, wonderful. I'm planning to go to Northern Rhodesia.' Out of a
desk drawer he pulled a map that was crumpled from
being repeatedly folded and unfolded. 'The capital is
Lusaka.'

I repeated the name. 'Lusaka. I like that. What is it
like?'

'Beautiful. I've never been there, but look, here's a book about it. Take it home to read.' The enthusiasm in the tall man's eyes sobered. 'But it's very difficult to get a visa. Rhodesia is a British colony and the embassy here is closed.'

I knew that. Dr Mossadeq, the new Iranian prime minister, was a liberal who opposed the hereditary power of the Shah and the ruling aristocratic elite of Iran. He had come to power by mobilizing a refusal in the Iranian parliament to grant an oil concession in northern Iran to the Russians. He was immensely popular and responsible for many reforms. He had put an end to official persecution of Bahá'ís. His political power had reached the point where he was able to nationalize the British petroleum company that was exploiting the enormous oil reserves of Iran with little profit to the Iranian people. The British were furious over the loss of their company and had cut off all diplomatic ties.

'I know it is going to be difficult to get a visa,' I said. 'I don't have the solution yet but surely something will turn up. My mother says that if it's God's Will, it will surely happen.'

Aziz shook my hand. 'We are certain to see each other over there. You'll meet my wife, Soraya. She's a wonderful girl, even more excited than I am about going.'

I took the book home and devoured it. Besides the films from Hollywood about white hunters and wild animals and naked black men who carried lances and danced to the maddening beat of drums, I knew very little about Africa. In the Dark Continent of the movies it always seemed to be night. The book told about a land of flowers and sunlight, mountains, lakes and rich, productive farms. I was enchanted by the green and fertile land in the photographs. I read the book from cover to cover, trying to imagine what my life would be like there, staring at the pictures, wondering what the people were really like.

Back in Tabriz I discussed my project with friends, but no one knew how I could get a visa to a British colony. Ali Akbar was very upset when he learned that I planned to leave. He could not understand how I could willingly give up such a promising partnership to go and live with 'cannibals'. He was convinced that Bahá'í leaders were forcing me to leave Tabriz. He offered to buy off my obligation to serve so that someone else could go in my place. When I explained that I was under no obligation, that it was my own choice to leave Iran, Ali Akbar proposed that I go to Germany. We could open up an office in Hamburg, where several well-to-do Iranians had established branch offices, and I would be the head of all our European ventures. By then I was so focused on going to Africa that I turned down his offer without even thinking it over.

All the arrangements had been made for Ali Akbar's trip to Mexico City with Nobari. I called Mr Krauthamer to inform him of the plane schedules and to suggest an agenda for discussions. The Mexican exporter told me that there was a change of plans. He would not be able to receive Ali Akbar in Mexico City because he had to go to Europe for personal reasons. His wife was ill and was going to be operated on by a famous French specialist.

He suggested that we meet in Paris to settle our differences.

I couldn't believe my ears. Even after I hung up I wondered if I hadn't misinterpreted Mr Krauthamer's proposal. But within a few days a telegram came to confirm that hotel reservations had been made for Mr Zahrai and Mr Ali Akbar at the Hotel Commodore, Boulevard Haussmann, Paris.

I felt as if my obedience had been rewarded. Not only was I going to travel abroad as I had dreamed, but also it was possible that in Europe I would be able to obtain a travel visa for one of the British colonies in Africa, removing the main obstacle to my pioneering project.

On 1 June 1952 Ali Akbar and I boarded a Constellation aircraft belonging to Scandinavian Airlines. We flew first to Damascus and then to Geneva, Switzerland. Our connecting flight to Paris was not until the next day, so I had time to meet Dr Shapour Rassekh, a friend from the early days of *The New Melody*, the magazine I had edited as a student. Shapour, a sociology student at the University of Geneva, showed me around and took me to the office of the Bahá'í International Bureau. There I met two American women, Miss Lynch and Miss Honor Kempton, who maintained correspondence with all the Bahá'í Assemblies. With very little equipment and a great deal of devotion, they managed to keep Bahá'ís scattered around the world informed about what was happening in their community.

The following day Ali and I flew to Paris. Our plane arrived at Orly airport on 3 June. Teodoro Krauthamer invited us to lunch in a prestigious restaurant in the Eiffel Tower. I was impressed by the splendid view, which showed the orderly way Paris was laid out. City planning in Iran, particularly in Qazvin, was far more haphazard. Now I realize that Mr Krauthamer had wanted to impress two young businessmen who had never been out of Iran before. The week was taken up in business meetings and with sightseeing. Ali Akbar wanted to see the famous Folies Bergère, so I accompanied him. Coming from a country where women in public were often hidden under chadors or long black robes, we were amazed to see beautiful young ladies with no clothes dancing on the stage. Like other tourists, we sat in the sidewalk cafés, visited the Eiffel Tower and the Louvre, and admired the tree-lined avenues and the well-dressed women. My time was so taken up with accompanying Ali, who did not speak French, that I had very little time to contact the French Bahá'ís. I did, however, find a brief opportunity to meet Miss Sanderson, one of the early believers in Paris.

When the differences with Belmartex were settled to our mutual satisfaction, Ali Akbar flew back to Tehran. I stayed on, determined to see as much of Europe as possible and to obtain a visa to one of the British colonies in Africa. On the 12th of June I flew to Rome, accompanied by some young Bahá'í friends that I had met in Paris. Through them I met Professor Bausani, an Italian scholar who specialized in the Middle East and spoke excellent Persian. He had become a Bahá'í after meeting Dr Ugo Giachery, a well-known Italian Bahá'í.

Professor Bausani invited us to his home for dinner

where we met his new bride. She had prepared pasta. I thought it was very good and helped myself to three servings. Then the young bride brought in another dish and I belatedly realized that the pasta had been a starter. I had difficulty honouring the main dish after my three plates of spaghetti, but I assured the hostess that everything was delicious and ate as much as possible to prove it. The dinner party was very cheerful and we stayed up talking and laughing until midnight.

The following day my friends took me to Milan by train. There I met Miss Dägmar Dole, an American of Danish extraction who had pioneered in Copenhagen during the Bahá'í Seven Year Plan. At that time Shoghi Effendi had asked American Bahá'ís to pioneer in the country of their family origin. It was for the same reason that Dr Giachery had come to Italy as a pioneer.

While I was in Paris I had not been able to celebrate the 19 Day Feast, but in Milan Dägmar Dole said prayers with me and a young Persian student, then we went out to a sidewalk café in the Plaza Douma and had ice cream. We sat and chatted and enjoyed the warm summer evening while being faithful to one of the commandments of our religion, to meet in fellowship once every 19 days.

From Milan I went alone to Florence by train. Coming from a land that is mostly desert, I was fascinated by the green hills of northern Italy. I noticed the ancient irrigation ditches and the terracing on the mountainsides that made the land so productive. I saw buildings that were centuries old, but no traces of the war and no ruins. In my hometown in Persia there were ruins everywhere one looked and I wondered what would have remained of my homeland if the war had raged there as it had in Italy.

I had been given the address of Marion Little, an American pioneer in Florence. I went to the Hotel Berchielli where she was staying and requested the manager to say that there was a gentleman from Persia who wished to see her. Marion asked me to come up. When I stepped off the elevator a woman about 40 years old opened her door and said, 'Alláh-u-Abhá, God is Most Glorious.'

It warmed my heart to hear the greeting that all Persian Bahá'ís used on the lips of an American lady in a faraway country.

'Alláh-u-Abhá,' I replied.

Marion welcomed me into her sitting room and introduced an elderly gentleman as Charles Mason Remey, the President of the International Bahá'í Council. They were having dinner together and invited me to join them. I stayed a couple of hours, and learned about the teaching work being carried on in Europe by dedicated pioneers like Marion Little. When I excused myself, saying I was tired after the long train trip, Mr Remey invited me to have lunch with him the next day. We exchanged business cards and I saw that the address on Mr Remey's card was '10 Persian Street, Haifa'. It was the address of 'Abdu'l-Bahá's house in Haifa, known to all Bahá'ís.

The next day I met Mr Remey at ten o'clock. When I said, 'Good day,' Mr Remey replied, 'Alláh-u-Abhá.' He was a charming dinner companion, friendly and spiritual. He had served 'Abdu'l-Bahá faithfully for many years and Shoghi Effendi had named him President of the International Bahá'í Council. He was known as someone who never criticized others behind their backs. 'Abdu'l-Bahá had said that 'the most great sin is backbiting'.[3]

Mr Remey told me that he had visited Iran 43 years before and had many good memories of the country and of the Bahá'ís he had met there. He particularly remembered a doctor from Qazvin whom I knew.

After an excellent lunch, Mr Remey suggested that we have coffee in a café. We crossed the Ponte Vecchio and sat by the river, talking. The old gentleman explained that he was in Florence on a mission for Shoghi Effendi. The Guardian wanted an Italian artist to make a model of the Bahá'í International Archives building in Haifa to present to the National Spiritual Assembly of the United States.

Marion Little asked me to be her escort to a party she was giving for the foreign students in Florence.

'You'll have a chance to meet a lot of young people your age, and we'll have opportunities to talk to them about our Faith.'

The party was in a palace that had once belonged to Dante. A wealthy American socialite, a friend of Marion, had rented it. I enjoyed the party and the cosmopolitan blend of guests from many different countries.

Marion also introduced me to a group of ten or twelve friends who got together every Monday to discuss the Bahá'í Faith and its principles. She asked me to talk to them about the activities of the Bahá'í youth in Iran. I told them about the magazine, *The New Melody*, and friends who had volunteered as pioneers in Iran, Afghanistan and in the Persian Gulf. I spoke in English and a woman professor translated into Italian.

I also was able to meet Mrs Giachery, who invited me for tea. Her husband was in Haifa. They had moved to Italy five years before and were encouraged by the progress the Faith had made in such a short time. A Local Spiritual Assembly had been formed in Rome. Mrs Giachery introduced me to Professor Fiorentini, the secretary of the Local Assembly.

One of the things we talked about was racial prejudice in the United States. I came from a country where prejudice was based on religion rather than race, and had difficulty understanding how strong racial hatred could be. I had always considered prejudice as an attribute of backward countries and was surprised that it could still exist in the modern American civilization. Mrs Giachery told me a story about her husband. He had once gone out walking in the streets of New York with an old Bahá'í friend of his, Mr Louis Gregory. When he returned, some friends ran up to him, saying how shocked they were by his behaviour.

'How could you go out in public like that with a Negro? What will people think? Have you no pride?'

With an ironic twinkle in his eye, Dr Giachery apologized.

'The man was so kind and lovely that, believe me, I completely forgot that he was black.'

I returned to Rome and went to the Iranian embassy. Very few Iranians travelled in those days and the ambassador was glad to meet me. He advised me to go to the British consul for my visa. The local consul had a reputation for being helpful.

I went to the British consul's office and applied for a visa to Tanganyika, now Tanzania. I was nervous but tried not to show it as I explained to a consular official who seemed quite friendly that I had some savings and wanted to see if there was a possibility of setting up a business. I was given a three month entry visa with little ado, as if it was a very run of the mill operation.

I smiled and shook the official's hand, trying to be as casual about it as he was. As soon as I was out of the building, I jumped in the air and laughed out loud. Italy was a beautiful country and it was a beautiful day and I was going to Africa!

Back in Tabriz, I settled my affairs and drew all of the money out of my savings account; it amounted to more than £3000. Then I began making arrangements for a one-way trip to Africa. I could have flown all the way but the cheapest way to reach East Africa was to fly to Bombay and sail by ship from Bombay to Dar-es-Salaam. I knew that my savings had to last me until I could find a job and a regular salary. Unlike missionaries, Bahá'í pioneers have to earn their living by finding jobs in the countries they go to.

One day in early November 1952, I stood on the airfield outside Tehran watching porters load a four-engine former military transport airplane that had been left behind by the Allied forces stationed in Iran and converted into a makeshift commercial airliner. The

November sun was still warm but dry yellow leaves from a stand of birch trees were swirling across the runway, carried by a cold wind from the north. I looked at the distant stand of trees and wondered if there would be birch trees in Africa.

The plane was scheduled to take off around noon. A small tanker truck finished fuelling the plane and backed away. A crowd of well-wishers clustered around the travellers. It was easy to pick out the passengers. They clutched their hand luggage and wore a look of repressed excitement. In those days travelling abroad was still a major event and no one pretended to be blasé about flying.

Ali Akbar was there to see me off. During the five years that we had worked together, the mutual respect that we had started with had developed into real affection. He may have been hoping that I would change my mind at the last moment, but I was excited and happy about the adventure ahead of me. Through the years we have kept in touch and I still consider him a true friend.

There were also many Bahá'í friends. They all had friends or relatives who were pioneers but in those days very few Iranians went to Africa. Although it was not that far away, in our minds the 'Dark Continent' remained a mystery, the fantastical setting for adventure movies.

My brothers were there with their wives and children. Aziz's son Fuad was five and Ehsan's daughter Zohreh was two. I embraced the children, knowing I would miss them, and I kissed my sister goodbye and shook hands with her husband. I remember I was holding my briefcase in one hand and my mother held on to my other hand as if she would never let me go. Although her eyes were red as if she had been crying, her smile was calm and serene. When the passengers were told to board, she looked up at me and said, 'I will manage. You do what God wants you to do.'

Now that the moment of departure was near, I had mixed feelings. Ali Akbar's business promised to become very important. Perhaps I should have waited and got married before leaving for Africa. But what Persian girl in her right mind would want to go to Africa? We Persians are proud of our ancient culture; there was nothing about the untamed jungles of Africa to attract us. I did not know when I would return, when or where I would see my loved ones again.

I walked up the gangway, turned to wave goodbye one last time and found my seat. The propellers began to turn slowly, then accelerated. Like a reluctant bear, the big heavy plane began to move down the runway, then it was moving along, its powerful motors roaring, there was a bump and suddenly the cumbersome plane was weightless in the air. Through the porthole I saw a flash of barren plains, a distant glimpse of Tehran, a little cluster of buildings nestled against the side of the mountain. After that I could see nothing but yellow desert, miles and miles of dry, sandy plains.

We landed in Karachi for a 24-hour stopover. As the passengers left the air-conditioned plane we were hit by the hot, humid air of the low-lying coastal region. An old bus transported us to a nearby hotel. On the streets I saw a wide variety of costumes, races and nationalities. There were Afghan mountaineers wearing their traditional robes, Sikhs in turbans, Pakistanis in their pyjama-like suits and even a few Tibetans.

In the hotel restaurant a large overhead fan turned slowly. It was so hot that the waiters were dripping with perspiration. Seated with a German businessman on his way to Bombay, I ate a very spicy curry which made me sweat even more. After supper the rooms were too hot for sleeping, so I stayed on the terrace with my dinner companion and chatted. When I went to bed, I lay awake, listening to the sounds coming from the street. Watchdogs barked and an occasional voice spoke words I couldn't understand. The early morning call to prayers from a nearby minaret woke me up. Shortly afterwards someone knocked on my door. It was time to leave for the airport.

The plane took off and the stewardesses served breakfast. I dozed off. When I woke up the plane was circling over Bombay. I saw a vast agglomeration of tiny shacks and the wide muddy river flowing to the sea. When I stepped out of the plane, the first thing that struck me was the stuffy, humid heat and the stench.

I took a taxi to the hotel. The streets were crowded with multitudes of people of different nationalities, castes and creeds. I saw women in brightly-coloured saris and women in black chadors, bearded Sikhs in ''
priests in flowing robes, naked beggar
with parasols and a few Englishmen
The odour of multitudes of unwashed b

garbage was laced with peppery sauces cooking on char-coal braziers installed beside the curb. Sidewalk vendors hawked their wares in a dozen languages. A turbaned traffic officer in shorts was trying to regulate the movements of cars, push carts and zebus without any apparent success. I was reminded of Tehran's Lalezar Street where no one respected traffic lights, but the clothes were more varied and colourful.

I had seen Sikh soldiers with the British army in Iran, but in Bombay I saw their women and children. The little boys wore a simple net over a bunch of hair the size of a ping pong ball. Young boys wore brightly-coloured turbans like those of their fathers. Women sitting beside the sidewalk sold oranges, mangos, bananas, samosas, candies and cigarettes.

My hotel was the cheapest one listed by the travel agency, a shabby old building in a poor section of Bombay. Its only furniture was a bed and a sink. A large fan hung from the ceiling, languidly stirring the hot air. When I saw that the door had no lock, I began to worry about being robbed because I was carrying all my money in traveller's checks. Before going to sleep I wrapped the pouch containing my traveller's checks in a scarf and tied it around my waist under my pyjamas. I thought of the Arabian proverb attributed to Muhammad, 'Trust in God but tie up your camel.' In spite of the large fan squeaking overhead, the heat was intense and the noise from the street dwellers outside went on undiminished all night. I lay awake, too excited to be able to sleep. Around twelve 'clock I got up and walked outside. To my surprise the streets were full of people. Hundreds were stretched out on the pavement, sleeping. Others were talking quietly, sitting around their little fires, cooking food. I had never dreamed there could be so many poor people in the world. I walked among them until early morning when I returned to the hotel and finally fell into an exhausted slumber.

At nine o'clock a.m. someone knocked loudly on the door and walked into my room. I sat up in bed, startled out of my sleep. The visitor introduced himself as Mr Ardeshir, sent by the travel agency to make the final arrangements for my trip. He was a friendly young man, an Indian Parsi. He spoke English, of course, but also a dialect of Farsi that I had no trouble understanding. He checked my papers and pointed out that I had no yellow fever vaccination. No one in Tehran had told me it would be necessary.

'Your ship, the SS *Kampala*, leaves in 48 hours. Unless you have your vaccination papers, the shipping company won't issue you a ticket. The vaccination is given only in certain centres on certain days and is valid after two weeks. Without the certificate you will have to wait and take the next ship for Dar-es-Salaam, which may be a month from now.'

A month's wait in Bombay would have used up all the money I had saved by not flying. But I felt certain that if it was God's Will that I go to Dar-es-Salaam we would be able to solve the problem. I dressed and ordered tea for two.

A small boy carried up the tea. It was a lukewarm

mixture of milk, water, tea and sugar that bore little resemblance to hot, fragrant Iranian tea. While I was trying to drink my tea, Ardeshir summed up the situation.

'You do not need a vaccination. What you need is a vaccination certificate. Do you have any Indian rupees?'

'Yes, I have.'

'How much?'

'A hundred, two hundred rupees.'

'That may be enough to pay the doctor.'

I was surprised. 'Doctors are very expensive here.'

'No, they are quite cheap. But buying a false certificate is expensive. Come along, I think I know a doctor who can help us. He works in one of the city hospitals.'

When we got to the hospital, the doctor explained that the vaccination was valid only after a second shot taken two weeks after the first. He would give me a first shot and issue me a certificate testifying that I had had both shots, but I would have to be sure and get my second shot once I reached Dar-es-Salaam. Ardeshir explained that the doctor expected to be paid for his cooperation. I wondered which was worse, missing my ship or contributing to the corruption of a civil servant. Offering a bribe seemed like a poor beginning for my pioneering mission, but it also seemed too ridiculous to wait in Bombay for a month because of a technicality. Reluctantly I came to the conclusion that no one would be hurt by my action. Ardeshir realized I was having qualms.

'Don't worry,' he said. 'You'll get the second shot when you land and everything will be okay. The doctor trusts you to keep your word. It's not the first time he has rendered this service. Be thankful he's willing to help you.'

So I paid the doctor and the next day, 11 November 1952, I was ready to board the SS *Kampala*, a Union Castle liner, bound for Zanzibar, Dar-es-Salaam and Durban in South Africa. Ardeshir took me through customs and the immigration department. It may have been part of his job, but I was grateful for his company, for he was the only person I knew in India. Ardeshir seemed to understand and stayed with me until the last minute. He told me that he envied me. Someday he too would like to sail away to a foreign land, to visit one of the exotic names on the tickets he handled every day. I was reminded of my own childhood dream of being a sailor.

The wharf was crowded with relatives and friends waving goodbye to the passengers. A brass band was playing on the top deck and pink, yellow and blue spirals of paper confetti flew through the air. The confusion on the wharf was indescribable. Hindus, Pakistanis, Goans and Ceylonese were shouting in a dozen different dialects. There were sari-clad mothers with babies tied behind and fathers who seemed to be carrying all their household furniture on their backs. They gripped their cardboard suitcases tied shut with ropes and belts and argued with the Indian police constables in khaki uniforms who were vainly trying to maintain order. Two officials in civilian clothes stood by the gangplank and checked the papers of boarding passengers. There was so much pushing and shoving going on that it seemed a miracle no one fell into the dark, oily waters between the ship and the wharf. Sometimes someone tried to board without the right papers and was pushed back into the crowd, adding his cries of protest to the havoc.

'Where are they all going?' I asked a tall, grey-haired man standing beside me.

'They are Indian labourers who are going to work in East Africa with their families. Some of them are legal immigrants and have contracts with the railroad or construction companies. Others are illegal immigrants and hope to find work. They have forged papers, bought in the market at a high price, and are willing to do any kind of work.'

We second class passengers embarked with slightly less pandemonium from a different part of the wharf. I shook hands with Ardeshir and waved goodbye as I went up the gangplank. Further down the wharf I saw the first class passengers leisurely boarding the ship. They were all Europeans, mostly British civil servants and their wives and families.

The whistle blew and the SS *Kampala* began pulling out of the port. An hour later Bombay's tall buildings were spread out on the horizon and for the first time I realized how enormous the city was. The sky was clear and cloudless.

Once we were on the high seas the band stopped playing. Pink and blue tapes hung from the first class passenger deck, gleaming in the afternoon sun. Cool breezes ran over the waves, lifting the strips of confetti and carrying them away, like housekeepers cleaning up after a party. The ship's powerful motors churned away, pushing it through the high seas. I stayed on deck, watching tall purple clouds pile up in the west.

Overhead a squadron of seagulls accompanied the SS *Kampala*, their shrill cries adding to my feeling of loneliness and my anxiety. Was I doing the right thing in leaving not only a lucrative business but also my family and friends? After all, I had been serving the Cause in Tabriz. Other Bahá'ís could teach in Africa. The Europeans were familiar with their colonies and would have much less trouble fitting in. I couldn't pretend that it was going to be easy to live in and adapt to a culture that I knew almost nothing about. Then the sun sank into the western ocean, sending golden rays across the ocean surface. Its beauty brought me a sense of calm and the inner joy of setting out on a great adventure.

To save money I was travelling second class, sandwiched between the top and lower decks. I shared my cabin with five others, three Indians and two Goans. I soon made friends with Mr Nair Patel, the tall man I had talked to before boarding. He was an Indian lawyer, about 50 years old, who lived in Durban. Courteous and well-educated, he could talk intelligently on almost any subject and knew a lot about Iran, although he had never been there. During the long days of the crossing I spent many hours listening to him tell about his life in Africa. Mr Patel was curious to know what an Iranian intended to do in Africa. The only Iranians he knew of there were diplomats. In need of labourers, the British colonies brought in Hindu, Pakistani and Chinese workmen, tradesmen and middle-class professionals but there were almost no Persians.

My other berth mates were young civil servants and bank clerks. They were very friendly and in spite of the crowded conditions in the tiny cabin we got along quite well. All of them had been born in Africa and had gone to visit relatives in India in the hope of finding a bride. They told me all about their adventures and misadventures and close calls with a great deal of humour. But I particularly enjoyed my long conversations with Mr Patel and spent a lot of my time with him.

Every evening around six o'clock we saw European women in long dresses and men in tuxedos taking the air on the first class deck, waiting for the cocktails to be served while the band played dance music.

Most of the second class passengers were middle-class Indians going back to Africa after a holiday in their native land. There were no Europeans. One man that I had taken for a European was 'half-caste' according to Mr Patel. Of mixed blood, he was not readily accepted by either race and spent most of the trip alone.

The third class passengers were lodged in the depths of the ship, next to the engine rooms. They were mostly new immigrants and small shopkeepers returning to Africa with merchandise they had bought in India. They were packed in like cattle and the sanitary system, barely adequate when they left Bombay, soon degraded.

The second day out the young purser announced that fresh water was to be used only for drinking. For the rest of the journey the lower class passengers had to take showers and brush their teeth with briny sea water.

The food was Indian curry or a tasteless imitation of

English cooking, but it was regular and nourishing and no one was getting enough exercise to be really hungry. At lunch and dinner time the ship corridors were filled with the spicy odour of curry coming from the lower deck. The strong smell would last until late at night when the evening breeze blew in some fresh air.

I spent as much time as possible on deck, watching the vast, empty ocean that stretched to the horizon. I liked to say my prayers there early in the morning. The ship seemed a tiny island of humanity afloat in an immense universe, a blue infinity that only God could comprehend. I was reminded of the verses of my daily prayer:

> Too high art Thou for the praise of those who are nigh unto Thee to ascend unto the heaven of Thy nearness, or for the birds of the hearts of them who are devoted to Thee to attain to the door of Thy gate.[4]

I often went to the stern of the ship and looked for the dolphins that seemed to accompany the SS *Kampala* on its crossing. Frequently the siren would wail a greeting to another liner or a freighter that came over the western horizon, passed and disappeared in the east. For the passengers in their deck chairs who found the crossing long, watching the lonely vessels slowly approach and then dwindle out of sight was an occupation that took up several hours of the day.

One day while I was sitting on deck with Mr Patel, I asked him why he was travelling in the overcrowded second class. From some things that Mr Patel had said, I understood that his practice in Durban was prosperous and it seemed that the price of a first class ticket would not have been an obstacle. The Indian gentleman looked at me; he may have wondered how innocent my question was. Then he told me that living in the British colonies I would soon become familiar with the 'colour bar'. If Mr Patel had requested a first class ticket he would have been told that there was no room left. If he had managed to buy a ticket through someone else, his fellow passengers would have ostracized him for the entire 12-day crossing, making him understand that he had overstepped the bounds. He described his life in Durban. There were hotels and restaurants for 'whites only' where he could not go. He could not send his children to school with white children; they did not even use the same beaches.

'Because of the colour of my skin, I am a second class citizen,' he said. 'I have been told by friends who live in East Africa and Rhodesia, where you intend to go, that segregation is as strong there as it is in South Africa. The only difference is that in South Africa it is written into the constitution and in the other colonies it is an unwritten law.'

I wanted to comfort my friend.

'There will come a day when there will be no more segregation. Bahá'u'lláh, the founder of the Bahá'í Faith, said, "The earth is but one country, and mankind its citizens."[5] One day men will live in peace and harmony on this earth, one united family.'

Mr Patel smiled. 'Those are wonderful ideas. Unfortunately I have seen enough of the world to know that there is little chance of their ever being put into practice.' He looked across the sea. 'Yet I have no desire to return to live in India. My parents came from there as railway workers. In their native land I would never have had the opportunities I had in Africa, receiving an education, becoming a lawyer. I may suffer from prejudice, but I still love the land I was born in. Africa is beautiful. You will see. After a while you too will love it.'

Then Mr Patel smiled, as if afraid he had been too serious.

'Don't worry. With your fair skin and blue eyes, you will have no problems. Do many Persians have blue eyes?'

I laughed. 'No. But they say that my paternal grandfather had blue eyes and was nicknamed "the Russian".'

Afterwards I thought a lot about Mr Patel's description of racial prejudice. In Iran I had seen a few black people, descended from slaves that had been brought to Iran in ancient times. As house servants and nannies, they were considered members of the family, to be loved and cared for in their old age.

After nine days on the high seas we had our first sight of land, Zanzibar, the fabled land of cloves. The SS *Kampala* docked and the passengers were allowed to visit the island during the half day it would take the ship to unload cargo.

The first thing I noticed was not the fragrance of cloves but the odour of highly spiced curries cooking in homes all over the town. The dark-skinned people were tall and slender with handsome faces. They wore long, ample Arabian robes and headgear. The traders in the small shops and the restaurant owners appeared to be Indians.

In a small side street I saw a sign that said 'Persian Restaurant'. Delighted at the idea of having some real Persian food and meeting a fellow countryman so far from home, I walked in. A large portrait of the old Shah adorned one side wall. A young man hurried from the back to greet me. I asked him in Farsi. 'Are you Iranian?'

The restaurant owner looked bewildered and then surprised.

'Yes – no,' he stuttered. 'Wait.'

Then he disappeared in the back of his shop. After a while he returned with his father, who spoke in a southern Persian dialect that I recognized. The old man was very happy to meet someone from Iran and we had a long talk. He explained that his son had been born in Zanzibar and understood very little Farsi. He had not heard about the old Shah's abdication and wondered where he could find a portrait of the new Shah to put up in his restaurant. He had originally come from a small port in southern Persia where since ancient times small *dhows* travelled back and forth across the Persian Gulf, trading between the Arab countries and the African coast. He told me that Persians had settled in Zanzibar long before the Arabs and many of the oldest families still called themselves Shirazi, after their original home. The Sultan of Zanzibar was said to be of Shirazi descent.

The next day we reached Dar-es-Salaam in the British colony of Tanganyika. The port being too shallow for its tonnage, the ship anchored beyond the bar in deep water. Immigration officials boarded and began checking the documents of the disembarking passengers. I stood in line for what seemed a very long time, waiting my turn. I worried that the travel agency, which had not informed me about the yellow fever vaccination, might have forgotten some other necessary document. I heard someone saying that if a passenger's papers were not in order, the immigration officials would make him return to India on the same ship.

Finally it was my turn and I stepped up to a young, red-faced officer who looked more bored than threatening.

'What are you going to do in Tanganyika?' he asked, glancing at the tourist visa delivered in Rome.

'Visit with some friends,' I replied.

The Englishman nodded, stamped my passport and handed it back.

'Your visa is valid for one month. If you stay longer you will have to have it extended.'

Boats came out to take the passengers ashore. There was a spacious launch for the first class passengers, while the other classes were packed into small, unreliable-looking craft. I heard someone shouting my name and saw a dark-haired man in a motorboat alongside the ship. Informed of my arrival, the pioneers in Dar-es-Salaam had sent Jalal Nakhjavani to meet me. Jalal worked for a ship chandler, so he was able to use his company's boat to pick me up. I clambered into the little motorboat and had an exciting ride across the harbour. Looking back, I had my last glimpse of the SS *Kampala*. It was continuing its journey to Beira, Lorenço Marques and Durban. On the second class deck I thought I saw Mr Patel waving goodbye to me.

Jalal Nakhjavani had arrived in East Africa in 1951, the first pioneer to settle in the region. He and his wife received me with true Persian hospitality in the house they rented from an Indian trader. The other pioneers in the small Bahá'í community were eager to meet me. I brought news and messages from Iran and they had many things to tell me about life in Africa. After dinner we sat on the veranda where it was cool, drinking tea and talking late into the night. Jalal related funny stories about his adventures and misadventures in Africa. Hassan Sabri, an Egyptian engineer and his American wife, Isobel, told me they had a spare room I could use. The pioneers were not numerous and they had little money, but they were all excited at the idea of conquering a new continent for their Faith.

Kenya

. . . religious, racial, political, economic and patriotic prejudices destroy the edifice of humanity.[1]

'Abdu'l-Bahá

The next morning I had an early breakfast of mangoes, hot Quaker Oats and tea with Isobel and Hassan. We sat in front of an open window that let in the cool morning air, then Hassan left for the automobile agency where he worked. Afterwards I looked over the house, a delightful hybrid of American ingenuity, Oriental comfort and African colour. Built in a European style with whitewashed, cement-plastered adobe walls, the house had high ceilings under a thatched roof.

With simple furnishings Isobel had made a clean and comfortable home. There were bookshelves with books in English, Persian and Arabic. Cushions in bright African prints made the rattan furniture more comfortable and the same colourful prints hung as curtains at the windows. Woven mats were spread on the floor. In the living room there were rattan armchairs, an American rocking chair and goatskin cushions. A portrait of 'Abdu'l-Bahá hung on the wall.

Isobel proudly showed me her garden. The house stood on a hill in the outskirts of Dar-es-Salaam, which

I could see in the distance. Isobel had planted a dozen varieties of hibiscus plants and red bougainvilleas along the fence. In front of the terrace grew red and yellow cannas and orange lilies. While she showed me around we talked about the pioneers' life in Africa. She gave me several health tips.

'You must be sure that your drinking water is boiled and filtered. Never drink water in the villages, but tea is all right if the water has boiled a good five minutes. Sleep under a mosquito net and take your quinine and salt tablets regularly. Malaria is no joke. Be sure you look in your shoes before you put them on. Scorpions like to hide in shoes.'

Isobel and Hassan had met while Hassan was a student in London. She had come from the States to work with the British Bahá'ís. When Hassan finished his studies they married and volunteered as pioneers.

Since I was eager to have my first good look at Africa, Isobel suggested that I walk into town while she cleaned house and prepared lunch. As I walked along the dusty road, I met people coming from the market. The women carried their purchases in shopping bags balanced on their heads. Both men and women greeted me with friendly familiarity. 'Jambo. Jambo.' I smiled back at them and replied, 'Jambo.' Goats and pigs grazed by the side of the road, searching piles of garbage for anything edible. Little brown toddlers wearing nothing but a string around their waists stopped their games and stared at me in unabashed curiosity.

The native market was a collection of tiny booths

selling canned goods, cloth, shoes, patent medicines and soap. Market women sat on the ground beside their produce piled on spread-out leaves. They sold eggs, small black chickens, green bananas, and mysterious tubers of different shapes and sizes. Rice, millet and tapioca were heaped in shining piles and measured in old tin cans. I bought a pineapple from an old woman with gleeful black eyes. She spoke only Swahili, holding up her fingers to show me the price. Whatever she was saying, her neighbours thought it very witty. I suspected that it was the price of the pineapple that made them laugh.

Beside the native market there were many small stores run by Indians, reminding me of Bombay. They sold a wide variety of imported goods, textiles, patent medicine, soap, toothbrushes and kerosene lamps. Downtown the buildings were larger and more modern. There were comfortable hotels, restaurants, department stores and showrooms for modern appliances and automobiles. When I had finished looking around, I walked back to the Sabri house, carrying my pineapple under one arm. Now that the sun was up, it was getting hot. After lunch Isobel advised me to follow the local custom and take a nap.

That evening the Sabris and I went to visit the Nakhjavani family. A pretty young Englishwoman named Hazel also stopped by. Her husband was an Indian lawyer. She was not a Bahá'í but enjoyed the Nakhjavanis' company and often came to see them. Later in the evening an elderly gentleman came by. He was one of the first African Bahá'ís and had translated *Bahá'u'lláh and the*

New Era, a book by a British author, into Swahili. I had several Bahá'í books in Persian and English in my luggage and thought that it would be a good idea to obtain books and pamphlets in Swahili.

After dinner we sat out on the terrace with a kerosene lamp. Dr Farhoumand, a Persian doctor who had recently joined the pioneers, came by with another Persian, Mr Yazdani, and their families. Soon the mosquitoes began to bite. Jalal set out burning coils that gave off an acrid smoke; he reminded me to take my malaria tablets.

Looking up, I saw a strange, transparent lizard hanging upside down from the ceiling. 'What's that?

Everyone laughed.

'That's a gecko,' replied the Persian doctor. 'They're friendly and you don't want to chase them away because they eat mosquitoes.'

Most of my new friends had come to Africa within the last year. They enjoyed telling me horror stories about their many encounters with snakes and scorpions.

'Do you know how to tell how long someone has been living in Africa?' asked Jalal with a grin.

'No,' I replied.

'When a newcomer finds a fly in his drink, he pours out the drink and asks for a clean glass. After a year, he just flicks the fly off and swallows his drink. After five years he wrings the fly out before he throws it away.'

When I went to my room that night, I carefully inspected my suitcase and put the underclothes I was to wear the next day under my pillow, where the scorpions couldn't get into them, then crawled under the mosquito net and tucked it in. This was to become my standard procedure for the next several years.

The pioneers were all excited about the coming Bahá'í conference in Kampala. At that time there was only a handful of newly arrived pioneers living south of the Sahara. They were expecting visitors from Haifa, England, Iran and the United States. It was to be a great event for those who lived in lonely outposts. They were looking forward to being able to share their problems, their worries, their difficulties, their joys, their little victories, their hopes.

I stayed with the Sabris for a month and they kindly helped me adapt to life in Africa. Before my visa expired, I was able to obtain another visa for Kenya.

By then Aziz Yazdi, whom I had met in Tehran, and his family were living in Nairobi. The tall, enthusiastic pioneer had gone to Northern Rhodesia but had not been able to obtain a residence permit. So he had rented an office in downtown Nairobi and was developing a business representing pharmaceutical companies. He and Soraya were living with their children in a boarding house where several other pioneers had rooms. There was Ted Cardell, an Englishman who was a professional photographer, and two other Persians, one of whom was married to an Englishwoman. I enjoyed the Yazdis' company and frequently accompanied Aziz on trips into the bush where we were able to meet with Africans in their villages and talk about our Faith.

I learned a great deal about teaching on the trips I made with Aziz. My tall friend was friendly and relaxed in his teaching. He would stop in a village and introduce himself to the headman. No matter how poor the village was, we were always greeted with African hospitality. The chief offered us warm beer or soda pop. We gently refused the beer and accepted the soda pop. We kept the conversation general until a crowd of curious listeners had gathered. Then we explained that we were Bahá'ís, that we had come to share our beliefs with the Africans. We gave a brief description of Bahá'í principles and asked if the headman would like us to return another day to talk about our religion. Sometimes we met with suspicion, sometimes with indifference and sometimes the villagers were afraid of offending the local missionaries. Yet often there was enough curiosity that we were invited back, and Aziz and I would continue visiting the village as long as we felt we were welcome. We gave out brochures and willingly answered questions, praying that some of our listeners would decide to declare their belief in Bahá'u'lláh. We never told our listeners that their former beliefs were wrong. On the contrary, we stressed that Bahá'ís recognize both Jesus and Muhammad as divine Messengers. I repeated to myself the verse from *Gleanings from the Writings of Bahá'u'lláh* which says,

> Whoso ariseth among you to teach the Cause of his Lord, let him, before all else, teach his own self, that his speech may attract the hearts of them that hear him. Unless he teacheth his own self, the words of his mouth will not influence the heart of the seeker.[2]

During this time I did not attempt to find work, for I

thought that after the conference in Uganda I would have a better idea of where I could best serve the Cause.

In Nairobi I soon encountered the colour distinctions which Mr Patel had warned me about. The few Iranians then living in British East Africa were considered Europeans, like the Lebanese. The arbitrariness of these supposedly racial distinctions was visible in the fact that Parsis from Pakistan and India, Persian by race and language, were 'Asians' while blacks coming from the British Honduras were classified as 'Europeans'. If you were considered European, you automatically received better pay and housing. As a measure of survival in a society which defined different degrees of citizenship, the Persians had to maintain their standing as 'Europeans' to be able to send their children to the better schools and to be allowed to go into all the quarters of the cities. As 'Asians' it would have been difficult to visit the restricted quarters and to find jobs which could give them the financial means of continuing their work for the Faith.

In Nairobi I had the opportunity to meet a remarkable Bahá'í, Richard St Barbe Baker. He was known around the world as 'the man of the trees' because he travelled all over the globe teaching the basic principles of conservation, fighting against deforestation and encouraging villagers to plant trees. He had first come to Kenya in 1920 as an Assistant Conservator of Forests for the colonial administration. He worked among the native Kikuyu, creating a society that he named 'The Men of the Trees', whose members pledged to plant trees and protect the forest. In a project in Nigeria he developed the concept of sustainable yield, convincing lumbermen that they were destroying their capital when they clear cut the tropical forests and advocating selective tree felling, a method now widely practised in West Africa.

St Barbe Baker had lost his job with the colonial government for taking the defence of an African being beaten by a European. Shortly afterwards he encountered the Bahá'í Faith and became a believer. In 1929 he went to Palestine to meet Shoghi Effendi and organized a conference of representatives of the major religions to promote a plan to reforest desert areas.

I met St Barbe after he had created the World Forestry Charter, a forum to provide for an exchange of ideas among the representatives of countries around the world. He had set the organization the task of reclaiming the Sahara Desert, making a 26,000 mile exploratory trip across the Sahara in a secondhand yellow army Humber. He knew the roads of East Africa as well as he knew the Bahá'í scriptures.

When St Barbe offered to take me to the conference in Uganda in his old Humber station wagon, I was delighted. It was a memorable trip and a wonderful opportunity to make it in the company of a man who knew the region so well. We travelled by night, when there was less heat and traffic. The sky was beautiful. Far from the pollution of artificial city lights, the stars appeared with an immediacy and brilliance I had never seen before. St Barbe asked me to chant a prayer in Persian. I recited the lovely words by heart and got so carried away that he finally told me to stop, that that was enough.

He told fascinating stories about his adventures. In the middle of the Sahara desert, at the well of Ekker, he had met an old rest house keeper who described 'the Last Forest', a vast wooded area that had existed around the well when he was a boy. The Englishman was convinced that the desert had once been wooded savannah and could be reclaimed. He explained to me that when he travelled in the desert the only supplies he carried were water and nuts, which were nourishing and took up little space.

I asked him how he had become a Bahá'í, and St Barbe chuckled.

'How not to? When I met the Bahá'ís I recognized a world vision that I had been struggling to articulate all my life. What other religion integrates science and religion in one truth? Who else has a concept of "a planetary civilization based on ecological and spiritual principles"?'[3]

In Kampala I saw Jalal Nakhjavani's brother, Ali. We had met before in Tehran and fell into each others' arms like lost brothers. Ali's father-in-law, Musa Banani, had been a prosperous businessman in Tehran when he learned that Shoghi Effendi wanted pioneers in Africa. He sold his company and moved to Kampala. His daughter Violette, her husband Ali and their daughter, Bahiyyih, moved with him. Mr Banani had just been given the title of 'Hand of the Cause' by Shoghi Effendi.[4]

It was both a great honour and a great responsibility, for the Hands of the Cause were teachers who dedicated their lives to travelling throughout the world, working for the Cause. I also had the chance to meet Philip

Hainsworth, a young British pioneer, and Clair Gung, who wanted to open a school.

The pioneers of Kampala were bubbling with enthusiasm. The first African Bahá'ís had declared their belief in Bahá'u'lláh just a year before. I met one of them, a remarkable young government employee named Enoch Olinga. He was a husky young man with a wide grin who shook my hand with enthusiasm. His intelligence and his profound devotion to the Faith impressed me.

Before becoming a Bahá'í, Enoch had a drinking problem which eventually cost him his government job. A friend of his had introduced him to Ali Nakhjavani. He began going regularly to meetings at the Banani house, attracted by the warm fellowship. After one meeting he returned late at night and asked Philip Hainsworth and Ali to answer some questions that were bothering him. He went home and sat up all night, thinking over all he had learned about the new religion. Early the next morning he went to Ali's door with a letter declaring his belief in Bahá'u'lláh. He stopped drinking and when his wife saw the change in his behaviour, she too became a Bahá'í. Enoch decided to leave Kampala and return to his home town of Teso. Since then, through his enthusiastic teaching, entire villages had been brought to the Faith. Over two hundred new believers came to the conference from Teso, three hundred kilometres away. Enoch Olinga was planning to accompany Ali on a trip to West Africa to open to the Bahá'í Faith territories where there were no Bahá'ís. He was later to become the first African Hand of the Cause.

From Haifa Shoghi Effendi was closely following the

events of the Intercontinental Conference in Kampala. He had sent a message outlining the Ten Year Crusade, a plan to spread the Bahá'í teachings around the world. The plan was breathtakingly ambitious, for in 1952 the Bahá'ís were a small, insignificant community, persecuted in their homeland and little known elsewhere. There were only twelve countries with National Spiritual Assemblies. Shoghi Effendi's plan was nothing less than to spread the Bahá'í Faith to every country, territory and island in the world.

The Guardian had also sent a portrait of the Báb to bestow a spiritual blessing on the gathering and as a special honour to the newly-enrolled African Bahá'ís. The painting, the only one made during the Báb's lifetime, was usually kept in Haifa and shown only to pilgrims. The new believers were deeply moved by the Guardian's attention and the opportunity to view the painting of the young prophet.

Whenever Bahá'ís gather, you can expect diversity. In Kampala there were Americans, British, Persians, Indians, Belgians and many Africans. The white population of Kampala was shocked to see whites and blacks meeting as equals, eating together, sharing their homes, greeting each other in public with hugs and kisses of welcome. We were regarded suspiciously as some kind of political movement and several critical articles appeared in the local newspaper concerning 'This Bahá'í Business'. The colonial authorities considered radical and dangerous any movement which proclaimed racial equality and publicly practised what it preached.

But we Bahá'ís had survived far more violent persecutions than raised eyebrows and a few critical articles in the local press. We went on planning the spiritual conquest of the 'Dark Continent'. Shoghi Effendi had named 33 virgin territories in Africa which needed to be opened to the Faith.

I and the other young pioneers, and some pioneers who were no longer very young, were eager to put Shoghi Effendi's plan into operation. We all gathered around a map of Africa which showed where the present pioneers were living and looked for the empty spaces, the countries listed in the plan. Someone would put a finger on the map and say, 'I'll go here'. And what had been a strange name and an empty space on a map became their home for years, sometimes for the rest of their life.

No Bahá'ís were then living in the Portuguese colony of Mozambique, although a travelling teacher had visited and made a few contacts. I had dropped my original idea of going to Rhodesia and thought Mozambique sounded interesting. Soheili, a young Parsi whom I had become friends with, also thought he would like to go there, so we divided the country between us. I would go to the capital, Lorenço Marques, in the southern lowlands, and Soheili would go to Beira, the main port in the northern highlands. I left the conference full of enthusiasm. I was young and healthy, I had no immediate financial worries and I had a worthy purpose to strive for.

In Nairobi I obtained a tourist visa to Mozambique valid for one month. When I flew to Lorenço Marques my first goal was to find a job that would allow me to stay in the country.

Someone had told me that the Polana Hotel was the best in town. I thought that staying there would allow me to get acquainted with people who could help me find a job and obtain a residence permit.

The Polana Hotel had an orchestra, a swimming pool and a good restaurant but I quickly realized that if I stayed there long, my savings would soon be gone. I looked around and found a comfortable boarding house run by a Portuguese family.

I soon made friends among the other boarders and occasional travellers. One of them, Gordon Kallen, a businessman from Salisbury, said that he had a job for me in his commission agency in Southern Rhodesia. I thanked him but hoped to find something in Lorenço Marques. Friends in the boarding house in Nairobi had given me the address of their Portuguese contacts in Lorenço Marques. They in turn had introduced me to a lawyer who suggested I create an import–export company. The lawyer said that it was difficult for foreigners to settle in Mozambique, but not impossible. In the meantime I refrained from teaching activities.

I received a cable saying that a group of pioneers on their way to South Africa would be stopping over in Lorenço Marques. I checked with the shipping company and was in the port to greet them when they arrived on 14 April 1953.

Fred Schechter was a young American travelling with an older couple, Mr and Mrs Laws. Fred and I quickly became good friends. Fred told me about his experiences as the first pioneer to Djibouti. Shoghi Effendi had named him a Knight of Bahá'u'lláh, a distinction given to pioneers who opened new territories to the Faith. Before he left, Fred offered me a prayer book in English, writing on the inside cover, 'To Ezzat, with prayers for countless confirmations throughout Africa'.

After a day I accompanied my friends back to their ship and they continued on their journey to South Africa.

One morning shortly afterwards I was woken up by someone banging loudly on my door. I looked at the alarm clock and saw it was only six o'clock. When I opened the door I found myself face to face with a tall, stern-looking man wearing a police uniform and carrying a pistol in a holster on his belt.

'Are you Mr Zahrai? You are under arrest. Get dressed, we're taking you to headquarters.'

Another officer followed him into the room and they confiscated my books, letters, papers, photographs and camera. As soon as I was dressed, they took me downstairs. I felt bewildered and humiliated at being hustled along in front of the boarders just rising for breakfast. I could only imagine that it was some kind of ridiculous mistake. The police officers told me to climb into the back of a military jeep parked in front.

As we drove through the streets, I grew dismayed and a little frightened. I did not know what I had done to attract the attention of the police nor what they intended to do with me. Iran had no diplomatic representation in Mozambique, so I could not expect any aid. If they were going to expel me, my African adventure was at an end.

In the headquarters of the Portuguese secret police, I was left sitting on a bench for over an hour. After a while a clerk told me I could leave but that I must return at two o'clock p.m. He handed me a written summons and said they were keeping the books, papers, photos and other belongings which they had seized in my room.

At two o'clock I returned and was ushered into the office of a Portuguese officer who spoke English. Once again I was asked to give my name, age, place of birth and state my business in Mozambique. My interrogator wanted to know about the conference in Kampala and who had been present. He wanted to know what the Bahá'í Faith was.

'We believe in one God, one religion and one world,' I replied.

'What does that mean?'

'We believe there is only one God, though men worship him with different names in different manners. There is only one religion, for all the divine Messengers have tried to teach men to love one another, to live in peace and harmony. And there is one world, for all men are brothers.'

The police officer frowned.

'Are you Catholics?'

'No, but we respect the Pope and all Catholics who honestly try to practise their religion.'

'Then why aren't you Catholics?'

'We have no priests, no hierarchy. We believe that the Bahá'í Faith is the spiritual renewal of all religions.'

'So you're communists?'

I shook my head, depressed by the turn the conversation was taking.

'No. Communists are atheists. We believe in God, in the same God you believe in.'

'Who is Shoghi Effendi?'

'The great-grandson of Bahá'u'lláh.'

'Who is Bah . . . babala?'

'In 1844 a man we call the Báb, the Gate, declared that God had sent him as a divine Messenger to announce a new era. The Báb said that He would be followed by one greater than He. He was executed by order of the Shah of Iran and nine years later Bahá'u'lláh declared that He was the one that the Báb had announced. He was put in prison, exiled and then imprisoned in St Jean d'Acre, in Palestine. When He died, His son, 'Abdu'l-Bahá, carried on His work. When the Turkish Ottoman Empire fell 'Abdu'l-Bahá was at last free to leave Palestine. Although he was an old man, He went to Europe and the United States and many people listened to His message and adopted His faith. When He died, He appointed His grandson, Shoghi Effendi, Guardian of the Faith.'

'Where does this Shoghi Effendi live?'

'In Haifa, on Mount Carmel.'

The officer pulled my English prayer book out of a drawer and pointed at the dedication Fred Schechter had written.

'Who wrote this? What does he mean by countless confirmations in Africa?'

The interrogation went on and on in this manner until five o'clock, when the officer told me I could leave but that the police would keep in touch with me. They returned most of the articles that had been confiscated but kept all my pictures, my books and my papers, including a letter addressed to me from the Africa Committee in London. To this day I regret that they did not return the letter from the Iranian National Spiritual Assembly saying the Guardian wished me to go to Africa.

I returned to the boarding house feeling very low. I had never before had anything to do with the police and did not know what to think about my situation. I wanted to explain to my boarding house friends why I had been arrested but I found it difficult to justify, since I did not really know myself. My explanations sounded lame, even to my own ears.

Two days later I was again called to the police station by the chief of the secret police. I obeyed the order and was questioned again.

'Who is your God? Allah or the Heavenly Father?'

'Those are names that have been given to God by men. God is above all names, above all that man can conceive. Some men call him Allah, some call him the Heavenly Father.'

During the days that followed, twice I was woken up at six o'clock in the morning and bustled off to the police headquarters. Each time my room was searched and my correspondence confiscated. I wondered if visits were intended to catch me unawares with compromising doc-uments that I might have hidden. A foreigner in a strange land with no one in whom I could confide, no compa-triot, no consul to represent me, I became depressed when I realized that the other boarders seemed to be avoiding me.

The police found among my papers the name of an American Bahá'í living in Lisbon. They wanted to know who she was, where she came from. I answered as honestly as possible. The Bahá'í were not spies nor were they a secret society. Wherever possible our Centres were listed in the telephone book. Once more I was asked who Shoghi Effendi was.

'Is he your God?'

'No. He is the Guardian of the Bahá'í Faith. He has the authority to interpret our sacred scriptures.'

'Who are your friends in Mozambique?'

'I have no friends here.'

'What is that newspaper?'

'It is the *Keyhan*. It is printed in Iran.'

'Is it in favour of Mossadeq or against him?'

'In favour of him.'

'Give me the names of the countries you have visited.'

I listed all the countries I had visited in Africa and in Europe.

'How long did you stay in Austria?'

'I did not stay there. I just passed through on my way to Italy from Germany.'

'Have you been to Sweden?'

'No, sir.'

'Your letters mention the Stockholm Conference. Is that a peace conference?' (In the fifties any activity that was associated with the peace movement was assumed to be inspired by 'Reds' and KGB agents. As long as the cold war lasted, those who were in favour of peace were open to accusations of siding with the enemy, on both sides of the Iron Curtain.)

'It is not a peace conference,' I replied for the tenth or twentieth time. 'It is a Bahá'í conference.'

'Why do you want to "open up" Cape Verde and Mozambique?'

I tried to explain that the cause I represented had no political goals, that we were a spiritual movement, but my interrogator seemed to consider my religion as nothing more than a cover for more material aims. Finally he said that I could leave but that I should be out of the country by the 23rd of May.

I walked out of the police headquarters feeling exhausted. Then I noticed a well-dressed man who had been strolling along behind me for some time and realized that I was being followed. I decided to send a cablegram to my brother in Tehran asking for a transfer of money I had left on my account there. I did not want to use up my travellers' cheques and having to wait for money would give me a reason for staying longer in Mozambique. My cable was also destined to inform my family of my whereabouts.

In the days that followed, every time I left the boarding house I was followed. Sometimes the police were in uniform, sometimes they wore civilian clothes. As a result I stayed in my room whenever possible, not wanting to create problems for the few people I might have visited.

One early dawn the police came to my room again and confiscated the few books and papers I had left. They told me to report immediately to the chief of the secret police. I found my patience wearing thin. I felt angry and wanted to yell at them. If I had committed some crime, broken a law, even unknowingly, why didn't they say what I had done and put me on trial? If not, why didn't they leave me alone? Obviously these repeated arrests were intended to harass me into breaking down and confirming their suspicions.

After my first arrest I got into the habit of reading the Tablet of Aḥmad, a prayer that Bahá'u'lláh gave to one of the early Bahá'ís when He was being persecuted by enemies. As I read it over and over, its words spoke to me:

> And if thou art overtaken by affliction in My path, or degradation for My sake, be not thou troubled thereby. Rely upon God, thy God and the Lord of thy fathers.[5]

I remembered how others had suffered far more than harassment for their beliefs. I took a deep breath and went to the station with the police. There I was left standing in front of the chief's office door. It was eight o'clock in the morning when I arrived. Secretaries and clerks were busy at their desks but no one seemed to take any interest in me. A fan turned slowly overhead, lethargically stirring the hot air. Big, lazy black flies landed on my face, but somehow anticipated my swats. There was no place to sit, so I began pacing from one window to another. Outside I could see nothing but a dirty wall spotted with urine and a dusty road where a thin, mangy dog was nosing a pile of garbage.

An hour passed. Then another. No one called me, no one seemed to be watching me. I found myself wondering what would happen if I just walked out. Perhaps that is what they hoped I would try. Or perhaps there had been some confusion about my summons. They might have made a mistake.

By the time it was eleven o'clock, I told myself that if at half past eleven I had not been called, I would ask permission to leave. I watched the minute hand of the clock on the wall creep slowly forwards.

Finally the tip of the minute hand touched the six and I walked over to the nearest desk. Using my very rudimentary Portuguese, I asked, 'Can I go home?'

The officer looked up as if seeing me for the first time. He took out a piece of paper. 'Your name?' I gave my full name, spelling it out and then he wanted to know my father and mother's names. The officer was impressed by the number of consonants in Persian names. He stood up and walked out of the room. In a little while he returned with a pink slip in his hand. He said something I didn't understand. Then, with gestures, he made me understand that I was to empty my pockets. I put my keys, loose change and wallet on the table. He put them into an envelope, then gestured that I should follow him. I stared, flabbergasted. It wasn't possible that they were going to put me in prison. The officer frowned. Not wanting to provoke him, I followed him out of the room.

We went through a narrow, smelly corridor, crossed a dusty courtyard and entered another building. All the upper storey windows had bars. In the entrance two armed guards were chatting, sniggering at each other's jokes. My escort spoke to them in Portuguese. I thought I understood that he was telling them that they should watch me carefully. I was a clever man and spoke several languages: Russian, English, French and German. I wasn't sure why this made me dangerous, but the two guards gave me a wary look. They took my tie and belt. Then I was escorted up a stairway and put in a small cell. The iron door clanged shut. I listened to the rattle of the keys locking the door, too stunned to really grasp what was happening. Then I looked around. Except for a cot so filthy that I hesitated to sit on it, the cell was empty. A low wall in one corner half masked a Turkish toilet and a wash basin. A bit of blue sky shone through the bars of a small window set high in the wall.

'I am in gaol,' I thought, staring at the bars, 'like any common criminal.' My mouth felt dry and I struggled to remain rational and keep my fear under control.

Suddenly the small window reminded me of Bahá'u'lláh and His imprisonment at St Jean d'Acre. I remembered the stories that were told of Persian pilgrims who made the long, weary journey across the desert on foot, just so they could catch a glimpse of Bahá'u'lláh's hand waving from a small barred window. 'Abdu'l-Bahá had described their imprisonment as a time of meditation, love and fellowship in spite of the hardships. The Master, as He is called by Bahá'ís, had said the years spent in a prison cell had been one of the happiest times of His life because He had been put in prison for the sake of truth.

I went over to the window and stretched to reach the

bars. The Manifestation of God had spent most of His life as a prisoner without having ever committed a crime. As I meditated on the long years of His life that Bahá'u'lláh had spent in prison, I began to feel calm and serene. Compared to what the early Bahá'ís had suffered and what believers are still suffering in the Islamic Republic of Iran, my imprisonment was very light. I chanted a few prayers, spread my jacket on the stained mattress and sat down. I wondered how to go about informing the Africa Committee in London about my mishap. When it was lunchtime the gaolers opened the little window in the door, then brought in my lunch, Portuguese rice and shrimp. I was hungry and thought such a dish was surprisingly good fare for prisoners. Later a nun came by, visiting the prisoners, asking if they needed anything, if they wanted to confess. I thanked her for her concern and said, no, I had everything I needed. I felt fine and smiled at the kind woman. She must have thought I was out of my mind.

Late in the afternoon the guard came and took me back to the office. Once again I was made to wait. After half an hour the chief of police stepped out, looked at me and said, 'Come back to see me tomorrow morning.'

'I can go home?'

'Yes, yes. Just be sure and be here tomorrow morning.'

I breathed a short prayer of praise and gratitude. The clerk gave me back my belongings and I left.

The next morning I was interrogated by the chief of police. He spoke excellent English.

'How old are you?'

'Twenty-seven.'

'Where were you before coming to Lorenço Marques?'

'Nairobi.'

'You reject Christ, don't you?'

'No, sir. We believe in Jesus Christ.'

'Who have you met here?'

'Very few people. A lawyer.'

'Who introduced you to the lawyer?'

I knew they had found the names of my contacts in my correspondence. I gave their names, saying they were friends of friends and that I had never met them before coming to Mozambique.

'Who is your god?'

'The unique God, the Heavenly Father, Allah. He is called by different names, but He is the same.'

'Where does your god live?'

'That is a strange question. God is everywhere.'

'Where have you travelled in Africa?'

'I have been in Kenya, Uganda and Tanganyika.'

'Who do you know in those countries?'

I gave the names mentioned in my correspondence, certain I was not giving away anything they did not already know. I was asked to specify the nationalities. The police officer seemed to find the diversity extremely suspicious.

'Obviously you love Iran more than any other country.'

'Bahá'ís love all humanity. Bahá'u'lláh said, "The earth is but one country, and mankind its citizens."'[6]

'Do you mean you are not a patriot?'

'Loving humanity doesn't mean hating my country. If

you love Mozambique, it doesn't mean you hate Lorenço Marques.'

'You seem to be a cultivated man. You speak well. You came here saying you were a businessman. Business and religion are contradictory. You were lying. In reality you have come here to teach your religion. Isn't it so?'

'Yes, I came here to teach. But a Bahá'í is not a missionary; he must work and earn his living. I am a businessman, but if someone asks about my religion, I try to answer their questions. It is true I came here as a pioneer for my faith but I don't stand in the street shouting that I am a Bahá'í.'

'What do you think is the cause of the Mau Mau upheaval in Kenya?'

'I don't know much about it. They say they want more land.'

'Don't you think they have other reasons?'

'I don't know. I'm not familiar with their politics.'

'Do you think the Africans are doing the right thing, taking up arms to obtain their rights?'

'No. They can obtain more through non-violence. I am against taking up arms.'

'You are against taking up arms?' The officer's eyes gleamed. I had just admitted I was a pacifist. 'Without arms there would be chaos. Crimes and robbery.'

'I did not say that the police, who are responsible for our protection, should not be armed. Force is justified when it is needed to restore order and protect us from thieves.'

The telephone rang and the inspector answered it. The conversation was in Portuguese but I caught the words 'communist' and 'communist movement' several times.

From the glances the officer gave me, it was easy to guess that I was the subject of the conversation.

I waited for him to hang up and tried to appease his fears.

'Sir, the Bahá'í Faith is a world religion, not a political movement. The United Nations has recognized us as a non-governmental organization. You can check this.'

'What are your political opinions? Are you in favour of Dr Mossadeq?'

'He has done some good things and some bad things. But I believe he is sincere.'

Finally the officer said, 'You can go. You are free, but you must leave the country before May 23rd.'

I explained that I was expecting money from Iran, and that if possible I would like to stay until my money arrived. I showed the papers I had from the bank to prove what I said. The officer said, 'If your money has not arrived by the 23rd, I'll extend your permit. But it would be best to leave as soon as possible.'

The following day I went to the Swedish consulate which represented Iran while diplomatic relations were cut off with Britain. I explained what had happened. The Swedish consul said that it would be impossible to get permission to stay in the country but that if I were put in prison again they would intercede on my behalf.

Several days passed without incident. Then once more I was summoned by the chief of the secret police. He wanted the names of Bahá'ís living in Nairobi. Knowing that the British accepted the Bahá'í Faith, I complied. The names were written under the photographs they had found in my belongings and the pictures were numbered. In many of the photographs blacks and whites were standing together, often with their arms around each other. While the Portuguese were not racially prejudiced, they seemed to find so much interracial friendliness suspicious.

I saw them put my photographs into a large file, about two inches thick, containing the documents they had taken from me, including the letter from the Persian National Spiritual Assembly which quoted Shoghi Effendi's advice to go to Africa to teach. The letter was very precious to me, but it was not returned. On the file's cover were two pictures of me and my visiting card.

Back at the boarding house the businessman from Southern Rhodesia was sympathetic and suggested once more that we might work together. I asked the police for an extension to the deadline that had been set for me to leave the country in order to have time to obtain the visa and receive my money order from Iran. I wrote a long letter in Persian to the Africa Committee in London, asking that Hasan Balyuzi translate it.

I worried about Soheili, my friend in Beira, for I had heard nothing from him for some time. The police had confiscated several letters from him, so they had his address and knew he was in Mozambique. I later learned that Soheili had also been arrested, interrogated and told to leave the country. He eventually settled in Southern Rhodesia.

I remained hopeful about the future. Knowing that there was no justification for my imprisonment and expulsion, that I was being treated wrongfully, made me feel strong. I was in the right and those who oppressed me were mistaken.

Obtaining the visa for Southern Rhodesia turned out to be far more complicated than Gordon Kallen, my boarding house friend, had expected. I was told that applications for permanent residence had to be made outside of the country and applicants were not allowed to enter until the immigration department authorized their entry. Such an arrangement would have put an end to my African adventure. Unless I obtained a visa I would have to return to Iran.

I was summoned one more time to the police headquarters on 23 May. By this time I considered the chief of police an old acquaintance and our conversation was almost friendly. After some quibbling I was given permission to remain until my money arrived from Tehran. Then, turning the tables, I began questioning my interrogator.

'Sir, what are my chances of obtaining a residence permit?'

'We have enough businessmen. We don't need any more.'

'I have another question which is very important to me. After all the information I have given you concerning the Bahá'í Faith, what do you think of it?'

'I am not interested. Your Bahá'í Faith seems very suspicious to me. All religions say they are not involved in politics, but are they telling the truth?'

'You have our documents, you have read them. Bahá'ís are not allowed to participate in political activities. If they disobey this rule they lose their membership.'

The officer made a doubtful grimace.

'There is no difference between religion and communism. Communism is a religion to those who follow it.'

'There is a difference between religion and a man-made ideology. Communists are atheists. Their only concern is with material well-being. My interest is in our spiritual well-being.'

'There are many religions in Africa who are merely paving the way for communism. Even the Mau Maus claim to be a religion.' He continued talking about various movements in Africa of which I knew nothing.

For a while we discussed freedom of religion and the situation in Portugal. The officer stretched his legs and said, 'We are Catholics and do not want to see a new religion imported into our colonies. The Africans are naive and soon become attached to new ideas.'

I remembered that the first Christians had been naive fishermen but I said nothing. The police officer seemed to have some regrets about how I had been treated and attempted to justify himself.

'We don't even allow Seventh Day Adventists to come here. As an individual, I trust you and respect your ideas. As the chief of the secret police I cannot. Are all Iranians Bahá'ís?'

'No, sir.'

'Is Dr Mossadeq a Bahá'í?'

'No, sir. He is a Muslim.'

'Why don't you teach the Persians instead of coming all the way to Mozambique?'

I realized that I was being teased and felt hardy enough

to ask more questions of my own.

'Why did you put me in gaol when you knew I was not a criminal? It was unjust.'

'I can put anyone in gaol and keep them for eight days without trial. You are lucky. You stayed only a few hours.'

The next day I was summoned to a different department. They took my fingerprints, measured my height, weighed me and took pictures from different angles with a metal sign hanging from my neck that said, 'No. 303'. Fortunately they didn't think it necessary to shave my head. While they were taking the pictures I saw my file containing letters from the American woman who lived in Lisbon. Her name and that of Soheili had been underlined in red. Then they asked me where the world centre of the Bahá'í movement was. I gave the address in Haifa.

On 29 May I received an encouraging telegram from the Africa Committee in London. It was a relief to know they realized what was happening and were praying for me.

A few days later I received the money I had been expecting from Tehran. I had managed to obtain a tourist visa for Northern Rhodesia while I was in Nairobi as a matter of precaution. I did not want to go to Northern Rhodesia but I asked the British consulate for a transit visa through Southern Rhodesia.

They granted me a transit visa that authorized me to stay only 24 hours. Once I reached Bulawayo, I would have to use my wits to stay in Southern Rhodesia. I booked a place on the next plane and said a prayer.

6

Wandering

Just as the plough furrows the earth deeply, purifying it of weeds and thistles, so suffering and tribulation free man from the petty affairs of this worldly life . . .[1]

ʿAbdu'l-Bahá

As the plane flew towards Bulawayo, the second largest city in Southern Rhodesia, I looked out at the clear blue African sky and wondered what I was doing there. Had I done the right thing in giving up my position in Tabriz? Would I ever be able to settle down and begin teaching? Or was my destiny to wander from place to place, unwanted, an eternal exile, a foreigner whose language no one understood, carrying a message no one cared to hear?

I felt very sad. It was one of the first times in my life that I felt so alone, with no one, neither family nor friends, to share my feelings with. I opened the red prayer book in English that Fred Schechter had given me. Its pages were stained with chemicals that I suspected the Portuguese had used to see if it contained secret messages. I read over the Tablet of Aḥmad, praying for assistance and guidance. The last words of the prayer were:

Should one who is in affliction or grief read this Tablet with absolute sincerity, God will dispel his sadness, solve his difficulties and remove his afflictions.

Verily, He is the Merciful, the Compassionate. Praise be to God, the Lord of all the worlds.[2]

As always the prayer gave me a feeling of strength and I felt better prepared to face the future. I remembered that my fellow pioneers had encountered situations much more difficult than mine. I was not the only one to have to deal with humiliations, obstacles and setbacks. If this was what God intended, His Will would prevail.

When we landed in Bulawayo, I followed the other disembarking passengers off the plane and across the runway to a small building with a sign saying 'Colonial Administration – Police Formalities'. I was dreading the moment when an immigration official would look at my transit visa and tell me that I had to take the next plane to Northern Rhodesia, so I hung back at the end of the line.

Slowly the line inched forward and I racked my brain unsuccessfully for some excuse that would allow me to stay in the country. I watched the officer, a heavy, red-faced Englishman, examine the passports and vaccination certificates. Sometimes he asked a question or two, then he stamped the passport and directed the passengers who had reached their destination through one door and those who were in transit through another.

Finally it was my turn and I still had no valid reason for staying. Even if I had thought of something, my throat was so tight and dry that I couldn't speak. Mutely I handed my passport to the officer.

After a surprised glance at my passport, he looked

at me and smiled. 'You're from Iran? I haven't met any Iranians since I left Tehran years ago. What brings you here?'

'A . . . a visit,' I managed to croak.

'I enjoyed my time in Tehran very much. It is a lovely country.'

Because I was last in line, he had time to chat. He talked about Tehran and we decided that we might have seen each other there since he had been a customer of the Imperial Bank at the time I was working there. He had worked for the Anglo-Iranian Oil Company. He was so friendly and genuinely delighted to meet an Iranian that I began to relax. My new friend flipped through my passport, not even glancing at the transit visa, and asked, 'How long are you going to stay with us?'

'Twenty days,' I said, scarcely daring ask for more, delighted at the opportunity to stay even that long.

The immigration official stamped my passport 'Valid for 20 days' and told me that I could extend my stay if I wished. I thanked him and shook his hand enthusiastically, saying I hoped we would meet again, then I followed the other passengers who were going to take a connecting flight to Salisbury.

I went to the Grand Hotel and found Gordon Kallen had reserved a room for me. He had left a message saying he would come and take me to lunch the following day.

The first thing I did the next morning was to go to the post office, rent a mail box and send a cablegram to Haifa announcing my arrival in Salisbury. At that time I did not realize that I was the first Bahá'í pioneer in the Ten

Year Plan to have reached Southern Rhodesia, a country among 131 'virgin' territories in which Bahá'ís had been asked to settle.

After a good lunch, Gordon took me to a law firm, Danziger and Lardener-Burke. He explained to them that he wanted to hire me but that I did not have a permanent residence permit. One of the junior lawyers, Mr Guthrie, was put in charge of obtaining the permit. He was quite optimistic. Seeing that I was not penniless, that I disposed of an investment capital, that I was sponsored by Mr Kallen and belonged to the 'white race', he was quite sure the Immigration Board would accept his application, after the usual delays. I remembered Mr Patel's prediction that I would have no trouble obtaining a residence permit as long as I was considered 'white'.

Gordon Kallen offered me a form of partnership, hoping that I would be able to help him to open up contacts with the Middle East. So that I could obtain my residence permit, Gordon wrote out a contract stating that he was willing to pay me a salary of 100 pounds a month, a considerable amount in those days. The terms were quite fair, and although the contract would not be official until my residence permit came, I went to his office every morning. In the afternoon there was little to do, so I would go to a movie or stroll around the city, observing and trying to learn as much as possible about life in Rhodesia. I would often go to the city park and sit there with my prayer book, praying and imploring divine assistance so that the doors would open so the message of Bahá'u'lláh could reach the people of this country.

Everywhere I went, in all the hotels, restaurants and public facilities there were signs stating, 'The Management reserves the right of admission'. It was all too obvious how the management decided who would be admitted and who would not, for there were no Africans or Indians in those establishments. In South Africa apartheid was a legal institution; in Kenya and in Rhodesia it was an unwritten law that was just as effective. At the movie theatre the tickets were stamped 'This ticket valid for whites only'. Blacks and Asians had to sit in the balcony. The ticket taker would look at the ticket and then examine me closely before letting me enter.

Several days after my arrival in Salisbury I received the following telegram from Haifa: 'Fervently praying success: Shoghi.'

It touched me deeply to know that the Guardian was praying for me. I hoped someday to be able to go on pilgrimage to Haifa, to meet Shoghi Effendi and to be able to tell him about my work in Southern Rhodesia. As long as my status was uncertain, I refrained from teaching, but every evening I went to the park, sat on a bench, and prayed that the city of Salisbury would come to know the Bahá'í Faith.

I checked in regularly with Mr Guthrie who was able to renew my 20-day visa. Then, when the extension was almost at an end, he informed me that the Immigration Board would not decide on my case while I was in the country. I would have to leave Southern Rhodesia and wait for their final decision.

I came out of the lawyer's office feeling stunned. I

feared that if I left the colony, there was no telling when or how I would return. I had become very confident, certain that I would soon be established as a permanent resident and able to begin teaching. The news that I would have to leave shattered my hopes. I stood in the street and looked out over the city of Salisbury, spread out below. I had actually started to think of it as my city, my home. Was I going to lose it? I had never felt so discouraged; I had come to believe that the trials I had encountered in Mozambique were designed to send me to Salisbury to teach. This new setback made them seem pointless.

Suddenly I looked up and saw 'Abdu'l-Bahá. The old man with His long white beard and oriental robes filled the whole vast African sky. He looked down at me and smiled. The vision of the kindly expression on His face seemed far more real and tangible than the streets and buildings below me. I felt as if He was saying, 'It's all right. Don't worry about it. It's all right.'

After a while I looked around and to my surprise I was still standing in the street outside the law office. I took a deep breath and looked up at the sky. It was vast and blue, no longer empty, but full of promise. I vowed then and there to trust in God without expecting things to follow my own plans and expectations.

I told Mr Kallen what the immigration officer had said and he advised me to go to Elizabethville in the Belgian Congo and wait there. After my problems with the Portuguese police, Mozambique and Angola were out of the question. The Congo was the closest non-British colony. It was not far by plane and I had no difficulty

Aziz Yazdi, *second from left*, with Knight of Bahá'u'lláh Fred Schechter, *far right*

Bahá'ís in Nairobi, including Soraya Yazdi, *standing third from left*; Ezzat, *standing far right*; Aziz Yazdi, kneeling, *second from left*; and Knight of Bahá'u'lláh Ted Cardell, *kneeling far right*

Bahá'ís in Kampala, including Ezzat, *far left*; Aziz Yazdi, *centre*;
and Richard St Barbe Baker, *seated*

Teaching trip in Mackinnon Road, Kenya,
with Knight of Bahá'u'lláh Ted Cardell, *centre*

A fireside in a village outside Mombasa

Some of the
members of the
first Local Spiritual
Assembly of
Mombasa

Ezzat and friends relaxing on Nayali Beah, Mombasa

Ezzat in the heart of Africa

Baháʼís of Mogadishu, Somalia, including Ursula, *standing left*, and Mehdi Samandari *standing right*, whom Ezzat first met in 1953

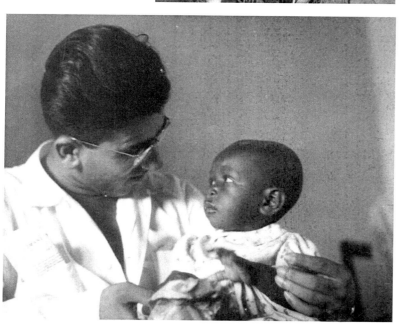

Ezzat meets a baby in coastal Kenya

Hands of the Cause at the conference in Kampala, 1953

Hands of the Cause Leroy Ioas and Hasan Balyuzi
at the Kampala Conference

With Mr and Mrs Vahdat in the Belgium Congo, September 1953

Ezzat's office in Mombasa

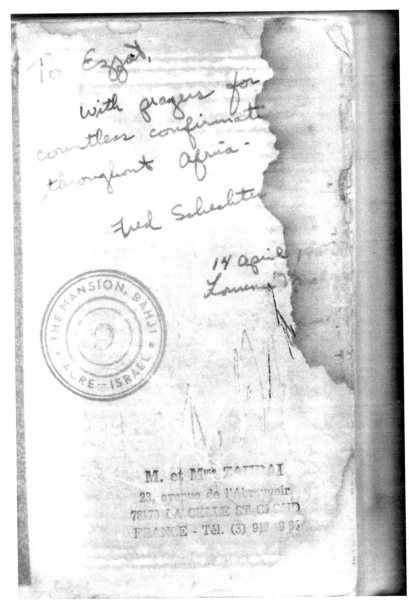

To Ezzat,
with prayers for
countless confirmati..
throughout Africa –

Fred Schechter

14 april
Loureng..

THE MANSION · BAHJI · ACRE – ISRAEL

M. et Mme ZAHRAI
23, avenue de l'Abreuvoir
78170 LA CELLE ST. CLOUD
FRANCE – Tél. (3) 918 19 35

Cover of the prayer book given to Ezzat by Fred Schechter showing
stains from the chemicals used by the Portuguese secret police in
Mozambique in examining it

obtaining a tourist visa from the Belgian Consulate. Mr Guthrie promised to keep me informed by telegram.

As soon as I arrived in Elizabethville, I went to the post office to register and telegrammed my general delivery address to the law firm. I stayed in a good hotel in Kasai Avenue, for it seemed important to maintain my standing in order not to be considered a second class citizen in case I needed to obtain a resident permit. But in meals and everything else I was very thrifty, aware that my savings were dwindling.

For the first time I found myself in a French-speaking country. I brushed up on my high school French and soon, with practice, was making myself understood. It was intriguing to see how the Africans had adapted to the culture of their colonial masters. In Kenya and Rhodesia men were called John, Henry and David and wore shorts. In Mozambique they had Portuguese names and sang fados. In the Congo they were called Jean-Marie, Michel and Pierre and wore pointed shoes.

Once again I found myself with a great deal of time on my hands. I went to the post office twice a day and inquired if there was any mail for me. The clerk came to know me and as soon as I walked in would say, '*Non, il n'y a rien pour vous*, there's nothing for you.' After that I spent the rest of the day in a café reading the papers, writing letters and striking up conversations with other customers just to practise my French.

Before the Ten Year Crusade there were only a few Bahá'ís registered as living in Africa south of the equator. One of them was an Englishwoman who lived in

Durban and another was Mr Vahdat, a Persian married to a Belgian woman. I knew he lived in Kamina, a small township in the Belgian Congo, more than 600 kilometres away. I did not have his exact address but I learned that the train to Leopoldville went through Kamina and I decided to try to visit Mr Vahdat while waiting for a reply from Mr Guthrie.

The clerk at the train station told me a train went to Leopoldville and returned once a week. I could go to Kamina and come back the following week. I wanted to write to Mr Vahdat to announce my visit but learned that my letter would go on the same train I intended to take. And without an exact address I wasn't sure my letter would reach Mr Vahdat. I was too impatient to see a fellow Persian to wait two weeks for a reply.

The train I took was pulled by a wood-burning locomotive supplied by three wagons full of firewood that followed the engine. It progressed very slowly and sometimes when the track went uphill the passengers could get out and walk for a while, easily keeping up with the train. Knowing that I had to be careful with my money until I could start working, I had paid for a second class ticket. People stared at me as I entered the coach as most Europeans travelled first class. I found myself squeezed onto a tiny bench between a wide-hipped market woman dressed in a gorgeous African print and a little man with glasses wearing a Tergal suit and tie. My neighbour was a native civil servant and asked me many questions about my travels. He asked me where my wife was, and when he learned I was a bachelor, he shook his head and clucked his tongue in sympathy. It was a terrible misfortune and I should get myself a wife as soon as possible.

After many long hours the train reached Kamina. I was glad to get off the train and stretch my limbs, but when I looked around I was dismayed. Kamina was a mere hamlet, lost in the middle of the tropical rain forest. There was a market place with the usual skinny, hairless dogs and rotting piles of banana leaves and a small administrative district with half a dozen brick houses for the Belgian civil servants. Beyond lay the African quarters, a huddled mass of wooden shacks that seemed propped up against each other, ready to tumble like dominos if one collapsed. A wide road, like a red laterite wound, cut through the forest, leading to a guarded military base.

I asked a small boy where Mr Vahdat lived and the lad pointed towards the red brick buildings. Soon a crowd of joyous children in rags were accompanying me, chattering to each other excitedly in Lingala. A stranger asking for Mr Vahdat seemed to be a major event in their lives.

The dirt of the road was soft and thick, a fine powder that rose in a cloud with each step, and settled on my legs and shoes. A military jeep passed me, leaving a trail of red dust that completely covered the pedestrians. I felt its grains in the corners of my eyes and snorted to clear my nostrils.

Mr Vahdat's house was a small bungalow. The shutters were closed. I knocked on the door and waited. No one came. I knocked again; the children were chattering and gesturing among themselves but seemed too intimidated to give any information. Then a girl who was older than the others spoke angrily to a little boy, who scampered off to the neighbouring house and soon returned with an African wearing a houseboy's uniform, white trousers and white T-shirt.

'*M'bot*, M'sieu.'

'*Bonjour*,' I replied. 'I am a friend of Mr Vahdat. Do you know where he is?'

'M'sieu Vahdat is on a trip. He left last week.'

'And Mrs Vahdat?'

'Madame Vahdat, she's with M'sieu Vahdat.'

'And their daughter? I think they have a daughter.'

'M'selle Vahdat, she's in Belgium.'

I thanked the man, wrote a note to Mr Vahdat and stuck it in the door. Then I turned back to the train station. I remembered seeing a small hotel next to it. There was nothing to do but take a room and hope that Mr Vahdat would soon be back from his trip in the bush.

At the hotel I was surprised to learn that all the rooms were taken. I offered to sleep on the floor in the dining room but the owner, a red-headed Belgian woman, told me I could find a room at the Catholic mission, about five kilometres from Kamina.

There was no solution but to hoof it out to the mission. The road was long and hot and dusty and by the time I reached the mission I was covered with fine red dust, my skin caked with red clay where I had perspired. Even my eyelashes were coated with red dust. I felt doubtful of the reception my disreputable appearance would get. I saw that the mission was a large one, with a church, a dispensary, a school run by nuns and other buildings set on green lawns amid well-tended flowerbeds. It didn't appear to be the kind of place that took in vagrants.

The Belgian mission priest had red hair and a goatee. He wore immaculate white robes that seemed a minor miracle in such a setting. Sitting on his well-shaded verandah, served by an old African whose back seemed permanently bent in an attitude of humble respect, he told me that he knew Mr Vahdat well. They had a few extra rooms for travellers but I should not expect any luxury. I assured him that the only luxury I wished for was a shower. The priest offered me a drink; there was a bottle of whiskey on the table beside him. When I thanked him, explaining that I did not drink alcohol, he asked the servant to find something non-alcoholic. After some searching the old man returned with an almost empty bottle of mint syrup and some soda water. The resulting mixture was cold and sweet; I downed it in one go and sincerely thanked my host.

The servant led me to another building and showed me to a small room with a cot and a shower. The sheets on the cot were dark with dirt and the symbolic mosquito net had large, gaping holes, but I was grateful that at least I had a place to sleep. As soon as I had set down my suitcase and closed the door, I took a shower. The thin, sluggish stream of tepid water that came out of the pipes was pink with either rust or laterite dirt, maybe both. After my shower I felt a little cooler and slightly cleaner.

The next day I had to walk into town to buy food for my meals. In a small shop next to the hotel I found some cans of corned beef and sardines to make sandwiches. I bought several loaves of under-baked bread with the unmistakable flavour of manioc flour. I bought a case of lemonade because I dared not drink the pink water that came out of the faucet. When I returned to the mission the priests were having their lunch served on the verandah. I went to my room and took another shower.

Sunday came and I didn't go to church. The priests took no interest in me. In the evenings I could hear them entertaining guests. Servants carried the dishes from the kitchen to the dining room in what seemed a continual stream. Alone in my room with cold sandwiches of canned meat I imagined I could smell the odours of fried potatoes and roast meat. I was angry with myself for not having written before making the trip and feeling lonely and dejected. I remembered the Persian poet who wrote that he was so alone there was not even a pistachio nut to smile at him. Then once more I remembered the other pioneers who were suffering in lonely outposts. I told myself that my problems were nothing compared to what some of them were enduring.

The week went by without any news of Mr Vahdat and the train to Elizabethville was due the next day. I regretted having come. Tomorrow I would take the train back and the entire journey would have been a waste of time and money. It was foolish to get upset about the mishap, but I realized that I had been counting on meeting a fellow countryman and a fellow believer. Since I had left Kenya I had not once been able to carry on a conversation in Farsi. Wherever I went I was considered a foreigner, someone strange and different. As I sat on the verandah in the dark, wondering how long I would be able to endure such isolation, a car drew up in front of the building and stopped. In the dark I saw someone get out and look in my direction.

'Ezzat Zahrai?'

Only a Persian would pronounce my name that way. I jumped to my feet.

'Mr Vahdat?'

The man who walked up the steps holding out his arms was a short, middle-aged man. He had a dark tan from years of working outdoors in Africa. He gave me a big hug and told me to pack my things; he was taking me to his home right away.

I hesitated. 'I must tell the priests that I'm leaving.'

'Don't worry about them. I'll stop by in the morning and explain.'

It took two minutes to get ready and then I was in the big American car, on my way to Mr Vahdat's house. I felt like I had been rescued by a friendly angel. The sudden transition from feeling lonely and abandoned in a foreign country to being warmly, kindly welcomed in Farsi by a fellow countryman almost overwhelmed me. Mr Vahdat had just got back from his trip and had come to fetch me immediately without waiting for the next day. He too was glad of a chance to speak Farsi and talk to someone from Iran. When we reached the little red brick bungalow his wife, a very kind Belgian, had prepared a delicious meal of rice and pork in a steaming sauce. I joked about the combination because while rice is a favourite dish with

Iranians, the Muslims never eat pork.

'This is an Irano-Belgian association,' I said.

Their daughter was away for her studies, so Mrs Vahdat put me up in her vacant room. It was clean and pretty, decorated in the European style, and had its own bath with a tub.

The following week went by swiftly. Mr Vahdat was an agricultural expert and made many trips into the bush, teaching the Africans how to cultivate coffee, cocoa and other money-making plants. He had studied in Belgium where he had met his wife and become a Belgian citizen. Since he had not been back to Iran for many years, I told him what was happening there, the reforms Dr Mossadeq was trying to put through and how the Bahá'í community was doing. I told him about my experience in Lorenço Marques and why I was in the Congo, waiting for a reply to my application in Southern Rhodesia. He was a pleasant man, easy to get along with, and we never seemed to run out of things to say to each other.

We were able to go to some movies and one day we went to see a soccer match. While we were watching the game a Belgian man drew Mr Vahdat aside and talked to him for a while. When he left, I noticed that Mr Vahdat looked a little worried.

'That was a friend of mine. He is a police officer and he says they have you on their index. The Portuguese police must have given them your name.'

This news bothered me because if I didn't hear from Mr Guthrie soon, I would have to renew my tourist visa. Mr Vahdat wrote a very kind letter of introduction to a friend of his in Elizabethville, a civil servant who worked in the immigration office, and advised me to pay him a visit to see about renewing my visa.

When the train came down from Leopoldville, I took it back to Elizabethville. I felt that I now had friends I could count on in this vast country. Mr and Mrs Vahdat were planning a long overdue holiday in Belgium. I didn't expect to be there on their return but I hoped that we would meet again someday.

July went by and then August. The rainy season came, turning the fine red dust into slick rusty mud. Almost every day a heavy downpour would begin early in the morning and continue through the day and then, sometime in the night, stop, as if someone had turned off the tap. There were no storms, no lightning or thunder, just warm, monotonous, unceasing rain. The streets were muddy, the sidewalks pocked with puddles. It was an exploit to make my daily walk to the post office without being splashed by a passing car. On 18 August, as soon as I walked into the post office the friendly clerk greeted me with a big smile.

'There's a cablegram for you!'

He was so obviously happy that my long wait had finally been answered that I supposed that he had seen the contents. If so, his wide grin must mean that my application had been approved. I thanked the man and left. I went to a café, the only one in town, and sat down, staring at the pale yellow paper that would decide my fate. I opened the telegram with fingers that trembled and read:

REGRET ADVISE APPLICATION REFUSED ON GROUNDS
QUOTA AND ASSIMILABILITY.

Assimilability. What did that mean? Did it mean that if
my name had been Jones or Smith my application would
have been approved? The Immigration Board had never
met me, but they had made a decision that would affect
the rest of my life, that destroyed all hope of my carrying
out my mission in Southern Rhodesia.

I ordered coffee which I didn't really want and I read
over the telegram several times. I tried to think of what
could be done but the disappointment was too raw. After
a while I saw the café owner looking at me and realized
my cup had been empty for some time. I didn't feel like
leaving and I didn't want to impose on the owner, so I
ordered another cup of coffee. Finally, after a third cup, I
left the café and returned to my hotel.

I had dinner alone in the hotel restaurant that night.
There were few other customers and the rain was still
falling, a steady drumming on the roof. I could hear
the big, fat drops splattering on the walk outside, beating down everything, relentless. I wasn't hungry and left
early to go to my room.

In my room I tried to say a prayer for assistance but I
found it very difficult to concentrate. I went to bed but
couldn't sleep. The rain finally dwindled away and I could
hear water dripping off the eaves and the wet trees. The
hours went by and my brain raced, like a car that's not
in gear, going round and round my situation and getting
nowhere. I couldn't sleep. In the courtyard two men were

speaking softly. I couldn't understand their words; they were probably speaking in Kikongo or Lilanga. Their voices sounded sleepy. I supposed it was the night watchman and a friend who had come to keep him company. From time to time a car would go by, its wheels splashing through the puddles.

Long after midnight the Belgian in the room next to mine returned, cursing loudly but not very distinctly in French. I listened to him drop his keys and knock his shins against the furniture. Through the thin walls I could hear the bedsprings squeak and a little later I heard the man muttering, getting out of bed and stumbling around. Then came the sound of the toilet flushing. After that my neighbour was quiet. The night watchman and his friend seemed to be making humorous comments.

I closed my eyes, trying to talk myself into sleep, then stared at the stripes of moonlight coming through the shutters. I smiled. In French they were called Persiennes. I wondered why. I heard a rooster crow and glanced at my watch. It was only three in the morning. My body ached with a desire to sleep. I tried to force myself to relax, tried to empty my mind, but the thought of the telegram kept returning, its words ran through my mind, the humiliating 'assimilability', the 'regret advise' too professional to be sincere.

Morning found me exhausted. I got out of bed as soon as I heard the cooks preparing breakfast, feeling like a prisoner being let out of his cell. I felt a little better after my morning prayers. I decided to write to Mr Guthrie and ask why my application had not been accepted.

Could it be appealed? Soon my tourist visa would expire. If it wasn't renewed, where could I go? Once again I was in danger of being sent back to Iran with nothing to show for the ten months I had spent travelling from one colony to another, using up my savings while I was living in expensive hotels with no prospect of a job in view.

I bought a newspaper to read and went to the café. I wasn't very hungry, so I had only a sandwich for lunch. Feeling tired, I ordered a cup of coffee after my lunch. It was good coffee and I was learning to appreciate it. The café owner had started to consider me a regular.

'You don't look well,' he said. 'I hope you're not coming down with malaria. Have you been taking your Nivaquine?'

'Yes. I'm just tired. Didn't sleep last night.'

That evening it was raining again. I felt so tired that I was sure that I would fall asleep as soon as I got into bed. But once more I spent a sleepless night. I got up several times to count over my travellers' cheques, wondering how long I could make them last. Should I look for a room in the African quarters? There I could live for years with what I had, but who would take me seriously and give me a decent job if they knew I was living there? I had been in Africa long enough to know that the European community never forgave a white man who went native.

Dawn came slowly, grudgingly, and I heard the tinkling of bicycle bells as dozens of 'boys' pedalled in to the European district to make breakfast for their white employers. I got up and showered and shaved. My eyes were red and bleary, my hands so shaky that I cut myself.

I went to the hotel restaurant and had breakfast, tea and freshly baked bread with butter and jam. The other guests were mostly young bachelors like me, Belgians who had come to the Congo in the hope of making a fortune. Meeting every day at breakfast, we had become friendly and one of them asked politely, 'Did you sleep well?'

'Yes, just fine.'

Again I spent the day in the café, reading newspapers, unable to recall what I had read. I felt abandoned. I had been so confident that I was carrying out God's mission that I could not understand why so many doors had been slammed in my face. Had I done something wrong?

I went to a movie in the evening and then went back to my hotel room, dreading the ordeal I was to face, knowing that once again I would not be able to sleep. Before I went to bed I counted my travellers' cheques over once more. I tried to think what to do but I was too tired. My mind seemed to go around in aimless circles, repeatedly coming back to 'assimilability' and my dwindling stock of travellers' cheques.

I lay on the bed, listening to the now familiar night sounds, the night watchman making his rounds, the shrill singing of frogs, the occasional barking of a dog, and far away the drums and music of the African quarters where someone was always being buried or married.

In the middle of the night I remembered that 'Abdu'l-Bahá had revealed a prayer to be said at midnight. I got up, turned on the light and found the prayer in my prayer book.

O Lord, I have turned my face unto Thy kingdom of oneness and am immersed in the sea of Thy mercy. O Lord, enlighten my sight by beholding Thy lights in this dark night, and make me happy by the wine of Thy love in this wonderful age.[3]

I read over the prayer several times and meditated on it. I was indeed in a dark night of doubt, doubting my mission, doubting my ability to complete it. I went outside on the veranda and looked up at the sky. The rain had finally stopped and the night was beautiful. Somehow in Africa the stars seem much closer than they are anywhere else. After staring at them for some time, I went back in and began to say my morning prayers. I had given up any hope of sleeping, so I spent the rest of the night meditating on my situation. Why was I so concerned about my travellers' cheques? I had been relying on them instead of relying on Bahá'u'lláh. I said another prayer, asking forgiveness for having doubted. When I heard the bicycles of the 'boys' coming to prepare breakfast, I took a shower and dressed. I still felt tired but my head seemed to have cleared.

The first thing I did after breakfast was to go to see a doctor who told me not to drink any more coffee and prescribed a sleeping pill. That night I took the pill and woke up in the morning feeling refreshed. In *Gleanings* I came across a passage that said our trials are given to us according to our strength.

I decided that I should start looking for work. It might be possible to find a job here in Elizabethville. I put an ad in the local newspaper, *L'Essor du Congo*. The ad read:

Young man 11 yrs experience clerical work, correspondence in English, familiar with bank and business
operations, speaks French, seeking job. Good refer-
ences. Write c/o paper.

I received a package of mail that had been forwarded from
Southern Rhodesia. In the *Bahá'í News* was a message
that Shoghi Effendi had sent to all the National Spiritual
Assemblies concerning the World Crusade, the Ten Year
Plan, informing them that it 'has been befittingly ushered in through successive, magnificent victories won
by Bahá'u'lláh's crusaders in virgin territories in every
continent of the globe'.[4] In less than four months 28 territories had been opened. To honour the pioneers who
sacrificed the comfort of their homes to go to lands
where the Bahá'í religion was unknown, the Guardian
had created a Roll of Honour 'designed to perpetuate the
memory of the exploits of the spiritual conquerors'. The
pioneers whose names were listed on the Roll of Honour
were given the title 'Knight of Bahá'u'lláh'. I read through
the list and saw Fred Schechter's name and that of Amin
Banani who had gone to Greece. Then I read 'Izzatu'lláh
Zahrai, Southern Rhodesia'.[5]

Years later Amatu'l-Bahá Rúḥíyyih Khánum, Hand of
the Cause of God, explained why the Guardian chose the
title 'Knight'.

We had the ten year plan, which was the conquest of
the whole globe in the name of Bahá'u'lláh, 1953 to
1963. He called it a decade-long, world-embracing,

spiritual crusade, arduous, audacious, challenging, unprecedented. He said we should plant the banner of the Cause on the highest mountains, and spread the message in the deserts and in the islands of the sea and all over the world. That vocabulary of Shoghi Effendi I think was one of the things that carried us through to victory. Because he had such a marvellous command of English that it just pulled you up, and made you see the vision that he was seeing and made you realize that you had to do something about it. Shoghi Effendi said that posterity would be proud of these souls who were the spiritual conquerors, his own term, of the entire globe. And on whom he conferred the unique title of Knights of Bahá'u'lláh. I remember when he devised this title, how astonished I was that he should go back to the middle ages . . . (When) you received your knighthood, you had certain oaths of allegiance and service to take. It's not a light term, knighthood. Shoghi Effendi attached tremendous importance to the Knights of Bahá'u'lláh.[6]

I was astonished to see my name listed among the Knights, wondering if it could be a mistake. As it turned out, I had actually been the first Bahá'í pioneer to go to Southern Rhodesia with the intention of finding work and teaching the Faith. But I considered the title more as a challenge to be lived up to than an honour.

A few days later I received a reply to my newspaper ad from Georges Antoniades, a Greek businessman who ran a successful import–export company and had an automobile dealership. I had noticed the big showroom on the main street of Elizabethville with its beautiful Packard sedans. I went to the office and introduced myself to Mr Antoniades.

Once he was satisfied with my credentials, Mr Antoniades invited me to have dinner with him. He lived in a comfortable villa not far from the showroom. Mrs Antoniades and their daughter Helena worked in the office. I enjoyed the delicious Greek food, a welcome change from the fare at the hotel restaurant. Helena was a pretty and very friendly girl. After dinner Mr Antoniades offered me a job working for him with a decent salary that he promised would improve once I had given the measure of my abilities. I accepted the offer at once.

The Greek began working on an application for a residence permit for me and once more I had to have my birth certificate and diplomas translated, this time into French. I went to the office every day and began making a list of potential customers and writing letters in English to enterprises in the Middle East. Mr Antoniades seemed to appreciate my work and frequently invited me to eat with his family. Occasionally we went to an expensive restaurant run by a French woman. The food was very good, living up to the international reputation of French cuisine, but one day I saw the bill and realized that what Mr Antoniades had spent would have fed an African family for months. Elizabethville was at the centre of the Belgian Congo's copper belt, and the Belgian engineers and other Europeans who lived there could afford elegant feasts in grand restaurants.

I could not help seeing how hard the Greeks worked, never taking a day off, not even on Sundays. They made no secret of the fact that they had come to Africa to make money and did not question the long hours their work demanded. I could foresee difficulties if I wanted to spend my evenings and weekends teaching and working with the African population. And I began to feel ill at ease about Helena. I think my employer expected me to take an interest in his daughter. She was an attractive, pleasant girl, but I didn't feel particularly drawn to her and wanted to avoid any misunderstandings. I could only hope that everything would eventually work out. For the time being, I was back where I started, in need of a residence permit that no one seemed to want to give me. Mr Vahdat's friend had been able to renew my tourist visa but my application to become a permanent resident was making little progress.

I was not surprised when Mr Antoniades called me into his office to tell me that my application for residence could not be considered while I was in the country. Once more I would have to leave.

I was able to get a tourist visa for Kenya and I thought it would be good to go back there and consult with my friends. There were no direct flights from Elizabethville to Nairobi but I could go by train to Ndola, in Northern Rhodesia and take a flight from there to Kenya.

Ndola lay in the heart of the copper belt, a major industrial centre. There were hotels to accommodate the British mining engineers and other technical experts. On the train I struck up a conversation with a businessman from South Africa. He had driven to Ndola from Johannesburg and left his car at the train station. He offered to help me find a hotel in Ndola.

We arrived in Ndola in the middle of a tropical storm with the rain pouring down so heavily that it was impossible to see the other side of the street. We drove all over town to find rooms but the hotels were full. Discouraged, we returned to the train station and asked the station master if we could possibly sleep in one of the Pullman wagons.

'Yes, you can. But I won't guarantee that you won't find yourself in Mozambique or Angola tomorrow morning.'

We made another round of the hotels, getting drenched every time we had to run from the car to a hotel lobby. At last we found one vacant room, which we decided to share. My roommate told me many stories about living in the bush in South Africa and was pleasant company. The next day he left and I remained to wait for my flight to Nairobi.

7

Mombasa

He, verily, shall increase the reward of them that endure with patience.[1]

Bahá'u'lláh

As soon as I arrived in Nairobi I went to see Aziz Yazdi. He had managed to obtain a residence permit and settle in Kenya. He was developing a pharmaceutical business, representing an American company, a German pain-killer and a popular laxative made in South Africa called SS pills. He had bought a car, a light blue Ford Consul, and he and Soraya were talking about purchasing a house. Aziz advised me to ask for a residence permit on the basis of 'assured income'. Thus even if my application in the Congo was rejected I might settle in Kenya. I wrote at once to my brother Ehsan in Tehran and asked him to obtain documents testifying that I could guarantee my income.

While I was waiting to hear from Iran, I was surprised not to receive any news from Mr Antoniades concerning my application in the Congo. Knowing how erratic the mails were, I feared that a letter had been lost and wrote to tell them I had heard nothing.

I soon received a letter from my brother in Iran along with a statement from a Bahá'í lawyer saying that I had revenues in Iran which would furnish me with £150 a month. If I should run out of money, my family and friends were willing to send me what I needed to continue my mission, a sacrifice I was determined not to ask them to make, but I was encouraged by their confidence. I hoped to find a job before I used up all my travellers' cheques.

When I furnished the documents proving that I had an 'assured income', the Immigration Office asked me to fill in forms concerning my work experience and education. I was called in for an interview by a civil servant. A couple of months went by during which I had no news from the Congo. I wrote several times to Mr Antoniades without receiving any reply. My folder of travellers' cheques was getting thinner and thinner.

Then one day I received a letter from the Immigration Office saying that my application to stay in Kenya on a permanent basis was accepted. I shouted for joy and ran to share the news with Aziz and Soraya. At long last I had acquired the 'permanent residence permit' which had been eluding me for over a year. Now I could set about finding a job.

Shortly afterwards I received a letter from Helena Antoniades saying that I should let the matter of a job with her father drop. I was very surprised at such an abrupt change in their attitude, for the entire family had treated me with great cordiality right up to the moment of my departure. I was grateful that I had taken Aziz's advice and applied for permission to stay in Kenya without waiting for a reply from the Congo. I also received a letter from Fred Schechter, forwarded to me from the Congo, asking where I was.

'What baobab tree have the authorities chased you up now?'

I put ads in the *East African Standard* and went to several interviews which were not satisfactory. I frequently came away with the distinct impression that though my papers said 'Caucasian race' the employers I met were looking for someone with pink skin and blond hair. Once or twice they proposed a job classified 'Asian'. If I accepted I would have a lower salary and fewer fringe benefits. I had already encountered Indian medical doctors, graduates from prestigious British universities, who were paid a much lower salary than their former classmates because their papers said 'Asian'. I vowed to hold out for a salary corresponding to my training and experience. Also there was the problem of housing. If I accepted being classified 'Asian', I would have to live in the noisy, overcrowded Indian quarters. As in Rhodesia, the unwritten law that kept the races separate was strictly observed. I prayed that someday this beautiful land would accept the message of Bahá'u'lláh, that all men, whatever the colour of their skin, were brothers.

I went into the African quarters with Aziz to distribute free samples of headache remedies and other over-the-counter products that his company imported. It gave us an opportunity to meet people and sometimes we were invited to return to talk about our Faith. Aziz had finished the negotiations involved in buying his house and I helped his family move out of the boarding house. Their new home had a large garden, a guest house and servant quarters. Soraya and Aziz told me I was welcome to stay in the guest house until I found a job. The Yazdis extended their kind hospitality to all the pioneers coming to settle in East Africa or just passing through Nairobi. Their home became a haven for many Bahá'ís faced with difficulties and loneliness far from their native lands.

Week after week I studied the classified ads and answered any that seemed suitable. On weekends Aziz and I went on teaching trips into villages around Nairobi. Although the Africans were hospitable, it took time for them to understand that the Bahá'ís were not one more Protestant sect. We told ourselves it would take patience and continued to visit, letting the Africans observe us, waiting for the time when someone would ask a thoughtful question. The local people never questioned or contradicted white men but Aziz and I were looking for more than bland, polite agreement. We insisted that belief in Bahá'u'lláh can only come after a personal quest for truth.

Often after one of our trips we would discuss the people we had met and wonder who would be the first Bahá'í. Sometimes we thought someone was very close to declaring their belief in Bahá'u'lláh, but nothing came of it. Then one day Francis Jumba, a young student, came to us and asked, 'What do you have to do to become a Bahá'í?'

'Do you want to become a Bahá'í?'

'Yes.'

'Why?'

'Because what they say is true.'

'Do you truly believe that Bahá'u'lláh is a divine Messenger, sent by God to speak to all mankind in this age?'

'Yes.'

'Are you prepared to follow the commandments which Bahá'u'lláh left in His writings?'

'Yes.'

Aziz opened his long arms and gave the young African an enormous bear hug.

'My friend, if you believe in Bahá'u'lláh, if you accept His teachings and obey His laws, you are a Bahá'í. That's all you have to do.'

Through Francis we met other young students and later on we were able to form the first Local Assembly in Nairobi.

Although we were living in a segregated society, we Persian Bahá'ís were not race conscious and frequently, in the enthusiasm of sharing Bahá'u'lláh's message, we forgot how pervasive the distinctions were. One day I went with Aziz on a teaching trip to a small town called Equator because it was situated on the equator. It was little more than a railway station. The station master had become a Bahá'í. He asked us to accompany a young friend of his who had also become a Bahá'í to another village to meet friends who wanted to know more about Bahá'u'lláh. The three of us set out in Mr Yazdi's car. It was a long way and a hot, dusty day. When we saw a roadside restaurant shaded by bright red bougainvillea creepers, Aziz decided to stop and have some tea.

We went in and sat down without noticing that our African friend had fallen silent and was no longer participating in the conversation. The waiter came over to us, took our order and disappeared. We waited some time. The tea didn't come. We called the waiter over and repeated our order. He merely nodded and then disappeared. There was still no sign of the tea. Finally I got up and went to the kitchen to see the English owner.

'My friends and I are still waiting for our three cups of tea.'

The owner looked me over carefully. Then he said, not unkindly, rather with an air of explaining something obvious to a slow child, 'As long as that nigger is sitting at your table, we won't serve you.'

I was stunned. It was my first direct experience of blatant racial prejudice. I turned around and walked back to the table. 'Let's go,' I said. 'This is not a Bahá'í restaurant.'

I explained to Aziz in Persian what had happened. There was no need to explain to our African friend. He knew. I regretted having unknowingly put him in an embarrassing situation.

Back in Nairobi I kept going to job interviews and kept getting negative replies. I thought how ironic it was that in Rhodesia and the Congo I had been unable to obtain a resident permit but had had no difficulties finding work. Now that I had the long-sought-after permit, I could find no one willing to hire me. I wrote to the World Centre, expressing how discouraged I was and asking permission to go on pilgrimage. I thought that my spiritual batteries needed recharging. About a month later I received a letter from Dr Luṭfu'lláh Ḥakím saying that it was not a good time to visit Haifa but Shoghi Effendi was praying for my success.

After reading the letter I took stock of my present situation. It was not brilliant but other pioneers had encountered greater difficulties and prevailed. My cousin Shahab had written from Kuwait where he was living in a town that, having no drinking water, had to bring in tank trucks hauling water once a week. He made it all sound like fun. Mr Faizi was also in the Persian Gulf, taking care of the pioneers who had gone there. Besides the great difficulties they had finding jobs and obtaining residence permits, the living conditions were harsh and as a result many of them had health problems. I realized that I had no right to complain. After a year in Africa, I had enough money left to last two more months, if I was thrifty. I kept in reserve enough to buy an air ticket back to Tehran. I recited the Tablet of Aḥmad, then I said a few more prayers.

Bahá'u'lláh, if it is your will that I return to where I came from, I will accept it. If you have something else in store for me, I hope you will manifest it now. I have gone through the tests; let not my hope of pioneering in Africa be shattered. I desire to participate actively in teaching your Faith to the people of this continent. O God, my God! Look not upon my hopes and my doings, nay rather look upon Thy Will that has encompassed the heavens and the earth.

That evening Soraya and Aziz invited me to go to the movies with them. I enjoyed movies but had stopped going in order to save money. I didn't feel like going out and thanked them, saying I preferred to stay at home. Aziz insisted that the outing would do me good and refused to take 'no' for an answer. So I went along with the two of them, telling myself it would do me good to forget my worries for a while.

As we were coming out of the movie theatre, I felt someone pluck at my sleeve. Turning around I saw Mr Baddeley, a man I had gone to for an interview some time before.

'Hullo there. Say, are you fixed for a job yet?'

I thought that my heart would stop. 'Not yet.'

'Well, here's my card. Come and see me tomorrow.'

I looked at the precious card, my ticket to a job and a chance to fulfil my mission in Africa. It read, 'Omni-Africa Trading Company, Managing Director, Victor Baddeley'.

I lay awake most of the night, thinking morning would never come. I kept telling myself not to get my hopes up, to be prepared for another rejection, but hope kept bubbling up, chasing off prudence. As soon as it was light I said my prayers, showered, shaved and dressed. I had to tie my tie three times before I was satisfied with the knot. I asked Aziz to drive me downtown.

Mr Baddeley explained that there had been nothing available in his company when I had come to see him about the possibility of a job.

'But now, if you are interested, there is a position open

as branch manager of our Mombasa office. You will have a "European" salary, a car and fringe benefits. All your travel expenses will be paid. The only drawback is that you must be ready to leave within the week.'

I would have been ready to leave the same day if necessary. Not wanting to seem too eager, I asked the usual questions about the conditions before accepting the job. Mr Baddeley told me to return in a couple of days to sign my contract. I shook hands with him and walked out a very happy, very grateful young man.

The following week I was sitting in my office in a big modern building in downtown Mombasa. I no longer had to count and recount my travellers' cheques; I had a salary of £70 a month and was a citizen in good standing. I had learned that God helps us when we have lost all faith in material means and rely only on Him.

Mombasa was an island city divided into white, Asian and black quarters. A bridge, a causeway and a ferry service linked it to the mainland. The settlement dated from the 16th century when Portuguese explorers had built Fort Jesus to protect the old port which had prospered during the slave trade. Located on the eastern side of the island, the original port had become too shallow to handle anything but light fishing craft and the Arab *dhows* that traded with the Persian Gulf since antiquity. The British had built a deeper, modern port on the western side of the island where ocean-going liners and freight ships could dock. Mombasa supplied most of British East Africa with imported goods.

Omni-Africa Trading Company had three main

branches of activity. It represented textile companies and sold cotton piece goods to local companies at wholesale prices; but it also supplied soft drink companies such as Coca-Cola with carbon dioxide. Its third branch imported bottles, labels, caps and syrups for soft drink companies.

For my work I had a company car, a small, two-door Anglia. It was dark blue, very old and had only three gears in working condition, first, third and reverse. It took me a while to learn to jump from first to third without any transition but I soon got the hang of it. The windows would never completely close at the top, so when it rained the seats got wet. Because of the bad roads, few cars in Africa had handbrakes that worked and the Anglia was no exception. I had to carry a rock with me to put behind the wheels when I wanted to park. The Anglia's speedometer was no longer working but I didn't worry about it because it was incapable of getting anywhere near the speed limit.

I had learned the rudiments of driving on army jeeps when I was working for Mr Hannibal, so I went to the British police and asked for a licence. The officer who gave me my test told me I needed practice. So I read the road regulations over carefully and practised on roads outside of the city where there was little traffic. The second time I went for the test I passed and was given a British licence.

My predecessor explained how the office ran and introduced me to the office boy, Moses. Coming from a culture which respects and honours old age, I was shocked to hear Europeans referring to an older man as their 'boy'. Moses told me that he was a Kikuyu who had come down to the city because he wanted to earn enough money to buy a guitar. That had been years ago but living in the city was so expensive that he still didn't have enough money for a guitar.

On first reaching Mombasa I registered at the Carlton Hotel. As soon as I had settled into my job I started looking for housing. I knew that living in the African quarter would look suspicious, not only to the Europeans but also to the Africans. I looked for something in the 'restricted area' reserved for Europeans that would allow me to maintain my status without using too much of my salary.

At the hotel I met a friendly young Dutchman named Jan who was also looking for a room. Eventually we were introduced to a rather mysterious American lady, Mrs Veynel-Mayo. She had a modern villa and was renting a large room that was big enough to share. No one knew exactly how or why she had come to East Africa but later she married a British doctor, Dr Walker. Her house, located along Mombasa Creek, was very comfortable and had a respectable address. The rent was quite expensive but by sharing the bill with my friend I was able to afford it. In general I got along well with my roommate, who worked for East African Metal Containers, which manufactured metal drums for Shell Oil Company.

Since there were no cooking facilities, I arranged to have my meals in town at a boarding house run by a Polish couple, Mr and Mrs Epstein. Actually, Mr Epstein rarely intervened; it was Mrs Epstein who gave the orders. She was a short, stout woman in her fifties with black hair that she wore in a tight bun. Glasses with rhinestone frames dangled on a chain around her neck. They seemed more a fashion accessory than a necessity, for I never saw her put them on. The large dining room had separate tables for families and married couples. The bachelors ate together at a large oval table in the middle of the room. I soon knew the menu by heart. Monday we had baked fish, Tuesday the leftover fish was served in fish croquettes and Wednesday the leftover croquettes were served in something called fish soup. On Wednesdays most of the boarders planned to eat out. Every now and then we did have some meat.

I became friends with the other bachelors, mostly young police officers or civil servants working in the port. I made no mystery of the fact that I was a Bahá'í but few of my friends were curious about what that meant. Anyway, pioneers were to give priority to teaching the Africans. Bahá'u'lláh had compared the black race to the pupil of the eye, through which spiritual light shines.[2] The Guardian was certain that the Faith had a glorious future in the great African continent.

Since my arrival in Africa, I had always worn a suit and tie whenever I presented myself to the authorities or went for a job interview. It seemed important to make a good impression. Now I began to dress like the other bachelors at the boarding house. I put my suit in mothballs and began wearing the colonial 'uniform': white shirt, white shorts and knee-high white socks. I even started smoking a pipe, and like everyone else, stuck it into the top of my socks when I wasn't using it.

I had not lived long in Mrs Mayo's house when I realized that there must be termites in the woodwork, for I was often kept awake by a gnawing sound that went on all night without interruption. I told Mrs Mayo about it and she came to inspect the room several times, looking everywhere, but she found no traces of termites. Yet the noise continued. One night I woke up around one o'clock in the morning. Outside everything was still but I could distinctly hear something gnawing wood. Exasperated and unable to get back to sleep, I got up and tried to locate where the noise was coming from. To my surprise I traced it to my roommate's bed. Listening carefully, I bent over the Dutchman and realized the gnawing sounds were coming from his mouth; he was grinding his teeth!

The next morning I told my friend about my discovery, and the Dutchman sheepishly showed me his teeth which were worn smooth from grinding together. It was a habit he had had since childhood, and though he had seen several doctors, they were unable to help him. I decided to try sleeping with earplugs.

As branch manager of Omni-Africa Trading Company, I was responsible for a sector that included all of Tanganyika (called Tanzania today) and stretched southwest to the copper belt of Northern Rhodesia (Zambia) and north along the coast up to Somalia. I enjoyed travelling across the vast African savannahs and learned a great deal about how the Africans lived outside the cities built by white men. The trips lasted several days. I sometimes covered thousands of kilometres visiting customers spread out all over my territory. Since my old car would not take me much further than the city limits, I usually travelled by train. When I had to go to Nairobi, the safest, most comfortable means of travelling was the Pullman. It left Mombasa in the evening and reached Nairobi early in the morning. There were two berths in each compartment, which meant sharing the compartment if you were travelling alone, and it was necessary to make reservations beforehand.

When I went to the train station to reserve my berth, I noticed that the Indian clerk who handled the reservations, a Sikh, examined the customers very carefully. Like many Indians, he was extremely respectful of the unwritten law of segregation. Blue-eyed blonds found themselves with another blue-eyed blond for a berth mate. Italians and Greeks were put in with Portuguese travellers. On my numerous trips to Nairobi, my companions were always dark-haired with fair complexions, Italian or Spanish. When I made a reservation by telephone, the clerk evidently decided that the name Zahrai sounded Italian, for I found myself with the Pirellis, the Hagikantakis and the Dos Santos, rarely with the Scotts, McPhersons or Butlers! Catering to their masters' prejudices, the Indian civil servants of East Africa, often victims of racism themselves, discriminated even more finely than their employers. (I heard of a hotel that had a sign reading, 'Dogs and Indians not allowed'.)

Sometimes I flew to Dar-es-Salaam on business. I occasionally found a ride with someone going my way. Europeans planning to make a long trip would put notices in the newspapers and up on bulletin boards in the hotels. It was always a good idea to have someone to share the driving and travelling expenses. I sometimes hoped that my companion would turn out to be a beautiful young lady, but young, eligible women were in short supply in the colonies. However, my travelling companions had many fascinating stories to tell about their experiences in Africa and I always enjoyed their company.

Later, when I had a new car, I made long trips on my own. I often drove to Dar-es-Salaam. On one trip I stopped for the night in Tanga. I found a hotel with a sign on the door that said 'Vacancies'. But when I went in and asked for a room, the young woman behind the desk looked me up and down and said, 'There are no rooms.'

'But the sign says there are vacancies.'

She looked at me again, her lips pursed with distaste, and pointed at a sign over the desk. 'Management reserves the right of admission.'

She made herself clear and I realized that I wasn't 'white' enough to rent a room in her hotel. For a second I felt furious. Then it occurred to me that there was no reason why I should feel insulted at being taken for an Indian. An Indian was as good as any other man. And if I had been an African? The incident helped me to better understand how angry and humiliated the Africans must feel, being treated as inferiors in their own land. I stared at the young woman, telling myself I should pity her. Her blind, stupid prejudice harmed her own spiritual growth more than it did me. I said nothing and went to look for another hotel.

I noticed that the English who had newly arrived were often shocked by the way the 'old hands' treated the Africans and had a tendency to stand up for the oppressed blacks and insist that they should be treated as equals. Young brides would ask their maids to eat at table with them, put vases of flowers in the servants' quarters and try to teach their old cooks to read. But after a few years, colonial life seemed to take the edge off their ideals and soon they accepted the traditional racial barriers.

Sometimes on a road across the savannah I had to stop the car at a zebra crossing. Tens, sometimes hundreds of striped pedestrians would leisurely stroll across the road, well aware that they had the right of way. Some came up to the car and sniffed, while the rest of the herd ignored it. At other times when I parked beside the road to rest and stretch my legs, a band of monkeys would jump on the car, bouncing up and down on the metal roof, apparently amused by the sound it made, then go on their merry way.

Once I drove beyond Dar-es-Salaam to Moshi and Arusha. There I stayed in a beautiful hotel, in a lodge halfway up Mount Kilimanjaro. The view was breathtaking. The hotel had been run by a German family since before World War I when Tanganyika had been a German colony. It was decorated with hunting trophies and a large fire burned in the diningroom fireplace. I was told that Princess Elizabeth had once stayed there. After living in the lowlands in Mombasa where the temperature was often 40 degrees C or more, it was a delight in the evening to snuggle under quilts and fur covers to keep warm. During the night I heard animals screaming in the dark. Occasionally I heard an elephant trumpet or the angry yowl of a great cat that had missed its dinner.

Strangely enough, although we heard many stories about the Mau Mau attacking settlers in the highlands of northern Kenya and the insecurity that was spreading, I felt perfectly safe during these trips. British law enforcement was effective and I didn't know any travellers who had been attacked or robbed, although the roads were long and lonely. Wherever I went the Africans were friendly and helpful, treating me with what appeared to be genuine respect. Certainly it wasn't the fear of prison that made them kind. I heard some of my African friends refer to the 'Hoteli Ya King George'. When I asked where this hotel was they told me that was what they called the state prison. Its prison cells, furnished with a cot, washing facilities, a toilet and regular, copious meals, were luxurious quarters compared to their shanty homes in the African quarter.

The Mau Mau uprising had begun before I reached Kenya. Essentially it concerned the Kikuyu tribe in the highlands and the European settlers who had taken their lands to build farms. Around Mombasa there were few Kikuyu but the Europeans were organized and prepared to defend themselves. At the boarding house, Mau Mau atrocities were a frequent subject of conversation.

In Nairobi Aziz Yazdi and his wife Soraya had a few tense moments when a group of excited young men that they took to be Kikuyu came to their house, but in the end they turned out not to be Mau Mau and afterwards my friends laughed about the incident. In Mombasa there seemed to be little danger.

Sometimes while on a trip in the lowlands I would have to stop for a bush fire. Seeing the wide savannah in flames, smoke broiling up to fill the dark night sky, was an impressive sight, but the Africans seemed to have everything under control. They burned the savannah at the end of the dry season so that they could plant for the coming rainy season. As the fire drove the game animals before it they were able to spear large numbers of small antelopes. The men smoked the meat to keep it from spoiling and then carried it back to the village. I began to get nervous when the flames were so close that I could feel their heat on my skin. There were always several jerrycans of gasoline in the car because gas stations in the bush were far apart. Yet, either because of my prayers or because of the Africans' care, the fires never came close enough to be really dangerous.

The month of March came and I began fasting. We Bahá'ís fast from the second of March through the 20th. I would wake up early in the morning while it was still dark, have my breakfast and say my prayers. Since my room did not have cooking facilities, my breakfast was just bread, fruit and an egg that I put in a thermos of hot water the night before. Depending on how big the egg was and how hot the water was, it was more or less soft-boiled by morning. I used the water in the thermos to make my tea. Since my roommate was still sleeping, I tried not to make any noise. I would get up in the dark and turn on the light in the hall so as not to disturb Jan and eat my breakfast by the light coming through the doorway. One morning I accidentally dropped a spoon and the noise woke up my roommate.

Jan was grouchy at being wakened so early. He glared at the alarm clock and shouted, 'I am fed up with your religion and your fasting. Why can't you live like any other human being?'

I just nodded. 'Yes, I can see that my fasting can get on your nerves. I'll tell you what. The day you stop grinding your teeth all night, I'll stop fasting.'

Jan got out of bed and stomped into the bathroom without another word. He was a long time in the shower. When he came out he apologized for his outburst. I apologized too, saying that the fasting period was meant to be a time of friendship and fellowship and I did not want to quarrel about it, but it was very important to me.

Once the sun came up I neither ate nor drank until it set, around six o'clock. Then I would stop in a cafeteria and have some tea and bread and butter. Later in the evening I had dinner at the Epstein boarding house, my one meal of the day. I did not suffer from hunger during the fast, but in the hot, humid climate of Mombasa it was difficult to drink enough to replace water loss from perspiration.

As a small child in Iran I had always enjoyed the yearly fast. In the preceding weeks my mother cleaned the entire house, took out all the carpets to air them and washed all the windows. Then she started planning menus, putting aside special treats and the ingredients for our favourite dishes. When the fast started, the whole family got up long before daylight, washed and had breakfast: yoghurt, bread, fruit, sweet syrups and jams, along with a cooked meal and lots of hot, sweet tea. Then we dressed and went to the home of Bahá'í friends to say prayers together. Only the adults fasted, and we children considered it a time of fellowship and special treats. I remembered the delicious meals that my mother prepared and the excitement of walking through the narrow, winding streets early in the morning, when the first birds were just beginning to stir. Sometimes in early March there would still be snow on the ground, which added to the mystery and excitement of getting up for the fast.

To me the yearly fast was a time of renewal and dedication. It was a time to forget physical hunger and think of spiritual hunger. The little bit of will power needed to hold off my appetite for a few hours was training for greater trials that we Bahá'ís would meet in upholding our Faith.

The fast ended on March 21st, the spring equinox and a major Persian holiday since antiquity, Naw-Rúz. To all Iranians, whatever their creed, it represents Easter, New Year's Day, Christmas and the 4th of July all in one. Schools are closed for an entire week. Most of the week is spent visiting relatives. First the younger members of the family visited their elders, then the elders returned their visits. We children received gifts of gold or silver coins which we saved until they were needed for something special.

For Naw-Rúz Iranian mothers prepared a special table of seven items, all beginning with the letter 'S'. The table decoration always included a bowl of gold fish and a mirror. Little bouquets of violets would be set out on the table if they were in bloom. A dish containing green lentil sprouts represented the new season.

Alone in Mombasa, the only Bahá'í pioneer within miles, I felt very lonely and yearned for companionship. I suppose that a Christian in a land where no one celebrated Christmas would feel the same on the 25th of December. I decided that instead of eating in the Epstein's boarding house that night I would go to a good restaurant and treat myself to a special meal.

I went to a restaurant that I had heard described as one of the best in town. A waiter seated me and I sat there, looking at my carefully set table. In spite of the vase of flowers, the snowy tablecloth, the gleaming silver, the crystal glasses and the tempting menu, I felt dissatisfied. Naw-Rúz was much more than an expensive meal. Naw-Rúz was a time for being with friends and celebrating spring, the rebirth of life, the end of dreary winter and the end of fasting, a spiritual victory. I looked around and saw another young man sitting alone at a table. I got stood up and walked over to him.

'Are you expecting company?' I asked.

The lonely diner looked up. 'No, why?'

'Would you mind if I ate with you? I'll explain why.'

'By all means.'

So I explained that I was Persian and what Naw-Rúz meant to me and why it didn't seem right to celebrate it alone. I learned that my new friend worked for the Cadbury Chocolate Company as a salesman. After dinner

I offered Brian a drink and Brian had some chocolate samples that he invited me to try. We became friends and saw each other often afterwards.

At the boarding house I met a friendly young man named Mortimer. He worked for the same pharmaceutical company that Aziz Yazdi represented. We got along well. One day Mortimer announced that he was going to be married and he asked me to be his witness. I was flattered at the request and glad to oblige my friend. When I went to the church for the ceremony, Mortimer introduced me to his bride. I thought that she looked familiar and she seemed embarrassed about something. Then I recognized her. Mortimer's new bride was the receptionist at the hotel in Tanga who had thought I was a bit too dark to be given a room. She had the decency to blush as we shook hands and I said nothing about our previous meeting.

I often had to go to the new port on business, but when I had some free time I enjoyed going to the old port on the eastern shore. By travelling a few miles I seemed to go back a hundred years. The Báb and His disciple Quddús had travelled from Persia to Mecca in a *dhow* just like those anchored in the old port. The Arab *dhows* had no radios, no engines and few sanitary facilities. They sailed across the Persian Gulf when the winds were favourable and sat at anchor when they were not. I spoke to the captains and crew members and found that some of them spoke Farsi with a southern accent.

One day I received a letter from Ali Nakhjavani in Uganda asking me to arrange to have a large quantity of flour shipped to a Bahá'í pioneer on Socotra Island in the Indian Ocean. It was a very isolated post and the pioneer was in need of financial assistance, but there was no way of sending him funds because there were no banking facilities on the island. Instead, the community had decided that if they sent him a large quantity of flour, he would be able to trade with the islanders for his basic needs.

I discussed the matter with an Indian brokerage firm in the old port. Since the business was urgent, I hoped that the flour could be sent by air freight. The brokers laughed out loud at the idea. No planes landed on Socotra Island. Then I supposed that it could be sent by freighter. Again the brokers found me amusingly naive and assured me that no respectable ocean-going freighter ever went anywhere near Socotra. They said that the only way the flour could be sent was by one of the *dhows* returning to Persia. They furnished me with insurance forms and bills of lading. Knowing that the pioneer in Socotra needed the goods urgently, I went to see the captain of the *dhow*. Walking through the narrow streets of the old city, I remembered that a two-metre-long python had recently been found in one of these old houses. I had seen a picture of three policemen holding up the monster in the newspaper.

The captain was a handsome, deeply sun-tanned man in his late fifties, with a magnificent yellow turban. He greeted me with courtesy and offered me some black coffee in the small porcelain cups used by Arabs.

'Sir, I'm the person who is sending a load of flour to

Socotra. Have you received the consignment?'

'I think so. If the broker said so, it must be so.'

'When are you sailing?'

'If Allah is willing, when the wind is easterly.'

'When will the wind be easterly?'

'Only Allah knows.'

'When will you arrive in Socotra?'

'It depends on the wind.'

'What happens if the wind is not favourable?'

'Then we will follow the coast to the Persian Gulf and we will deliver your goods in Socotra when we return to East Africa.'

'When would that be?'

'Next year, perhaps. Inshallah.'

'Inshallah, inshallah.'

I finished his coffee and went home, telling myself that I must remember the Bahá'í pioneer on Socotra in my prayers. To my relief, I later learned that the pioneer had received the flour after only one month.

8

Teaching

Once I had settled into my job, I began to look for opportunities to teach. The only Bahá'í on the island, I immediately began organizing teaching trips, hoping to see a Spiritual Assembly in Mombasa one day.

The International Bahá'í Council had addressed a letter on teaching to all the pioneers, stating quite clearly that we were to proceed with discretion and respect for the beliefs of others. The pioneers were not to 'sell' their religion but to look for people engaged in their own personal search for truth and to suggest that Bahá'u'lláh's message might be an answer.

I had the impression that part of the letter was addressed to me personally. It read:

> The Guardian realizes you will have many problems and difficulties, but he urges you to persevere under all circumstances; not to become disheartened in any way, but relying solely upon Bahá'u'lláh and His quickening spirit.[1]

We pioneers were not to use publicity, to put articles in newspapers or magazines, to contact authorities or political leaders concerning the Faith, to discuss government policies in any way or to seek a public proclamation of the Faith. We were urged to proceed with caution and discretion in presenting the teachings of the Bahá'í Faith.

> Make friends, and when these friends gain confidence in you and you in them, gradually confirm them in the Faith. What is needed is a complete reliance upon Bahá'u'lláh; pure consecration to the Faith, and then energetic but wise presentation of the Divine teachings. Such selfless sacrificial devotion will attract divine confirmations, and gradually you will confirm souls who will join you as strong supporters of the Faith in your area.[2]

One of the African paramedical students I had met in Nairobi, Jacob Kissombe, a friend of Francis Jumba, had originally come from the Mombasa area. I learned he was living in Mombasa and contacted him. Through him I met other young Africans who were interested in what I had to say about the Bahá'í Faith. Every weekend I would visit them in the African quarter. They lived in housing built for native workers, one storey brick houses with cold running water for showers and cooking but no hot water. They always welcomed me, asked me in and offered me something to drink. A little boy would scamper off to the nearest shop to buy a bottle of warm soda pop and I would sit and chat with my friends. After a while a neighbour would walk in, saying 'Jambo, jambo.' Then another, having noticed the Anglia parked outside, would come out of curiosity, then another, and when there was a sizeable crowd I would tell them about the Bahá'í Faith and the divine message that Bahá'u'lláh had revealed in Persia little more than a hundred years before. I described the terrible persecutions the early Bábís had suffered and my listeners groaned in sympathy, shaking their heads and clucking their tongues. I told them the stories of the early martyrs, of the heroic women who had marked the Faith at its very beginning and they listened with rapt attention. They were such an appreciative audience that I began to think I was a good storyteller.

They were awed by the story of Bahá'u'lláh, who came from a noble family and could have lived as a prince but instead accepted torture, exile, poverty and imprisonment in obedience to God. But best of all they loved the stories of 'Abdu'l-Bahá, who called Himself 'The Servant.' 'Abdu'l-Bahá, the son of Bahá'u'lláh, was born the day the Báb announced His mission. He was eight years old when He saw His father in chains in the Black Pit, the infamous prison of Tehran. He spent all the years of His youth and manhood in prison. When at last the Ottoman Empire fell, releasing Him from His gaolers, He was 65. An elderly man with no formal education, He set out to explain His father's message to the western world. And wherever He went, in the United States, Canada, England, France and Germany, crowds gathered to listen to the white-bearded old man in oriental robes who told them that women were the equals of men, that all races were one, that nations should disarm and form a world government, that there was a need for a universal language so that people from all around the world could communicate and understand each other, that conflicts between nations should be settled by arbitration rather than war, that religion was corrupted by men using it to satisfy their personal ambitions, that work well done was a form of prayer, that backbiting was one of the greatest evils a person could commit, that there can be no conflict between true religion and true science, which are but different perspectives of one, unique Truth.

'Abdu'l-Bahá had possessed the gift of expressing complex ideas in simple parables. He was sensitive to the question of race and went out of His way to honour the black people He met in His travels. I quoted from 'Abdu'l-Bahá's talks in Paris in 1911:

> We work and pray for the unity of mankind, that all the races of the earth may become one race, all the countries one country, and that all hearts may beat as one heart, working together for perfect unity and brotherhood.[3]

The Africans loved stories about 'Abdu'l-Bahá, and had no difficulty with the idea of fasting. Many of them were used to doing without meals. What they found hard to accept was the fact that alcohol was forbidden. Africans make beer out of coconut milk, whiskey from corn and wine with the sap of the palm tree. Drinking forms an essential part of all their traditional rites. Whenever someone dies or gets married or a child is circumcised, the first thing they do is to buy a crate of beer. I did not argue with them or try to convince them of the evils of drink. To me as a Bahá'í the matter was quite simple. If you believed in Bahá'u'lláh you obeyed His laws. If you didn't believe in Him, no one could expect you to obey Him and you were free to do as you saw fit.

One afternoon when I had been visiting the African quarter, I noticed when I got back into my car that the seat was very hot. I thought it was because I had left the car parked in the sun. It wasn't the first time I had had my thighs scorched by the hot plastic seat covering. Since the Anglia often refused to start, I had to park it on a hill and could not always find a nice spot in the shade. I drove off but the heat coming from the seat got hotter and hotter, burning my legs. Finally I could bear it no longer and had to stop. I got out of the car and saw smoke coming out of a small hole in the seat. The car was on fire!

Fortunately the seats were metal frames that could easily be removed. I was able to get the burning seat out and managed to extinguish the fire. It had burned a big hole in the seat, so I replaced it with the passenger seat. Now my car had no second gear, no hand brake and no place for a passenger to sit. Shortly afterwards I was given a pay rise that allowed me to buy a new car. I chose a white Volkswagen beetle and with it was able to make teaching trips outside of Mombasa, going to villages situated further inland.

Some of my young paramedical students became enthusiastic about the Bahá'í principles and declared their belief in Bahá'u'lláh. I organized 19 Day Feasts in the home of one of the new believers and we celebrated Naw-Rúz together. Within a year there were nine Bahá'ís in Mombasa, the minimum number needed to form a Local Spiritual Assembly. I wrote to Mr Banani in Kampala, informing him that there was now an Assembly in Mombasa. In those early days, the Hand of the Cause Mr Banani served as a clearing house, relaying messages between the Bahá'í World Centre in Haifa and all the pioneers. Later, when there were enough Local Assemblies, a Regional Assembly was established in Kampala that represented the Bahá'ís south of the Sahara. It maintained contact with all the pioneers and sent them *Bahá'í News* and messages from Shoghi Effendi.

One of the villages I visited was called Mackinon Road, 50 kilometres from Mombasa, on the road to Nairobi. The postmaster there declared his belief in Bahá'u'lláh and others followed his example. Soon a Bahá'í group was formed in Mackinon Road. I went there once or twice a month, for 19 Day Feasts and firesides, meetings at which people can learn about the Bahá'í Faith. When I went I would spend most of the day. My contribution to the potluck meal was always bread and butter, which were difficult to find in the bush. Sometimes Bahá'ís from Mombasa came with me. My little Volkswagen was indispensable for bringing those who lived far away to the meeting. A Local Assembly cannot vote or make any decision if there are not at least five members present. If my car broke down, there was no Assembly meeting. The little white beetle filled with most of the Local Assembly members became a familiar sight on the roads around Mombasa. I was very proud of my car and kept it clean and polished.

When there was no fireside planned and I found

myself with free time, I would drive north, south or west, leaving the main road and looking for new villages to teach in. I ranged widely on these trips. When I arrived in one isolated village the entire population turned out to stare at me. I learned that I was the first white man to pass that way since an assistant district commissioner had happened to pass by 20 years before. My arrival was quite an event and the little children stood around, staring at their first white man.

One day in a village when I was explaining that Bahá'ís did not drink, my listeners looked at one man and nodded their heads and grinned. Someone said, 'It won't be easy for him to become a Bahá'í.'

Later I asked why that particular man had been pointed out. They told me that he made his living by making palm wine and selling it. He supplied the whole village.

To my surprise, the next time I visited the village the same man came and sat down to listen to me. He said nothing but remained throughout my visit, obviously attentive to everything I had to say. The following week he was again present. When I had finished answering questions, the palm wine maker stood up.

'I have come to a decision,' he said. 'I am going to become a Bahá'í. I will stop drinking and will stop making palm wine.'

Everyone present understood that this was a momentous and courageous decision. There was applause and approving shouts. The man grinned widely.

'Come on, everybody!' he shouted. 'Let's go to my house and celebrate!'

As I left I hoped that they would not finish the entire stock of palm wine that night!

I continued working with the new Bahá'ís, explaining the scriptures, deepening their faith, teaching them the principles of consultation and decision-making in the Assembly. My goal was to make myself redundant, to see them develop as mature, autonomous believers. I did not tell those who had more than one wife that they must renounce all but one, as the missionaries did. On the contrary, I told them that they were responsible for all their wives and must care for all of them but that they should take no new wives and teach the next generation to give up polygamy.

Some of the new Bahá'ís, after an initial period of elation, became discouraged when they realized how difficult it was to live up to Bahá'í principles. I reassured them that I often had the same difficulties. No one becomes perfect the day they declare that they believe in Bahá'u'lláh. Becoming a Bahá'í is a lifelong project and no one on this earth attains perfection. What is important is striving to improve, bettering oneself just a little bit each day.

Hannah, a young woman who was one of the original members of the first Local Assembly, came to me and said that she was going to be married and would like to have a Bahá'í wedding. I read the prayer for weddings in front of the other Bahá'ís. It was the first Bahá'í wedding in Mombasa. Afterwards I couldn't help chuckling to myself. Through the marriage prayer the couple had dedicated themselves to God, saying, 'We will all, verily, abide by the Will of God',[4] but it was obvious from the bride's rounded shape that for the last six months they had been obeying their own will and desire.

Another day a Bahá'í named Joseph came to see me. He had been a paramedical student in Nairobi and was now working in the hospital in Mombasa. He said he had a major problem.

'I want to marry a girl. She is a laboratory assistant, an educated person like me and she wants to marry me. But our families will never accept the marriage if we don't follow the old customs. Before I can marry her I must offer her family the price of four cows. I have saved up enough to buy three but I don't have enough for the fourth cow.'

'How much do you need?' I asked.

'Forty shillings.'

'Okay. I'll lend you the money. You can pay me back later.'

So the traditional wedding took place with an enormous feast and music and dancing that lasted all night. Joseph kept his word and soon reimbursed the money he had borrowed for the cow.

Once, in a meeting in the African quarter, I was talking about my religion when a young man who had been listening intently spoke up.

'These things you are telling us are nice, but you are Persian and this is the religion of your country. Englishmen would never follow such a religion. All Englishmen are Christians.'

I understood what the man was getting at. The

European colonialists were powerful, they had taken away the land and made servants of people who had once been proud and independent. Therefore their religion must be powerful. Some Africans became Christians in the hope of sharing some of that power and were bewildered by the discrepancies between what the missionaries preached and the way they treated Africans in daily life.

'There are Bahá'ís in England and there are also English Bahá'í pioneers,' I replied.

The next day I wrote to Ted Cardell in Nairobi and asked him to come to Mombasa on a teaching trip. The following week I took my English friend to meet the Bahá'í group in the African quarter. Ted told them about 'Abdu'l-Bahá's trip to England and described how he himself had become a Bahá'í in England. The people present at the meeting were particularly dark, almost black, whereas most Africans are brown. I was fascinated by the scene of my very blond friend sitting in the centre of a group of black people. I remembered the words of 'Abdu'l-Bahá:

> Behold a beautiful garden full of flowers, shrubs, and trees. Each flower has a different charm, a peculiar beauty, its own delicious perfume and beautiful colour . . . So it is with humanity. It is made up of many races, and its peoples are of different colour, white, black, yellow, brown and red – but they all come from the same God, and all are servants to Him.[5]

I organized weekly meetings for the new Bahá'ís and anyone else who was interested. Outside of Mombasa Africans lived on small farms called *shambas*. They cultivated their own fields and kept a couple of cows and some goats. I became friends with an African who had a *shamba* close to a large market. I would park my car on the road, walk through the market and greet my friend, 'Jambo!' Stools would be brought out and set up under a large baobab tree and soon a small group of curious listeners would gather around. Traditionally the Bahá'ís call such meetings 'firesides' but I thought that 'fansides' would be a better name in Africa, for the heat was often excessive. At these meetings we had prayers and I talked about the principles I believed in and distributed pamphlets concerning the Bahá'í Faith to the few who could read English. Some of the new converts undertook to translate a pamphlet into Kiswahili, the lingua franca spoken all up and down the coast. I was able to distribute their pamphlet in the villages I visited on weekends.

I spent some of my weekends on the continent in small villages where white men were rarely seen and during the week I visited those who lived in Mombasa in the African quarter. There was quite a contrast between the two populations. The villagers maintained their ancient traditions, language and animist beliefs, while in Mombasa many of the Africans were of mixed blood, having been ruled for centuries by Arabs who came from the Gulf to trade. They spoke Kiswahili and wore shorts and trousers, following the European style. There were Muslim Africans in Mombasa but most of those that became

Bahá'ís had Christian backgrounds. Those who lived in town worked in factories, in the government administration or as servants, gardeners or cooks for white people.

The Bahá'í meetings were always held in African locations because I was not allowed to bring my friends to my room in the restricted area and the room would have been too small anyway. I regretted that I did not have a large home of my own to which I could invite them. I was aware that my Faith was being judged by my behaviour. It was not enough to proclaim my belief that all men were equal, I also had to demonstrate in my daily, professional life that I respected Africans. This sometimes caused me problems with the authorities.

One thing that shocked me was seeing that whites who had to drive their black servants somewhere did not allow them to sit up front. The Africans were put in the back seat, as if they were contagious, although they prepared meals for whites, made their beds and cared for their children. I believed that many Europeans were not really prejudiced but were unable or unwilling to fight the system that victimized the local people.

I always asked my African friends to sit with me up front in my car. This courtesy seemed to win over the carefully measured respect of Moses, my office boy. But one day I received a visit in my office from a police officer in civilian clothes who introduced himself as Mr Dixon.

'There have been some reports about an Iranian who goes into the African quarter and is frequently seen driving carloads of Africans around. What can you tell me about him?'

'I am the person you are talking about,' I replied. I explained that I was a Bahá'í and that I went to the African quarter to meet with other Bahá'ís. I showed the officer my papers. Mr Dixon came from the Criminal Investigation Department and was very surprised to learn that an Iranian could have a fair complexion and blue eyes. He decided that I was harmless and the matter went no further. I thought that it was both sad and amusing that the mere fact of being seen with a carload of Africans was suspicious to the colonial authorities.

Sometimes, with an African Bahá'í friend, I drove north along the coast and stopped at random in one of the villages. We would introduce ourselves to the headman and explain why we had come. Soon a meeting would be organized, seats would be set out under a tree and people would come to listen. I found it was easy to meet Africans, although in the city our relations were severely restricted. Those who had been taught Christianity asked me questions about Christ's second coming. Those who had come into contact with Islam asked me about the 'Mahdi'. But the one question that they all asked was whether or not there were any English Bahá'ís, as if they doubted that the white men they knew could accept a religion that practised racial equality.

'How can they deny it?' I asked. 'Look at that hen.' And I pointed at a little African hen scratching in the dust for her chicks. 'Her chicks are red and white and black but they all run after her and she cares for them all. Such are the races of mankind in the eyes of God.'

One day a man in a village stood up to speak.

'What you say is not new to us. We have heard about the Bahá'ís before.'

I was amazed because as far as I knew no pioneers or travelling teachers had come into the area. The man went into his hut and returned with a very professional brochure written in English and entitled *The Bahá'í Faith*. It began by giving an accurate and apparently objective description of the origins of the Bahá'í movement and its principles. Then, in the final paragraphs it attempted to refute the message of Bahá'u'lláh, particularly concerning the unity of mankind, on the basis of orthodox Christianity. The pamphlet had been printed, probably at considerable expense, by a group of Anglican missionaries. An African Bahá'í who accompanied me was amused by the incident.

'They have given a lot of these brochures to people who are illiterate, who will retain only the name Bahá'í and be curious to learn more about it from you. I talked to those who have read the brochure, and most of them did not read all the way to the end. So their impression is quite favourable. We can thank the missionaries for having prepared the ground for us.'

In 1955 letters from Tehran informed me that after Dr Mossadeq's fall from power the Bahá'ís were once more being persecuted. Their work ethics and their belief in education had helped the Bahá'ís to become a prosperous community. It is always easy for demagogues to turn the envious and often illiterate population against such a community and use it as a scapegoat.

Mullah Falsafi, one of the highest religious dignitaries

in the country, was inciting fanatical fundamentalist Muslims against the 'heretics', preaching in mosques and on national radio. The government supported his campaign and helped broadcast his sermons throughout the country. The young Shah, like his father before him, was courting the mullahs' favour in order to maintain his hold on the government, and once more the Bahá'ís were a convenient diversion. Military officials invaded the Bahá'í Centre in Tehran and gave orders to have it razed to the ground. The mullahs gathered an appreciative crowd and officers posed with sledgehammers for the photographers. A picture of Mullah Falsafi striking the first blow with a pickaxe made all the papers. Violent incidents took place in many parts of the country. Property belonging to the Bahá'í community was confiscated by the state, which officially refused to recognize the existence of the Bahá'ís.

Around the world Bahá'ís were mobilized in an attempt to put pressure on the Shah to stop the persecutions. Shoghi Effendi asked every community, no matter how small, to send a telegram to the Shah protesting at the unleashed violence and asking him to use his influence to stop it. In response to this appeal, I sent telegrams from Mombasa and Mackinon Road. The postmaster in Mackinon Road was thrilled. It was the first time he had sent a telegram to Iran and he half expected a reply from the Shah himself.

The Secretary-General of the United Nations, Dag Hammarskjöld, feared a large scale massacre. He convinced the Iranian representative that the world community would not close its eyes. The campaign against the Bahá'ís was called off and most of their goods were returned.

In addition to my job and teaching, I spent many evenings writing letters. I kept the Regional Assembly in Kampala informed of my progress and my problems but I also wrote to my mother and my brothers and friends in Iran, and to other pioneers in distant posts. There were times when I felt lonely and I always looked forward to the mail delivery, hoping to hear from faraway friends. When there were no letters there were the newspapers and magazines I subscribed to.

Mr Samandari, a Hand of the Cause from Qazvin, sometimes found time to write to me from Persia. His letters were written using Persian calligraphy and I treasured them both for the encouragement they contained and for their beauty. In one letter Mr Samandari told me that he had been talking to a group of Bahá'í youth, telling them about my work as a pioneer in Africa, and the work of his own grandson, Soheil, who was a pioneer in Somalia. Mr Samandari, who had dedicated his life to the service of the Cause, travelling all over the world, had been given the highest spiritual rank a Bahá'í could aspire to. Yet he wrote to me, 'How I wish I were in your shoes!' In spite of the hardships the pioneers encountered, their work was a glorious adventure for the Cause.

January 1956 came. I had been in Africa for almost four years. The Bahá'í groups I had formed were growing and becoming autonomous. The Omni-Africa Trading Company was also prospering and my employer was more than satisfied with my work. The routine that I seemed to be settling into was broken by the visit of two unusual Bahá'í pioneers.

Margaret Bates and her daughter, Jeanne, were well-to-do society women, well known in exclusive circles from California to New York. Today they would be called members of the jet set but in those days cosmopolitans travelled by ocean liner. Margaret and Jeanne had lived in Europe for many years, spoke several languages and were prepared to go anywhere in the world to share the message of Bahá'u'lláh. When they volunteered to be pioneers for the Ten Year Crusade, there were only a few goals that had not been met. One was in the Arctic Ocean and another was a small group of islands in the Indian Ocean. Shoghi Effendi suggested that they go to the Nicobar Islands. They travelled there with a mountain of luggage including ball gowns and dozens of matching hats and shoes and their dog, Muneca.

I was informed by the committee that the two ladies would be stopping over in Mombasa on their way to Bombay. So I met them when their ship came into port.

They were lovely, elegant ladies and I could not help being charmed by their enthusiasm for the Cause. And I was bewitched by their tiny, long-haired dog, the strangest looking creature I had ever seen. Jeanne told me that Muneca was a Lhasa Apso from Tibet.

I took the ladies to my favourite restaurant. It was near the port, the food was good and it was air-conditioned. The two ladies from New York were delighted to find so much civilization in the depths of Africa. After their lunch I escorted them to the native market near the old port, overlooking the graceful *dhows* at anchor in the bay. With its caged birds and monkeys, colourful cloths, bright piles of fruit and native sculptures, the old port of Mombasa was a fascinating combination of Africa and Asia.

Then I took my guests on a sightseeing tour. I introduced them to Hannah, one of the first women in Mombasa to declare her belief in Bahá'u'lláh. She explained to the new pioneers why it was so easy for Africans to accept the Bahá'í Faith. The Africans had their old, tribal gods, the Arabs had theirs, the colonists and their missionaries had other gods. The Africans had known all along that all gods were one, that all religions were based on the same truth.

I did my best to make the ladies' stay pleasant. Jeanne was attractive and I wished they were staying longer. I was worried about what would happen to two such elegant and cultivated women in the Nicobar Islands. The only thing they had learned about their future post was that the local people ate dogs. Yet they were determined to go there and do their best and I thought they would probably be able to charm their way out of any difficulties.

That evening I accompanied them back to their ship. Then I went home. From my bedroom window I could see the lights of the big ocean liner leaving the port. As I had promised, I began switching my light off and on. I found myself wishing I was on the ship, sailing into the dark in search of new adventures.

The following day in the market I saw a pair of lovely leopard-skin slippers. I remembered Jeanne complaining that her shoes hurt her feet. On impulse I bought the slippers and sent them to her hotel address in Bombay by air mail. And in a florist shop I wired her a dozen red American Beauty roses. I hoped that whatever hardships they encountered in their pioneering they would remember that their friends were praying for them.

After Margaret and Jeanne's departure, I realized that in spite of my many African friends and boarding-house buddies I was lonely. I sometimes felt the strain of living in two worlds. In my professional life I worked with Europeans and shared their advantages. In my teaching I spent all my time with Africans. I wondered sometimes if it would be more honest to move out of the restricted area and live in the African quarter. But I knew that the Africans themselves would be the first to condemn such a move as both hypocritical and condescending. I had met white men who had gone native and they were despised by whites, Asians and blacks.

I decided that it was time for a change. I had been working for four years without a real vacation, holding down a full-time job and spending all my spare time on Bahá'í activities. My contract allowed me only 'local leave', two weeks a year off work when I could go to Nairobi and spend some time with Aziz and Soraya. The two weeks went quickly and I felt a need for a longer holiday. I wanted to freshen my ideas, to have a change of scenery, to meet new friends.

Once again I wrote to Haifa, asking permission to go

there on pilgrimage. This time a favourable reply came through Mr Banani in Kampala. Since my contract with Omni-Africa Trading Company did not permit an extended holiday, I gave notice that I wished to resign. With my goal attained in Mombasa, I thought that I might be more useful elsewhere. Mr Baddelely was sorry to see me go and gave me a letter of recommendation saying that if at any time I wished to return to Kenya, he would be glad to give me a job.

The date was set. I would leave Mombasa in May 1957. While I was organizing my pilgrimage, I realized that it might be difficult to sell my Volkswagen. Cars were still a luxury in Kenya and there were few potential buyers. I put up notices and hoped to get a decent offer before I left Mombasa. In the meantime a Dutch friend, Joseph Hendricks, asked to borrow my car for a weekend trip to Tanga. I loaned him the car and was surprised not to see him Sunday evening. Monday morning my friend came to see me in the office, looking very nervous. He sat down and lit a cigarette, perspiring heavily.

'Joseph, what's the trouble?'

'Your car is a complete write off.'

'What happened?'

'When I was returning from Tanga somehow I went off the road and fell into a ravine and the car is completely wrecked; there's nothing left. I was lucky to come out of it alive.'

I was a bit concerned about the loss of the car but I did not want Joseph to feel too bad about the incident. He was a devout Catholic, never missing Mass, and we respected each other and had often had frank discussions about our beliefs.

'Okay,' I said. 'No problem. I'll call the insurance company.'

Joseph knew that I had always taken good care of my car. He felt miserable.

'If the insurance company doesn't pay, whatever the price, I'll pay the difference.'

But in the end the insurance company paid 350 pounds for the car, which I was able to add to my savings for my pilgrimage. I had an intuition that the loss of my faithful little white Volkswagen was a sign that I would not be returning to Mombasa. I knew that it would have been difficult to sell it at that price at such short notice. Before I left Mombasa, Joseph gave me a beautiful bound copy of the Bible which I treasured in memory of my friend for the rest of my life.

The next day I rode the train up to Nairobi and in a travel agency reserved an airplane ticket to Tel Aviv. Since there were no direct flights, my plane was routed through Athens. At last I was going to meet the beloved Guardian of the Bahá'í Faith, Shoghi Effendi, face to face.

9

Haifa

Render thanks unto thy Lord, O Carmel . . . Rejoice, for
God hath in this Day established upon thee His throne,
hath made thee the dawning-place of His signs and the day
spring of the evidences of His Revelation.[1]

Bahá'u'lláh

On the Italian airlines flight to Athens, I enjoyed the
comfort and appreciated the friendly stewardesses. The
very first Bahá'í pilgrims to St Jean d'Acre had travelled
for months through deserts infested with hostile tribes
and bandits. When their goal was in sight, the Ottoman
authorities refused to allow them to see the prisoner in
the old Crusaders' fort. They could only stand patiently
on the beach below and watch the barred window of His
cell until they glimpsed His hand waving at them. Then
they began the long journey back to Persia.

At the airport in Athens I met Dr Hermann Grossmann
and his wife, who were also travelling to Haifa. I had
met Dr Grossmann, a Hand of the Cause, in Heidelberg
during my European tour in 1952. Running into him
again seemed an auspicious beginning to my pilgrimage.

Our plane landed in Tel Aviv at one in the morning. The airport was far more modern than those I had
seen in Nairobi and Athens. Glasses of Jaffa orange juice

were passed out to the passengers waiting to go through customs. When it came my turn to have my baggage inspected, a rather stern-looking officer asked me why I had come to Israel. I replied that I was the guest of His Eminence Shoghi Effendi. Before I could open my suitcase, at the mention of the Guardian's name, the officer waved me on.

'That's all right, sir,' he said politely. 'You may go.'

I went directly to the Eastern pilgrim house and was soon asleep. At around one in the afternoon I was summoned to No. 10 Persian Street, which had been 'Abdu'l-Bahá's house in Haifa, to meet with the Guardian.

I wished I had had more time to prepare for the occasion. I was ushered into a plain sitting room where a gentle, smiling man immediately stood up and came forward to embrace me.

'Welcome, welcome,' he said in Persian. 'Come sit down.'

I was deeply moved. As a young boy living in Iran, I had dreamed of dedicating my life to the cause of the Bahá'í Faith and now I stood before its Guardian. My heart beat hard and fast with joy but also with awe. How could anyone with all my shortcomings measure up to the Guardian's expectations?

Shoghi Effendi led me to the sofa and sat down opposite me. He asked about my trip and said that he was glad to see me. About 60 years old, he had a gentle voice and kind eyes but there was about him an aura of natural dignity. He inquired about my life in Mombasa and his questions seemed prompted by more than simple courtesy. He wanted to know what my job had consisted of and said how pleased he had been to learn that I had finally found a job in Kenya. I felt as if I had come home and one of my brothers was asking about my trip and my work in Africa. I soon felt quite at ease. Whatever my failings, the man opposite me seemed to possess immeasurable quantities of love and understanding. The interview lasted half an hour and I came away with renewed respect and admiration, completely overcome by the Guardian's warm, compassionate personality.

Shoghi Effendi had a strange, unique destiny. He had learned to speak English when he was young. He studied first at the American University of Beirut and later at Oxford University. Utterly lacking in personal ambition, he had a quiet, shy, scholarly temperament. His only desire was to serve his grandfather, 'Abdu'l-Bahá, as an interpreter and to translate the writings of Bahá'u'lláh and 'Abdu'l-Bahá for the English-speaking world.

He was a 24-year-old student at Oxford when he learned of his grandfather's death. On his return to Haifa he was informed that 'Abdu'l-Bahá's Will named him Guardian of the Bahá'í Faith. Believers around the world were turning to him for guidance and the future destiny of the emerging world religion, less than a hundred years old, lay on his shoulders.

Older members of Shoghi Effendi's family refused to accept the young man's authority, in spite of the very clear and emphatic terms of 'Abdu'l-Bahá's Will. Shoghi Effendi was prostrated by grief over his grandfather's passing, by bitter attacks from members of his own

family and by the overwhelming responsibility of pursu-
ing his grandfather's plan for the expansion of the Faith.
Yet he took up the task and dedicated the rest of his life
to serving the Bahá'í Faith.

He brought to his role his own style and conception
of the job at hand. Unlike his charismatic grandfather,
he did not undertake speaking tours or in any way draw
attention to himself. He preferred to work through
others, encouraging each Bahá'í to develop his poten-
tialities to the maximum. He never spoke of his own
personal accomplishments, only of what the Baháís had
accomplished. Perhaps his greatest gift was his ability to
see what others were capable of. His vision and quiet,
behind-the-scenes efforts established the worldwide
organization that brought the Baháí Faith into the 20th
century, effectively preparing it for the 21st. In addition
to his administrative tasks he translated many major
texts of Baháʾuʾlláh and ʿAbduʾl-Bahá into English. He
lived modestly but for the construction of the magnificent shrines and administrative buildings in Haifa he
demanded exquisite quality. Nothing was too good for
the Cause.

Shoghi Effendi was interested in everything I could tell
him about the progress the Faith was making in Africa.
He asked detailed, informed questions and I was a little
bewildered by the fact that the Guardian seemed to know
the answers to some of the questions he asked.

I told the Guardian about a Baháʾí pamphlet that had
been translated into Griama, a tribal dialect of Kenya.
It was just a small brochure, no more than four pages

long, giving a brief description of the Bahá'í Faith and its founder. Yet Shoghi Effendi seemed to think that it was important and he mentioned it later to the other pilgrims. He became enthusiastic about anything that seemed to move the Bahá'í Faith one inch forward. I regretted not being able to give him more news of the growth of the Faith in my area, when I saw how much pleasure even small victories gave him.

I joined a group of pilgrims from Persia who met with the Guardian every afternoon. Shoghi Effendi received nine pilgrims from western nations in the evening and had dinner with them, usually speaking in English. In the afternoon, his secretary, Dr Luṭfu'lláh Ḥakím, would have chairs set up in front of the Báb's shrine and prepare tea for the eastern pilgrims returning from visiting the shrine. The Guardian sat with them and spoke to them in Persian for about an hour. He would answer their questions and speak to each one individually. Afterwards the pilgrims went to the pilgrim house and made notes about what had been said. Their notes, called 'pilgrims' notes', would be studied carefully by their local communities. Since the beginnings of the Bahá'í Faith pilgrims helped link the local communities with the founders of the Faith and their notes, although not authoritative, were invaluable guides to the local community's decisions, helping maintain Bahá'í unity around the world.

When I arrived in Haifa one group of pilgrims had just left. Another group was expected but they had had difficulties and had not been able to come. Shoghi Effendi chose to devote all the time normally allotted to eastern pilgrims to one young man from Kenya. I felt honoured by this unique opportunity to spend so much time alone with the beloved Guardian.

Shoghi Effendi told me that since the Suez war he had been unable to communicate with the sizeable community of believers in Egypt. He asked me to go there after my pilgrimage, to let the Egyptian Baháʼís know that they were not forgotten and to remind them of their pioneering goals. He wanted them to know of the progress being made in Africa and to encourage them to persevere in spite of their present difficulties.

As Shoghi Effendi explained the situation, I was walking behind him on the narrow path in the gardens around the shrine of the Báb and thinking about the task I was being given. At that time there were no diplomatic relations between Israel and Egypt and no direct flights. I would never be allowed to enter Egypt with a passport showing I had been in Israel. I would have to obtain another passport and be very careful that nothing in my luggage revealed I had been in Israel. Mentally I went over the things in my suitcase. Suddenly I became aware that Shoghi Effendi had stopped walking and turned to face me.

'Yes,' said Shoghi Effendi, 'you will have to be very careful.'

I stared at the Guardian. I had the impression that Shoghi Effendi had been listening in on my thoughts. I had heard it said that the Guardian could read minds but I had always assumed that the pilgrims, carried away by their love and admiration, had exaggerated mere coincidence. Now I began to have doubts.

Shoghi Effendi resumed his stroll through the garden. I followed him and heard the Guardian say, 'By going to Egypt you render a great service to the Cause.'

On another occasion the Guardian suddenly said, 'Dr Muhájir is a true pioneer.'

Dr Muhájir had been a friend of mine in Tehran. He had gone to the Mentawai Islands off the coast of western Sumatra, in Indonesia. He had given up his patients and a secure future in Tehran to be the first Bahá'í to reach the islands. Over a thousand local people had accepted the Faith. Their Assembly had been recognized by the government and he had founded a Bahá'í school. His name in Persian, Muhájir, means pioneer.

Nothing in the preceding conversation seemed to lead up to Shoghi Effendi's statement and I was struck by the way it seemed to come out of the blue. Dr Muhájir and I had served together on the youth committee but I did not know how the Guardian could know that.

Then the Guardian said to me, 'You are a Knight of Bahá'u'lláh. You too persevered in pioneering and succeeded. The young people of Iran and Europe must follow you.'

At these words I felt like a soldier that has just been decorated by his commander in chief. At the same time I felt unworthy, for I often wondered if I failed the Cause by not finding a way to stay in Mozambique or Rhodesia. I often told myself that if I had been more dedicated, more persevering, I would have accomplished more than I had. But I remembered a text from 'Abdu'l-Bahá which said:

Whosoever arises for the service of this building shall be assisted with a great power from His Supreme Kingdom and upon him spiritual and heavenly blessings shall descend, which shall fill his heart with wonderful consolation . . .[2]

The pioneers in Africa had given me messages, news and requests to relay to Shoghi Effendi. Philip Hainsworth felt that he had reached a stalemate in Kampala and wanted to leave.

'Philip must stay in Kampala,' replied Shoghi Effendi, 'especially now that the Regional Spiritual Assembly has been formed.'

After my audience with Shoghi Effendi I went to the pilgrim house to see Dr Luṭfu'lláh Ḥakím about obtaining a visa in Jerusalem. Dr Ḥakím had lived in England when Shoghi Effendi was a student and had served him faithfully ever since. He belonged to an eminent Bahá'í family, the descendant of the first Jewish Persian to accept the Faith. He was responsible for all correspondence from the eastern communities. Shoghi Effendi listened to the letters he read, gave his answers and Dr Ḥakím wrote the Guardian's replies in Persian. In this manner he had written and signed the letter to the National Spiritual Assembly in Iran which had urged me to go to Africa.

When I mentioned that I felt bad about Shoghi Effendi giving up so much of his precious time for just one pilgrim, Dr Ḥakím replied with a smile.

'No. You should not worry. He would come anyway. Whether there is one pilgrim or ten, he always comes.

And you are a Knight of Bahá'u'lláh. He is always glad to give his time to the Knights who come to Haifa.'

'But the pioneers in Africa have given me a lot of questions they want me to ask Shoghi Effendi. I'm afraid I'll tire him with all their questions. Isn't it too much for him?'

'You must ask questions,' replied Dr Ḥakím. 'You must ask as many questions as possible. And record the answers so that posterity will have the answers to those questions. Shoghi Effendi will not always be with us, and we will never have the answers to the questions you don't ask him. Many of the writings we have of 'Abdu'l-Bahá and Bahá'u'lláh are their answers to questions they were asked. Sometimes we regret that other matters were not brought up. The more questions you ask, the more answers posterity will have from Shoghi Effendi.'

He told me how meticulous and conscientious Shoghi Effendi was. When working on a translation he sometimes spent hours hunting for the one word that would give the exact sense of the phrase he was translating. He had personally designed the gardens and many of the decorations of the buildings of the Bahá'í shrines. He wanted the smallest details to be perfect.

During my stay I came to know several of the people who worked with Shoghi Effendi. They all received the same minimal salary and those who had the means forewent any payment for their services. Most of them toiled anonymously for years without any personal ambition, their only reward being the Guardian's gratitude. The Hands of the Cause did not consider their title as an honour but as a challenge to dedicate every moment of their lives to the Cause. They went wherever they were called, teaching, advising, carrying messages from the Guardian, truly acting as his hands, serving him with obedience, expecting only the reward of being allowed to continue to serve. I found their example inspiring.

Before the next group of pilgrims arrived, Shoghi Effendi instructed me to go to Bahjí to visit the house Bahá'u'lláh had lived in and to pray at the shrine. He said that I could spend two nights there.

Dr Ḥakím arranged transportation to St Jean d'Acre, now called Acco (Bahá'ís refer to it as 'Akká), on the other side of the bay, opposite Haifa. I went to the old fortress, which was still used as a state prison. The Israeli authorities allowed me to enter the cell where Bahá'u'lláh had once been held prisoner. I took off my shoes before setting foot on the sacred ground where Bahá'u'lláh had suffered. I looked at the only window and remembered the window in my cell in Lorenço Marques. I had spent only a few hours in gaol; Bahá'u'lláh had spent two years in this very cell, His family and friends crowded into other cells nearby. Several of them, including one of His sons, had died during their imprisonment.

I then went to Bahjí and walked through the garden to where Bahá'u'lláh was buried. Once more taking off my shoes, I said a silent prayer at His tomb, the most sacred of the Bahá'í shrines.

In Bahá'u'lláh's time, St Jean d'Acre had been 'a pestilential place, a home for criminals from all parts of the empire, a warren of labyrinthine alleys and damp crumbling buildings. Prevailing winds and tides washed the refuse of the Mediterranean onto its shores, creating a climate so unhealthy that a popular saying held that a bird which flew over Acre would fall dead in the streets.[3] After two years of strict imprisonment, the local Ottoman authorities required their prisoner to move from His cell to one small house after the other within the city walls, always under house arrest. Over time, the Ottoman authorities became more lenient and Bahá'u'lláh's son, 'Abdu'l-Bahá, worried about the fevers and diseases that were endemic in 'Akká during the hot summer months, looked for some way to move His father out of the city. Without His father's knowledge, 'Abdu'l-Bahá was able to rent a small house about four miles north of the city and had it repaired.

To test the injunction that Bahá'u'lláh and His family had to stay within the city walls, one day 'Abdu'l-Bahá did not ask permission to leave the prison-city but simply walked out. The guards made no objection and 'Abdu'l-Bahá went to the new house. The next day He left the city again, this time with a few friends, and again the guards did not stop Him. On another occasion He even arranged a banquet for town officials in a garden outside the city.

Eventually 'Abdu'l-Bahá went to Bahá'u'lláh and told Him that a new house had been prepared for Him in the countryside. Bahá'u'lláh refused to move, saying that He was a prisoner. Three times 'Abdu'l-Bahá asked Him and three times Bahá'u'lláh refused. Eventually 'Abdu'l-Bahá asked the Muftí of 'Akká to speak with Bahá'u'lláh and the Muftí was able to persuade Bahá'u'lláh to move to the new house. The very next day 'Abdu'l-Bahá drove Bahá'u'lláh in a carriage to the house in Mazra'ih.

Two years later 'Abdu'l-Bahá learned of a mansion for lease closer to 'Akká. The owner had fled an epidemic and was willing to rent cheaply. 'Abdu'l-Bahá leased the house, which was named Bahjí, which means 'Delight'. Here Bahá'u'lláh remained until His death in 1892.

That night I slept in the room that Shoghi Effendi used when he visited Bahjí. One wall was lined with bookshelves. Always a book addict, I looked for something to read. I chose *Christ and Bahá'u'lláh*, written by George Townshend, who had once been the Canon of St Patrick's Cathedral in Dublin.

After my return to Haifa, the Guardian asked me, 'Did you find something to read?'

Once again I had the uncanny feeling that the Guardian could read my thoughts.

'Yes. *Christ and Bahá'u'lláh*. I hope it was all right.'

'Of course.'

The Guardian added that it was a good book, explaining how he thought it could be used in teaching. Somehow, in addition to his work of translating the abundant writings of Bahá'u'lláh and 'Abdu'l-Bahá, corresponding with some 4,300 Bahá'í centres around the world, directing and coordinating the plans for the Ten Year Crusade, receiving pilgrims and other visitors who came to the World Centre, directing the construction of temples in distant lands and personally supervising the building of the Báb's shrine and the Bahá'í archives building on Mount Carmel, Shoghi Effendi had also found time to write a book about the history of the Faith, outlining the vision of its founders and its future development. I was impressed by the Guardian's capacity for work and his attention to the slightest details in everything he undertook.

On the afternoon of 11 May 1957, I had another audience with the Guardian. The two of us strolled in the gardens. Today thousands of tourists and Israeli schoolchildren who have never before heard of the Bahá'í Faith visit the gardens on Mount Carmel which surround the holy shrines and the Bahá'í World Centre. They are known locally as 'the Persian Gardens'. Shoghi Effendi, like most Persians, had a special love for flowers. While we were walking, the Guardian suddenly stopped and said, 'Those roses need cutting.' And he called over a gardener to give instructions. He wanted everything connected with the buildings and their gardens to be perfect.

While we were strolling past the rose bushes, Shoghi Effendi suddenly stopped and faced me.

'You're not planning to go to Iran after your pilgrimage, are you?'

'I had thought about it, just for a few weeks, although it might be difficult to get an exit visa to leave again. I haven't seen my mother for several years.'

The Guardian shook his head. 'Ask her to come to live with you in Africa. If it is possible.'

'But she doesn't speak any foreign language. It would be difficult for her.'

'You are alone; she could stay with you. If possible.'

As a result of this exchange I gave up any thought of going to Iran at that time. I wrote and encouraged my mother to come to Haifa on pilgrimage. There was a long waiting list and she was not able to come immediately but she did go on pilgrimage later. With time, I realized the wisdom and foresight of Shoghi Effendi's concern. If I had gone to visit my family in Iran at that time, they would have wanted me to stay, considering my mission as a pioneer finished. It was more than likely that I would have met an attractive young girl to make their arguments too convincing to resist.

On 12 May the first thing Shoghi Effendi said to me when we met was, 'How are you? You are alone again today, the other pilgrims have not yet arrived.'

I confided in the Guardian my disappointment over not having been able to obtain a residence permit in Southern Rhodesia.

Shoghi Effendi smiled. 'Today I have received a cablegram that the Assembly in Salisbury has been formed and registered.'

Indeed, after I was forced to leave the colony, other pioneers had arrived and managed to stay. Clair Gung came in October 1953, Eyneddin and Tahereh Alai in December of the same year and Kenneth and Roberta Christian in January 1954. I like to think that their work was made just a little easier by the many prayers I said in the park in Salisbury.

Shoghi Effendi told me about the map of the world he had drawn with the names of pioneers written in.

'It is in the mansion at Bahjí. Did you see it? Once all

the locations of the Ten Year Crusade have been conquered, a roll of honour will be prepared and it shall be put on a scroll and placed in the threshold of the shrine of Bahá'u'lláh. I intend this as an honour to the pioneers who obeyed my call to service.'

While we were walking, Shoghi Effendi stopped and rubbed his face and eyes.

'I am tired,' he said. 'Physically tired.'

At the time I thought that it was not surprising that a man with his workload should feel tired.

During another conversation I asked Shoghi Effendi if the pioneers in Africa should stay at their posts. The Guardian replied that they should work to delegate the power to the Africans, the sooner the better.

'Once they have taught, they should leave and go to other countries, even the most distant islands.'

Finally the group of pilgrims that had been expected arrived and Shoghi Effendi introduced me to the newcomers:

Mr Zahrai is a pilgrim and a pioneer from Africa. Five years ago when Mr Banani went to Africa, there was not even one single African Bahá'í there. As a result of his settlement, there are now more than three thousand Bahá'ís and all this happened in only five years' time.

The Guardian was very happy with the work accomplished by Mr Banani in Africa. I learned that Enoch Olinga, having opened the Cameroon territories to

the Faith where he had brought many new believers to
Bahá'u'lláh, had come to Haifa on pilgrimage in February.

The nine days of my pilgrimage drew to an end. I was
grateful for the opportunities I had had to pray at the
shrine of the Báb and to listen to the Guardian speak
about the work of teaching. I would treasure the memory
of the days of my pilgrimage for the rest of my life. I had
arrived in Israel thinking that my mission was accomplished. I left with a new sense of dedication, knowing
that my life's work had just begun. I was conscious of my
many imperfections but I made a promise to myself that
whatever the difficulties I might encounter, I would persevere in the service of the kind and gentle man who had
walked with me in the gardens on Mount Carmel, the
beloved Guardian of the Faith.

We had decided that Istanbul would be the first leg of
my journey to Egypt. I obtained a visa from the Turkish
consulate in Jerusalem. Turkey was the only Muslim
country that maintained diplomatic relations with Israel.
In Istanbul I would ask the Iranian consul for a new passport, then apply to the Egyptian embassy for a visa to
enter Egypt. I realized that it was going to be difficult and
had no idea how to convince the Iranian consul to grant
me a second passport. Persian diplomats rarely went out
of their way to help Bahá'ís. However, I felt confident that
if Shoghi Effendi wanted something to happen, it would
happen.

As soon as I reached Istanbul, I contacted the Local
Spiritual Assembly and gave its members messages
from Shoghi Effendi. It was a large, long-established

community. The first Bahá'ís to settle in Istanbul were faithful followers who had accompanied Bahá'u'lláh in His exile. On leaving Persia the Bábís had first gone to live in Baghdad. However, the Shah had become uneasy about their growing influence so close to his borders and he urged the ministers of 'Abdu'l-'Azíz, the Sultan of the Ottoman Empire, to have Bahá'u'lláh moved further away. The governor of Baghdad, Námiq-Páshá, held Bahá'u'lláh in high regard and reluctantly followed the orders that came down to him from his superiors to 'invite' Bahá'u'lláh to visit Istanbul.

Bahá'u'lláh and His family arrived in Istanbul in August 1863. Once settled, He was expected to call on the high officials. However, He made it quite clear that he had no interest in politics and no personal ambitions. His mission was spiritual and He did not hesitate to denounce the corruption and decadence of the Turkish court. Persian diplomats warned the Sultan that the movement was a menace to his empire and noted how Bahá'u'lláh's influence and popularity in the Turkish capital were growing daily. Hence, after only four months, Bahá'u'lláh was ordered to Adrianople, on the European continent, then, after five years, sentenced to life imprisonment in St Jean d'Acre.

I explained to the Bahá'ís of Istanbul that I needed to obtain a new passport and a visa to Egypt. They told me that it was impossible. The Persian consul general did everything possible to hinder the Bahá'ís in all their administrative requests.

'That's possible,' I said, 'but this mission was given to

me by Shoghi Effendi himself. I am to write a report to him and furnish him with the statistics he needs. I am determined to accomplish it, one way or another.'

A member of the Assembly said, 'Okay. Tomorrow morning I'll take you to the Iranian consulate. But that is all we can do to help you.'

The next morning in front of the consulate, my friend said that he thought he'd better stay outside. A known Bahá'í, his presence might indispose the consul before I could make my request.

So I walked into the consulate alone, smiled at the secretary and asked to see the consul general. Perhaps my good manners made a favourable impression. After a brief wait I was ushered into the office of the consul general. I explained that I had been in Israel and now wanted to go to Egypt but would not be allowed to enter with the Israeli visa on my passport.

'Why the hell did you have to go to Palestine?' asked the consul.

'I am a Bahá'í,' I replied. 'I went on pilgrimage to Haifa.'

The consul scarcely listened to my explanation and kept repeating angrily, 'Why the hell did you have to go there? Wasn't there any other place you could go?'

I refused to be intimidated. I remained polite but spoke with more confidence than I felt.

'Look, sir,' I said. 'I have to go to Egypt. I have important business to handle and with this passport I cannot go. So I would like you to give me a new passport.'

'Are you out of your mind?'

'No, I am not out of my mind. I could have come to

you and said that I'd lost my passport. But that would have been a lie. I'm telling you the truth and I would be very grateful if you would give me a new passport.'

The consul looked me over. 'Why did you leave Persia?'

I told him that I had read about the British colonies in Africa and wanted to find work there. I explained that for the last four years I had been living in Kenya. The consul asked if I had had any problems with the Mau Mau uprising and I repeated a few anecdotes that I had heard. The conversation went on and the consul seemed to relax a bit. I suggested that he read the book by Robert Ruark, *Something of Value*, about Kenya and the Mau Mau movement.

'If you like, I'll send you my copy when I get back to Mombasa.'

The consulate official suddenly seemed to remember that I had come to ask for a new passport.

'What you are asking me is impossible but let me see your passport.'

I handed it over. The consul looked through it and saw that I had a return visa for Kenya and had travelled a great deal in Africa. He was intrigued. He asked several questions about the countries I had visited. Then he mentioned that he had been to Palestine before the war and that he had visited the 'Persian Gardens' in Haifa.

Finally he said, 'Okay, I'll give you a new passport.'

He called in his second-in-command and asked for a blank passport. He filled it in himself and stamped it and handed it to me. I thanked him and left the consulate feeling very pleased with myself.

My friend was still waiting outside. I told him, 'I've got a new passport. Didn't I tell you that if Shoghi Effendi wanted something to happen, it would happen?'

We got into the car and I leafed through the document. Suddenly I realized that I would not be allowed to return to Kenya without my re-entry permit for Kenya which was in the old passport I had left at the consulate.

This time I was really worried. It seemed a minor miracle that I had obtained my first request. The consular officer might find me presumptuous and change his mind about letting me have the new passport. I decided not to bother the consul general again and asked to see his second-in-command.

I asked the official if he could cut the re-entry visa from Kenya out of my old passport and attach it to the new one. The Persian gave me a sneering look.

'No. I don't want to do that.'

'Very well,' I said. 'May I speak to the consul?'

Back in the consul's office, I explained my problem.

'Why didn't my assistant handle that?' asked the consul.

'He doesn't want to do it,' I answered.

'Never mind, let me do it.' And he took a pair of scissors and cut the re-entry visa for Kenya out of the old passport, glued it into the new one and put on stamps to certify its authenticity.

So I walked out of the consulate a second time, elated by my success. My Bahá'í friend was amazed that the consular officials had been so exceptionally obliging. Then we went to the Egyptian embassy and obtained a visa without difficulty.

That night I was lying in bed, drowsy but unable to sleep because of the heat. I noticed that the chandelier over my head was trembling. Gradually it occurred to me that chandeliers don't usually quiver. Then I sat up, wide awake. The entire building was being shaken by an earthquake. I opened the door and saw people in their pyjamas rushing down the hall. I followed them outside. Perfect strangers in their night clothes were standing around carrying on animated conversations; some said the earthquake was over, others said the worst was yet to come. The hotel was a modern building that showed little sign of damage but there were fires in other parts of the city and we could hear sirens in the distance. There was a great deal of confusion and panic but nothing seemed to be happening. After a few hours, I got tired of waiting. I went back into the hotel, dropped onto my bed and fell into a sound sleep.

Part III

Europe

10

Brussels

Among the people of Bahá, however, marriage must be a union of the body and of the spirit as well . . .[1]

'Abdu'l-Bahá

Two days later I was flying to Cairo on a four-engine, propeller-driven Pan American plane. I was surprised to see that we were only two passengers. After the Suez Canal was nationalized by Nasser in July 1956 there was little traffic to Egypt.

Since the war the Bahá'í community in Egypt had been completely cut off from Haifa. I was to be careful to appear to be meeting Bahá'ís for professional reasons and not to communicate the addresses I had to the police. As soon as I reached Cairo I went to the office of Aziz Yazdi's brother, Abul-Rahim Yazdi, a member of Egypt's National Spiritual Assembly.

Mr Yazdi was tall and friendly, like his brother. He called a meeting of the National Spiritual Assembly and introduced me to its members. I gave them the messages of encouragement that Shoghi Effendi had entrusted to me. They were relieved and thrilled by the Guardian's words, proof that in their isolation they were not forgotten and the rest of the Bahá'í world was praying for them. A member of the Assembly was chosen to accompany me on a trip all over Egypt. Before I left Cairo a gathering was organized in the Bahá'í Centre so that as many as possible could hear the news from Haifa. More than one hundred people were present. A professor at the University of Cairo, Mr Azzawi, translated my speech into Arabic. He had translated Shoghi Effendi's book, *God Passes By*, and knew all the Bahá'ís of Cairo by sight. They had agreed that if he saw a secret police officer or someone who was not a Bahá'í in the audience, he would say only things that could not be used against the Bahá'ís. Everyone was careful not to mention Israel or the Holy Land by name.

I read to the audience part of a message that Shoghi Effendi had recently addressed to all the Bahá'í world, commented on certain passages and answered questions concerning the implications of the message. I did not realize then that this particular message would be the last Shoghi Effendi would ever send to the Bahá'ís of the world. I also described the progress the Faith was making in Africa and talked about some of my own experiences as a pioneer. I relayed Shoghi Effendi's wish that they send pioneers to various locations in Egypt and to Tripoli.

After my talk cakes and tea were served. The Bahá'ís moved around, chatting with one another. A young couple came up and introduced themselves as my niece Aqdas and her husband, Enayat Akhavan, a student at the American University in Cairo. I hadn't seen Aqdas since she was a little girl in Qazvin and didn't know she had married Enayat. They invited me to stay with them while I was in Cairo and I was glad to accept. After the meeting I went home with Aqdas and her husband. They put a mattress down in the living room of their small studio for me to sleep on.

I spent the next two weeks travelling to the major cities of Egypt, meeting with Bahá'ís and telling them about the progress of the Faith and the work being done at the World Centre in Haifa. A member of the National Spiritual Assembly, Sabri Elias, accompanied me. We went by train from Cairo to Alexandria, to Port Said, to Suez. As in all Muslim countries the Bahá'ís of Egypt suffered from persecution and ostracism, yet they stubbornly clung to their Faith and I was profoundly moved by their spiritual attitude. Egypt had been open to the Faith very early in its history and was the first country to be visited by 'Abdu'l-Bahá when He was finally allowed to leave St Jean d'Acre. It was in Egypt in 1925 that a Muslim ecclesiastical court had ruled that the Bahá'ís were not an Islamic sect but a separate religion. To the Bahá'ís it was a landmark decision, proof of their independence, although its immediate effect was to have the marriages of three Bahá'ís annulled and for the Bahá'ís to be deemed heretics.

I took notes on my trip so that I would be able to make my report to Shoghi Effendi. My notes contained statistics concerning all the Egyptian communities, their numbers, locations, elected bodies and so on. When I was ready to leave Egypt I worried about this information falling into the hands of the police if I was searched at customs, but apparently I aroused no suspicions. I went through without any problems and boarded a ship to Italy. During the journey I wrote up my report and sent it to Haifa as soon as I reached Italy.

Later I received a letter from Dr Ḥakím saying that they were pleased with the information I had sent them. In reply to the Guardian's question, I had informed him that I intended to visit Scandinavia during my European holiday. Shoghi Effendi asked me to tell the Assemblies there how much he appreciated the services they had rendered to the Cause.

So I travelled north to Copenhagen, Oslo, Gothenburg, Stockholm and Helsinki. Everywhere I went I met with local Bahá'í communities to tell them about the Ten Year Crusade, the progress being made in Africa, my experiences as a pioneer and to share the news from Haifa.

I attended the Danish Bahá'í summer school in July. This gathering allowed Bahá'ís to combine their vacation time with deepening their knowledge of the Faith, its founder, its history and its principles. Talks were given in the morning while the afternoons were given over to fellowship and sporting activities. The Danish summer school was held in Aalborg and was attended by Bahá'ís from Sweden and Norway as well. Like many towns in Denmark, Aalborg was near the beach, so the young people often went swimming in the afternoon.

I made my first speech at a unity banquet in a hotel with about 50 people sitting around a U-shaped table. I spoke in English, which almost all the Scandinavians understood. After my talk there was music and singing.

I was struck by the variety of ages, social classes and

nationalities. The Bahá'ís came as families to the summer
school and there were activities for everyone and assis-
tants to watch the children while their parents attended
the lectures. One afternoon I saw a blond, enthusiastic
Danish youngster debating with a grey-headed Persian
pioneer and a black exchange student from the United
States. An elegantly dressed Swedish aristocrat was chatting with a janitor. In Persia and Africa there had been
mutual respect for different social classes but in the
European summer schools I first saw the Bahá'í principle
of 'unity in diversity' being most visibly put into practice.

I found the Danish girls friendly and very attractive.
In Persia, by tradition, a man had to count on his female
relatives to choose his wife. I couldn't help smiling at the
idea of going to matchmakers. By then I was 31 years old
and thought more and more often that I would like to
marry and start a family. In all my travels I had had few
opportunities to meet the kind of girl I dreamed of, a girl
who was well-educated, thoroughly modern, pretty and
stylish but dedicated to the Cause, and above all, a good
mother. I wondered when I would have a settled, secure
job that would allow me to start thinking about finding
a wife.

Summer schools sometimes provided the setting for
budding romances that ended in matrimony, and young
pioneers in isolated posts would plan their holidays to
coincide with the summer school calendar, making no
secret of their hope of finding a companion. But I had
a crowded timetable and stayed only a few days in each
of the summer schools I visited. The mission Shoghi

Effendi had given me took priority over any romantic hopes and wishes.

When I had completed my assignment, I decided to go to Belgium. I arrived in Brussels in late July 1957, hoping to find a position with a company that had offices in the Congo. Shoghi Effendi had suggested that I try to settle in the Belgian Congo where the need was greater than in Kenya. By then there was a large and flourishing Bahá'í community established in the British colony, whereas they were still very few in the Congo in spite of the much larger population. I intended to look for work with a Belgian company that would send me to Africa and help me obtain a visa and a residence permit. In general, employees hired in the mother country had a higher salary and better conditions than those hired locally. I thought friends in the Bahá'í community might be able to help me contact Belgian companies with offices in the Congo. If nothing came of it, I could always return to Kenya and ask Mr Baddeley to give me back my job.

The Bahá'í community in Brussels was willing to help me look for a job and also asked me to give a talk on my experiences in Africa and my recent pilgrimage to Haifa.

In October a cablegram for the community announced the Guardian's appointment of eight new Hands of the Cause. When I read the list I was delighted to see the names of two people I knew personally. Enoch Olinga, the enthusiastic young African believer I had met at Kampala, had done remarkable work in opening British Cameroon to the Faith. His appointment as a Hand of the Cause was a reward but also a sign of the Guardian's belief that he would continue to do great things in spreading the Faith.

The other name that I recognized immediately was that of my former teacher in Qazvin, Abu'l-Qásim Faizi. I knew that after extensive services to the Faith in Iran Mr Faizi had volunteered to pioneer in the Persian Gulf territories, areas where physical conditions were extremely difficult and where the animosity of fundamentalists frequently put the lives of pioneers in jeopardy. Mr Faizi was an inspiring example, not only to me, but to an entire generation of young Iranian Bahá'ís who today are spread around the world.

Some time later I received a letter from Gerd Strand, the secretary of the Scandinavian National Spiritual Assembly based in Norway.

'Your arrival was at a time when we badly needed encouragement. When you said that Shoghi Effendi appreciated what we had done, we asked ourselves what he meant. We had done nothing. So we felt obliged to begin doing things, in order to deserve his praise.'

At a 19 Day Feast in Brussels I met Mrs Marthe Molitor, a Bahá'í whose husband had been a civil servant in the Belgian Congo. When he was young Mr Molitor had gone to Iran with a Belgian delegation at the request of Reza Sháh who had asked Belgium for advisors to assist in modernizing the country. Mr Molitor had helped to organize the Iranian customs office and had many good memories of his stay in Persia. He liked to talk to me about his experiences there. Since his retirement the couple spent much of their time travelling and their apartment in Brussels was often empty. They told me I could use their apartment during my stay in Brussels.

I was very grateful, for once again I found it necessary to be careful with my money. I tried out half a dozen restaurants until I found one that offered a good, copious plate of spaghetti for a few Belgian francs and there I became a regular customer.

Early Tuesday, on the morning of 5 November, Mrs Lea Nys of the Local Spiritual Assembly of Brussels called me on the phone.

'Mr Zahrai, something terrible has happened. We have received a cablegram from Haifa. The Guardian has died in London.'

I dressed without even taking time to shave. I went to see Mrs Nys and we were joined by Mrs Dekonnick. We couldn't really believe that it was true but a telephone call to friends in England and another cablegram from Haifa confirming the first convinced us. The Guardian and his wife, Rúḥíyyih Khánum, had gone to London to choose furniture and decorations for the new archives building. Weakened by his heavy workload, Shoghi Effendi had caught the Asian flu which was sweeping Europe. He had seemed to be recovering satisfactorily when he died in his sleep of a heart attack.

We learned that the funeral would be held in London on Friday, 9 November. With other Bahá'í friends in Brussels we boarded a train for Ostend, where a ferry carried us across the Channel to England.

During the long trip, there was little conversation. We were not prepared to lose our Guardian so soon. Everyone

P.M.15517— '147G—1,500P—1.10.49

POST OFFICE TELEGRAPHS—S. RHODESIA

The first line of this Telegram contains the following particulars in the order named: Prefix Letters and Number of Message, Office of Origin. Number of Words. Date. Time handed in and Official Instructions—if any.

CIRCUIT	CLERK'S NAME	TIME RECEIVED	TIME SENT

T 2n.

STAMP

DATE
25 JUN
S. RHODESIA

R656 HXA153 HAIFA 9-25 1010 =

EZZATULLAH ZAHRAI BOX 2075 SALISBURYSOUTHRHODESIA

= FERVENTLY PRAING SUCCESS = SHOGHI ₥ 2075 ₥

If the accuracy of this telegram is doubted, enquiry should be made at the office of delivery. This form should accompany any enquiry.

Telegram from Shoghi Effendi received by Ezzat on his arrival in Southern Rhodesia

Ezzat, *far left*, with other members of the executive committee of 'Young Expo', Brussels, 1958

Annette Riis, around the time Ezzat met her in January 1960

Ezzat at work in his Paris office, 1960s

La Blanche, the Zahrai's farm in the south of France

Children's activities at La Blanche

Governing Board of the European Bahá'í Business Forum, with Muhammad Yunus, *seated centre*, founder of Grameen Bank, at a conference on Microfinance and Human Development, sponsored by EBBF, in Stockholm in 1998. Co-founders of EBBF George Starcher, *seated second from left*, and Ezzat Zahrai, *standing far right*

Knights of Bahá'u'lláh
gathered in Haifa
at the observance
of the centenary of
the Ascension of
Bahá'u'lláh, 29 May
1992

Ezzat and Annette visiting Mombasa in 1996

Harare, 2003: Local Bahá'ís and pioneers commemorate the fiftieth anniversary of the establishment of the Bahá'í Faith in Zimbabwe. Ezzat, *rear, far left*, and Annette, *front, second from left*

Ezzat with his wife, Annette, and children, 2009
and with his grandchildren, 2007

was shocked and overwhelmed at the loss. Those who had known him personally were completely demoralized and we were all apprehensive about the future of the Faith. Shoghi Effendi's vast capacity for service to the Faith and the energy with which he fulfilled his tasks had left us with the impression that he would always be there to watch over us and guide the young world organization that was taking shape. I remembered the quiet man I had walked with in the gardens of Mount Carmel, and I remembered seeing him put his hand to his head, saying, 'I'm tired. Physically tired.' I believed that though the immediate cause of death was a heart attack, the truth was that the Guardian had died of exhaustion and overwork. In his ceaseless, unstinting devotion to the Cause, he had worn out his terrestrial envelope.

When we reached London we went to the National Bahá'í Centre in Rutland Gate and found it crowded with mourners arriving from all over Europe. The telephone was ringing non-stop with messages and queries from Djakarta, Bombay, Kuwait, Israel and the United States.

Friday morning, shortly after ten o'clock, what seemed like an endless procession of cars left the Centre in the direction of the Great Northern Cemetery in New Southgate. I rode in a hired car with Mrs Nys and other friends from Belgium. Staring at the grief-stricken faces around me, I realized that each of my companions felt the Guardian's death as a personal loss, as I did. They were mourning not only the official representative of our Cause but also a dearly beloved friend who had watched over us, encouraged us and consoled us, who had known how to bring out in each of us hidden, unknown resources.

The casket, draped in a cloth of purple and gold, covered with an enormous wreath of scarlet roses and white gardenias, was carried into the chapel and installed on a dais. The prayer for the dead was read in Arabic, then other prayers were read in English. Suddenly I heard a familiar voice chanting a prayer in Persian. I looked up and saw Mr Faizi. My former teacher was still tall and athletic-looking but his hair was grey and thin on top. His deep, majestic voice chanted the words of the prayer with moving eloquence.

After the prayer the casket was carried outside and placed once more in the hearse. The limousine drove slowly to the burial site while the mourners followed on foot. Four young cypress trees had been planted at the corners of the large plot, recalling the many trees that Shoghi Effendi had planted in the gardens of the holy shrines. The tomb faced east, in the direction of Mount Carmel. When the flowers were removed, I could read the inscription underneath.

Shoghi Effendi Rabbani
First Guardian of the Bahá'í Faith
March 3rd, 1896 – November 4th, 1957

Rúḥíyyih Khánum informed the believers that we could render a last homage to Shoghi Effendi. For more than two hours the Baháʼís passed in front of the casket, one by one. Most of them knelt and touched their lips to the edge of the casket. Elderly men sobbed like children and even the British, known for their reserve, broke down and wept in public. A representative of the Israeli government paid his respects.

The last mourner was Rúḥíyyih Khánum. An erect, slender figure in black, she came forward and knelt in silent prayer. Then she covered the casket with a green cloth and a blue velvet brocade that had been brought from the tomb of Bahá'u'lláh in Bahjí. On top she laid an armful of jasmine flowers. The casket was slowly lowered into the tomb while prayers were said in Persian and in English. Then, slowly, the mourners withdrew.

I returned to Brussels determined to do what I could to further the Guardian's plans, to carry my little stone to build the new world order that Shoghi Effendi had described. The sacrifice of the life of the gentle man I had met in Haifa should not be in vain.

I continued going to interviews but I soon realized that the Belgian companies with offices in the Congo were not hiring. The independence movements made them very apprehensive about their investments in Africa. If I wanted to go there, I would have to accept any job I could find. Very little of the money I had saved in Mombasa was left. I spent almost all my time reading ads, writing letters and going to interviews. The pioneering committee gave me a loan of three hundred US dollars to tide me over until I could find work, which I was later able to reimburse.

To save money, I started doing my own cooking. I learned to cook rice with chicken bouillon cubes and found it to my taste. When Mr Khadem, Hand of the Cause, came to Brussels, I met him several times. I would have liked to invite him out but I could not afford a good restaurant and I was afraid that the little place that served spaghetti was too humble and noisy.

Mr Khadem was such a kind, friendly man, that I finally said to him, 'I would very much like to invite you to come to where I live, to eat with me, but I don't dare because I am not a very good cook.'

Mr Khadem smiled. 'By all means, let's go and see what you can make.'

I took him to the Molitor apartment and prepared a dish of rice cooked in chicken bouillon.

'This is marvellous, the most delicious food I have had for a long time. It has a Persian flavour,' said Mr Khadem.

Because of his kindness I gained new confidence in my cooking abilities. Yet I hoped that I would not always be obliged to do my own cooking. I was 32 years old and still a bachelor. Most of my friends had married and were raising families.

Belgium is a French-speaking country. Other than the three months I had spent in the copper belt area of the Congo, I had had few opportunities to improve on the French I had learned in school in Iran. I decided to sign up for evening classes. At the night school I met a nice young Canadian girl named Margaret. We quickly became friends and started dating. Wanting to make a good impression on her, I borrowed Mrs Molitor's car, a Volkswagen like the one I had had in Kenya, to take Margaret to a movie.

Margaret was a bright, witty girl who made me laugh with her stories about the other students in our class. We had a good time at the movies and I was driving her home, laughing at one of her stories, when all at once I heard someone screaming and a tramcar loomed up in front of us. I hit the brakes and stared in horror as the tram came to a shuddering stop. It took me a few seconds to realize that I was still alive and Margaret, the car and I were all intact. Having learned to drive in Kenya, I had completely forgotten that in Belgium you must drive on the right. The incident left me so shaken that it was the last time I borrowed Mrs Molitor's car.

Margaret returned to Canada soon afterwards and I went on looking for work. One day I received a telegram from an American company that I had applied to. It said, 'Come and see us urgently, Remington Rand.'

I put on my best suit and rushed to their office. When I got there I learned that they didn't have a job for me but they had a book that they wanted translated from French to English. They gave me a test that seemed to satisfy them that my knowledge of English was adequate for the job. They then explained that I could not take the book home. I would have to do all the work in their offices. I spent a month translating the book and was paid three hundred dollars for it. The manager was pleased with my work.

'You've done an outstanding job. In addition to your payment, we would like to offer you a Remington shaver.'

I thanked him but admitted that I already had a shaver.

'What would really be useful to me would be a type-writer.'

The manager ended up giving me a portable Remington typewriter which I was still using until my children declared that it was probably a priceless antique.

Word seemed to get around because one night shortly after midnight I received a call from a Canadian businessman who had heard that I was a translator. He explained that he had a contract to sign that he urgently wanted translated from Persian into English. The next morning I met him at his hotel for breakfast. The contract concerned construction work in Iran and was about four pages long. When the businessman asked what my price was, I offered to do the job for 50 dollars.

'Will 75 be all right?' asked the Canadian.

'Yes, of course.'

'In that case, I want it tomorrow.'

I went back to the apartment and stayed up until five in the morning translating the contract. I was back at the hotel the next day with the English translation. The Canadian paid me in travellers' cheques.

One day I learned that the Vahdats were in Belgium on home leave. I called on them and we had a pleasant time recalling my visit in Kamina. I assured them that at the time I little expected to ever look back on my stay at the Catholic mission with pleasure. Their description of recent events in the Congo was not encouraging. Many Belgian companies were closing down, fearful of what would happen when the colony acquired its independence.

In 1958 everyone in Brussels was preparing for the World's Fair. I heard that the General Commissioner of the Iranian pavilion was a Bahá'í named Azizbeglou.

When I met him, we discovered that we were related by marriage. I asked if he had any work for me and was hired immediately as secretary and second-in-command. The fair lasted six months. Almost every country in the world had a pavilion to display their goods and attractions with guides dressed in typical costumes to receive the visitors. In all there were over one thousand young people from around the world working at the exhibition. It was a rare opportunity to work among so many bright young representatives of virtually every country in the world.

A girl from Argentina tried to organize the young guides and pavilion employees into a club called 'Young Expo'. Unfortunately the cold war had contaminated the young people's attitudes and there was a lot of jealousy and misunderstanding between different groups, making it almost impossible for them to work together. A meeting was called in Argentina's pavilion to discuss what could be done. I went and listened to the complaints, criticisms and recriminations being tossed back and forth across the hall. After a while I raised my hand and stood up.

'I'm Ezzat Zahrai from the Iranian pavilion. I'm very surprised to see such disunity among young people. Our fathers have been fighting and killing for ages but we are the new generation. We should be setting an example of friendship and unity, yet here we are, fighting with each other, letting ourselves get caught up in the fire of political rivalries. Why not have a free election here and now and appoint a committee to organize things and sort out all the different suggestions? Can't we leave politics out of this and choose five or six people that everyone trusts?

Once they have listened to all the different points of view, they can propose a programme to be voted on.'

My suggestion drew some murmurs of approval and the motion was quickly made, seconded and voted. A Canadian, an American, a Czech, a Russian and I were elected by secret ballot. We met right after the assembly and to my surprise I was elected chairman. Used to consultation methods as practised in Baháʼí Assemblies, I applied the same principles to the governing board, encouraging the members to listen to each other's opinions without bias and making all decisions by a majority vote. I suggested that the girl from Argentina who had initiated the assembly but had not been elected to the committee be made our honorary president.

'Young Expo' organized social activities for the youth working at the fair. Most of the pavilions sponsored events; the Czechs had a magic lantern evening, the Americans gave a dinner party, the Russians a cocktail party. There were theatres, movies, luncheons and picnics. One of the most active members was a young Catholic priest, Father Verdoodt, from Belgium, who later became a good friend of mine. Each of the members wore a badge and we published a directory with the names and addresses of all members. Our profits were put into an account to be turned over to UNICEF. The organization generated so much good will that towards the end we learned that outsiders were trying to use the 'Young Expo' name to solicit members for other purposes. For that reason we voted to put an end to the organization when the World's Fair closed.

The experience proved to me that Bahá'í consultation methods were effective even when they were used with people who were not Baha'ís. I knew that it was not my skill that had made the committee work but the techniques of consultation we applied. When the fair was over it was sad saying goodbye to so many good friends but we promised we would write to each other and keep in touch.

Brussels was the European headquarters of the Coca-Cola corporation. I met a German Bahá'í who knew Dr Zimmerman, the head of Coca-Cola's legal department in New York. He wrote to the American lawyer and explained that I had experience working in Africa and was looking for work.

It so happened that when the general manager in Brussels received Dr Zimmerman's recommendation he had just had a letter from their African division saying they needed a manager for the Coca-Cola plant in Mombasa. He asked me to come in for an interview. While working for Omni-Africa Trading Company, I had supplied the Mombasa plant and was familiar with their set-up. My experience in Kenya, my banking and commercial knowledge and my linguistic abilities made it an ideal post for me.

I was hired, given a good salary and I spent three months in Brussels training for my new position, learning everything I could about the running of a plant before returning to Kenya. After completion of my training course I would be leaving for Africa within the month. I was very happy about the job, which promised to be more interesting than the one I had had with Omni-Africa. I was looking forward to returning to Kenya, seeing my friends and continuing my work for the Cause. With a secure job and an adequate salary, I would be able to think about marrying and raising a family.

One day, a few weeks before my departure, I was called into the office of the general manager of the European division who had interviewed me for the position of plant manager.

Mr Graf greeted me kindly and began by asking me a few questions about my training. Then he said, 'Mr Zahrai, I have some bad news for you.'

'What is it?'

'Well, I have received a letter from Mr Mansel, the general manager of Coca-Cola Africa Limited, who would be your direct superior. He lives in Southern Rhodesia and has studied your file. He has come to the conclusion that you are not suitable for the job we have been training you for.'

I was stunned into silence, trying to comprehend what was happening. Then I asked, 'Did he say why?'

I could see that the general manager was really embarrassed.

'He does not question your qualifications. It seems rather ridiculous but in East Africa the job is classified as 'European' and Mr Mansel claims that an Iranian manager, however well qualified he may be, would not be accepted by the other employees.'

He gave me a few minutes to take this in before going on.

'I may not agree with Mr Mansel but I cannot impose on him an employee he objects to, for whatever reason. He is not under my authority. If there were an equivalent position here in Europe, I would be glad to give it to you but unfortunately at this time there is nothing available.'

Although I was extremely disappointed, I realized Mr Graf's embarrassment was genuine. It would not do any good for me to get angry and shout about injustice and my rights. Mr Graf knew nothing about the unwritten race laws of the British colonies; he could not have foreseen Mr Mansel's objections. Even the Southern Rhodesian gentleman was but the tool of a system he had not created.

I stood up and shook hands. As I was leaving the office, Mr Graf took my arm.

'I am genuinely sorry about this. I'll see to it that you get generous severance compensation.'

And he did. I received three months' salary as compensation whereas I had only worked for the company for three months and could have been discharged without any severance pay.

Shortly afterwards I applied for a position with an American company that specialized in consulting work. Their headquarters were in Düsseldorf but they had a branch office in Brussels and worked with enterprises throughout Europe. Because the job involved constant travelling, they wanted a bachelor. I was interviewed by an American who found that my qualifications and experience met their requirements and I was hired as a consultant.

After a month's training I began working. For the next few years I carried almost everything I owned in two suitcases. I slept in hotels and ate in restaurants. My work was rewarding, involving all aspects of business operations, but also extremely difficult. My job was to go into medium-sized and large firms and analyse their requirements, studying how they operated in marketing, sales, management and production. After a week's study I would report my diagnosis to the management and suggest a programme to be undertaken by my company's experts to improve their situation.

This required the ability to rapidly assimilate business operations in widely different areas. One week I would go into a textile factory and the following week into a plant specializing in plastic materials, or a company which was service-oriented. When I presented my findings I had to show that I understood the technical jargon that was specific to each industry and be prepared to give knowledgeable answers to their questions, otherwise my recommendations were not likely to be taken seriously.

The other aspect of my work that was difficult was the constant travelling. Since the Molitors' apartment was no longer available, I rented a furnished attic room in Brussels but I was rarely at home. My first jobs were in Belgium and then I was often sent on missions to the northern part of France. Eventually my company decided to open a branch office in Paris and they asked me and several other consultants to move there.

I was not thrilled at the idea. My heart was still set on returning to Africa as a pioneer. I did not see living in comfort in a big city like Paris as compatible with the life of a pioneer. It did not seem that I could serve the Faith by moving to France. I wanted to turn down the job but my employers were adamant. They gave me the choice of going to Paris or looking for a new job. I told them that it would be very difficult for me to acquire a work permit in France but they said they would handle the authorizations. Within months I found myself in an office on the Champs-Elysées. It was merely a base of operations because I continued to travel as much as before, going all over France to give advice to customers who requested our services. I took a room in the Hotel Washington in Rue Washington, within walking distance of my office. When I realized that my stay in France was not going to be temporary, I moved into Le Petit Ritz, a boarding house in Rue d'Amsterdam, within walking distance of the St Lazare train station.

As soon as possible I met the French Bahá'í community, which was smaller than either the German or British communities. Now that I was settled into a steady job, I wanted to pay back the loan that had been given me by the pioneering committee. No one was able to find a record of the loan, so I gave the three hundred dollars to the National Spiritual Assembly of Iran as a gift.

I soon realized that working for the Cause in France was not an easy matter. Although French society was far more advanced and apparently more tolerant than those I had known in Iran and in Africa, the Faith had made little progress. Many of the French people I met were permanently soured on any form of religion after their childhood experience with Catholic catechisms. Others seemed to believe that religion was out of touch with modern life, something for children, old people and naive dreamers. I found it difficult to understand how some of the people I met could live so totally divorced from every spiritual aspect of life but there were many things that I liked about the French. I appreciated their elegance, their culture, their love of good food and I was amused by their worshipful attitude towards the great French wines.

I followed the progress being made in Africa where many of my friends were still working as pioneers. A Bahá'í temple was being built at Kampala for which the cornerstone was laid at the Intercontinental Conference held, on schedule, in January 1958. When I had first gone to Africa there had been a mere handful of pioneers in the entire continent. Now there were already thousands of registered believers and the number was growing daily.

In France also the Faith was progressing and in 1958 the delegates of the Local Spiritual Assemblies elected the first National Spiritual Assembly of France. The Custodians of the Faith in Haifa wrote to express their gratitude.

I met a young American Bahá'í working with a US company in France. John Bayers and his wife and two daughters lived near Paris in a big house in Le Vesinet that they had completely furnished with American furniture. I was invited to their home for dinner one evening in January 1960.

When I arrived at their home, I was introduced to

two attractive Danish girls. Susie was blond, short and a bit plump and very exuberant, the life of the party. Her friend was a tall, pretty, slender girl with curly brown hair. She was shy and spoke very little. I sat across from her at dinner and learned that Annette Riis lived with the Bayers as an au pair, looking after their two little girls who were seven and nine years old. She had been an exchange student at Harvard University in the United States, where she had studied history and English for a year. She had come to France to study French at the Alliance Française in Paris.

She was not only beautiful but she had what I can only call 'class'. It has something to do with education and up-bringing but it is more than that. Her clothes were simple but elegant, seeming suited to her quiet personality. I tried not to stare at her and listened to Susie's lively stories but when I went home that night, all I could think of was lovely Annette. The French have an expression for love at first sight, *coup de foudre*, which means struck by lightning. That's what happened to me at that dinner party in Le Vesinet.

It took me a couple of days to get up the courage to call her and ask her for a date. She seemed surprised but accepted to spend Sunday, her day off, with me.

For our first date I took her to Jour et Nuit, a very nice seafood restaurant near the Champs-Elysées. Later Annette told me she had never eaten oysters before but didn't want to seem provincial. So she forced them down, even one that tasted bad. Then we went to a movie but Annette started feeling sick. Before the end of the film she had to rush out and, unable to reach the ladies' room in time, threw up in a bucket in the hallway. I felt horrible that I had put her through such embarrassment and was sure she'd never want to see me again.

But as soon as she had freshened up a bit, she told me that she wasn't going to let a squeamish stomach spoil our date. She assured me that she felt fine and we went to visit the Palais de Chaillot and the History of Man museum on the Trocadero. Then we went to the Eiffel Tower to admire the view. It was a bright, sunny January day and Paris was beautiful. I talked about my life in Africa and by the end of the afternoon she seemed more comfortable with me and began to talk about her family in Denmark. Her father was a grain wholesaler who furnished oats for the horses of the Royal Danish Army. She confessed that she missed her brother and sisters very much. We spoke in English, for we both felt more at ease in English than in French.

Around five o'clock I asked her if she would like to go to a lecture at the Bahá'í Centre. I discovered that while Annette knew that her employers were Bahá'ís, she knew very little about their religion. She was curious and agreed to go. We took the metro to Rue de la Pompe where a ground floor apartment had been converted into a social centre. There were about 20 people present – French, Iranian and some Americans. Tea, cakes and cookies were served after the lecture and the young Danish girl seemed to be enjoying herself. Afterwards we went to a nearby restaurant for pepper steaks. No more seafood!

When I took Annette home that evening I asked if I

could see her again. I almost expected her to say no, after her disastrous introduction to oysters, but she agreed to see me the following Sunday. I spent most of the week travelling all over France and was only in Paris on weekends.

After that we saw each other every Sunday. We often visited museums and the Trocadero, the Arc de Triumph and other Parisian landmarks. We attended Bahá'í meetings regularly, for I wanted her to know that my Faith was an essential part of my life.

I learned that she was going to be 21 on the 16th of March, so I bought her a bottle of perfume as a birthday present and asked Mrs Bayers to give it to her at breakfast. I chose Femme by Rochas because the name means both woman and wife.

Shortly after we met, the French Bahá'í community received startling news from Haifa. In the hours following Shoghi Effendi's death, the members of the International Bahá'í Council in Haifa had sealed his apartments so that they would remain undisturbed until all the Hands could gather to consult on the matter of his succession. Bahá'u'lláh had left a testament naming 'Abdu'l-Bahá His successor, the Centre of the Covenant and the official interpreter of His writings. 'Abdu'l-Bahá had, in the same manner, left a testament naming Shoghi Effendi the first Guardian of the Faith, and, drawing upon texts left by Bahá'u'lláh, He had outlined the future world administration. Shoghi Effendi had dedicated his life to making those plans a reality. His grandfather had indicated that the Guardian's oldest son, if worthy, would inherit his rank. Unfortunately, Shoghi Effendi and Rúḥíyyih Khánum had no children. All the Bahá'ís expected to find in the Guardian's apartments a will appointing his successor and instructions to continue his work.

No such document was ever found and the 27 living Hands of the Cause of God that met in Haifa after the Guardian's funeral found themselves the temporary custodians of the Faith. Indeed, in his last message to the Bahá'í world, Shoghi Effendi had referred to them as 'the Chief Stewards of Bahá'u'lláh's embryonic World Commonwealth'.[2]

The Hands of the Cause recognized that as a body they did not have the authority to appoint a new Guardian. A decision regarding whether or not a new Guardian could be appointed could only be taken by the Universal House of Justice, and that did not yet exist.

At the same time, they realized that Shoghi Effendi had given them sufficient guidance in his instructions for the Ten Year Crusade to take the Faith forward until its conclusion. After that, there was no direct guidance. Thus the role of the Hands in his absence was to do everything in their power to establish the Universal House of Justice. Hence at their meeting in November 1958 they called for the election of the House of Justice at the conclusion of the Crusade, in 1963. An important decision made by the Hands of the Cause was revealing of their spiritual devotion. They declared themselves ineligible for election to the Universal House of Justice. It may be a unique example of a group of leaders at the head of a worldwide organization dedicating years of their lives to setting up an authority that would divest them of all power.

The Hands who met in Haifa in November 1957 elected nine of their members to remain in Haifa to serve as a permanent body of Custodians, handling the day-to-day affairs of the Cause. The entire body of Hands were to meet at least once a year. Their work programme had been clearly defined by Shoghi Effendi himself. In 1958 Intercontinental Conferences were to be held to bring together representatives of the more than 250 countries with established Bahá'í communities. The purpose of the Conferences was to promote unity and stir the believers to new efforts in order to attain the goals of the Ten Year Crusade launched by Shoghi Effendi.

In the spring of 1960 some of the American Bahá'ís in France began circulating a proclamation made by Charles Mason Remey, Hand of the Cause. Over 80 years old, he had come to the conclusion that his position as President of the International Bahá'í Council, a body established by Shoghi Effendi as the forerunner of the Universal House of Justice, made him Shoghi Effendi's successor and the second Guardian of the Cause. The other Hands of the Cause were deeply upset by Remey's claim and immediately and unanimously refuted it. He was plainly not a male descendant of Bahá'u'lláh, a requirement clearly stated by 'Abdu'l-Bahá in His Will and Testament. The American National Spiritual Assembly, to which his proclamation was addressed, immediately declared its unswerving loyalty to the institution of the Hands of the Cause. In the history of Mason Remey's claim to

complete, infallible authority over the entire world organization 'as Commander-in-Chief in all Bahá'í matters',
what is remarkable is the firm restraint and loving sadness with which the other Hands reacted, hoping that the
elderly Hand could be convinced of his error and brought
back into the fold. 'Abdu'l-Bahá had honoured Charles
Mason Remey with His friendship and Remey's lifetime
of service to the Faith had earned him the loving affection
of members around the world. They could only assume
that his great age and his grief at the sudden, unexpected
loss of the Guardian had affected his mind.

Cables from National and Local Assemblies around
the world assured the Custodians of their loyalty. The
only National Assembly in the world that accepted the
proclamation of the self-appointed 'Second Guardian'
was that of France. I suspected that some of its American
members had originally encouraged the elderly Mason
Remey to make his proclamation and used their pressure within the Assembly to have his claim accepted. The
Hands of the Cause met in Haifa and decided to send Mr
Faizi to France to represent them and reason with the
five members of the French National Spiritual Assembly
who recognized Remey's claim.

I then belonged to the local community of Paris,
which did not approve the proclamation. I met with Mr
Faizi and encountered several of the American Bahá'ís
living in France who had accepted Remey's claim, trying
to convince them of their error. In the Bahá'í religion
those who refuse the spiritual authority of appointed and
elected bodies are known as covenant-breakers. To my

deep sorrow my friends the Bayers were among those who rejected the authority of the Custodians.

I wrote them several letters, pointing out that according to 'Abdu'l-Bahá's Will and Testament, if the first Guardian's line was interrupted, he should choose 'another Branch', a translation of the Arabic word Aghṣán and it was applied only to the members of Bahá'u'lláh's immediate family. There were no living Aghṣán within the Bahá'í Cause for Shoghi Effendi to choose from and no texts that could justify applying the term to Charles Mason Remey.

The Will and Testament of 'Abdu'l-Bahá also specified that the Guardian's choice must be approved by nine Hands elected by the entire body of Hands, whereas none of the other Hands recognized Remey's claim.

I met with the Bayers several times but their minds were closed to my arguments and they eventually refused to see me again. Mr Faizi, acting under the authority vested in him by the Custodians, dissolved the National Spiritual Assembly of France and asked the Paris Assembly to serve as the central Assembly until elections could be held. The vast majority of French believers remained firm. The covenant-breakers were expelled from the Faith and the incident was quickly forgotten.

I continued seeing Annette for over a year. Then she told me that her parents had decided it was time they met me. In April 1961 Mr and Mrs Riis flew from Copenhagen to Paris for a short visit. I invited them to a very expensive restaurant that Annette's mother judged worthy of her fox stole. Although I did not drink wine,

I knew enough about it to order an excellent bottle for my guests. I hoped to impress them as a serious, hard-working young man but I think it was very clear to them that I was head over heels in love with their daughter. Before going back home, they let Annette know that they liked me very much.

That summer I took Annette to Bahá'í summer schools in England and Holland. While she was getting to know me better, she was also studying my religion. She told me that there were many things that attracted her in the Bahá'í teachings; she had not been completely at ease in the Protestant religion which sometimes seemed more of a social convention than a religion. Yet she took her time making up her mind. She knew then that if she declared herself a Bahá'í, it would be a lifelong commitment.

During the summer school in Holland we listened to a talk by Mr Ghadimi, a Persian who was then living in Liege, Belgium. He explained the concept of progressive revelation. Suddenly, as she sat listening to him, Annette seemed startled. Later she told me that she had remembered her communion ceremony in the Lutheran church of her childhood. The pastor had just declared that only through Christ could one be saved and had asked if there were any questions. It was part of the ritual so everyone was surprised when she stood up and said she wanted to ask something.

'What do you do with all the other children of the planet who happen to be born in China, India and Pakistan? Why should I be saved just because I happened to be born in Denmark?'

The pastor had frowned and mumbled something that failed to satisfy her. While Annette was studying in Cambridge, Massachusetts, she had met students from all over the world – Indians, Pakistanis, Japanese, Hindus, Muslims and Buddhists – who seemed certain that they possessed just as much of the truth as she did. In the concept of progressive revelation as Mr Ghadimi explained it she found that her question was answered. Throughout the history of man, God had sent divine Messengers to reveal His laws and commandments. Bahá'u'lláh had said, 'Every Divine Revelation hath been sent down in a manner that befitted the circumstances of the age in which it hath appeared.'[3] Many philosophers and theologians had realized that the fundamental messages of the different prophets and messiahs were the same. Bahá'u'lláh explained why. That evening Annette, with her usual calm air of knowing what she was doing, declared her belief in the Bahá'í Faith and made me a very happy man.

11

Paris

Consider these martyrs of unquestionable sincerity . . .
all of whom . . . have sacrificed their life, their substance,
their wives, their children, their all, and ascended unto the
loftiest chambers of Paradise.[1]

Bahá'u'lláh

I knew beyond the slightest doubt that Annette was the woman I had been praying for to share my life. I found myself thinking about her all the time, and at the same time I knew that my job involving incessant travelling would make me a part-time husband. Changing jobs seemed unlikely. The French government gave work permits to manual labourers from Africa and Asia for jobs that no one else wanted but management positions were reserved for French nationals. If I were to resign to take another job, my work permit would be revoked. It seemed unfair to ask Annette to become the wife of a man she would see only on weekends.

Throughout my life, whenever I faced difficulties and frustrations, I had learned that the first step was to pray about the situation. One morning I was alone in a small room that had been put at my disposal by one of my clients. I was drafting a new project for the company but my mind kept straying to Annette. I decided to pray. I had just finished when Mr Naintré, the client I was work-ing with, came to take me to lunch.

My host was an energetic, hard-working man in his late fifties. He had created Gamlen-Naintré and Company in association with Gamlen Chemicals Corporation, an American company. Gamlen-Naintré employed about 50 people and produced chemicals which improved com-bustion in boilers. They also manufactured speciality chemicals for industrial cleaning. I had made several sug-gestions in my role as a consultant. Mr Naintré liked my ideas and agreed to a contract with my firm. We had lunch together often and my respect for Mr Naintré had grown. If there had been an opening, I would have asked for a job but I knew they were not hiring any staff. Yet I had often had the feeling that Mr Naintré was observing me.

That day during lunch Mr Naintré seemed to have something to say that he found difficult to put into words. I began to wonder if he wanted to cancel our contract. I thought it was best to clear the air.

'Mr Naintré,' I said, 'I have a feeling there is something on your mind and you are not telling me.'

'Yes,' replied the businessman. 'I have had my eye on you for some time, longer than you know. I've noticed how you've been able to pinpoint our problems and find workable solutions. One day when I was taking the train to Marseilles with my wife, I saw you running down the platform with your briefcase in one hand and your suit-case in the other. I told my wife then, "That's the kind of man my company needs." Do you think you might come to work with me?'

I couldn't keep a big grin off my face.

'All this time I have been wanting to ask you if you had a job for me!'

I started work for Gamlen-Naintré in August 1961. As soon as my position was definite, I asked Annette to marry me.

She accepted my proposal but I explained that a Bahá'í marriage would require her parents' acceptance as well. I had already written to my mother in Tehran, who was delighted. Annette's parents consented and we decided on a wedding in Denmark so that all her family could be present.

Annette's parents were active members of their local Lutheran church. But they were tolerant and helped the Danish Bahá'ís organize the ceremony. I knew some of the local Bahá'ís because I had met them when I was in Denmark in 1957. When Annette went home for the arrangements she discovered that few of her friends and relatives had any idea what an Iranian looked like. Some of them feared that she was going to become part of a harem.

When we were sending out invitations, I sent one to Mr Faizi, who was living in Haifa. My former teacher replied with a lovely card on which he had written a prayer for our future in Persian calligraphy. He said he was looking forward to seeing pictures of our children.

We were married in Copenhagen on 23 December 1961. In many ways the ceremony was like any traditional occidental wedding. Annette had bought her bridal gown in Paris and her bridesmaids wore long dresses. Her father escorted her down the aisle to the strains of Mendelssohn's 'Wedding March'. The readings for the ceremony, on the theme of unity, were in Danish and English and taken from both the Bahá'í scriptures and the Bible. Some guests who had never before heard of the Bahá'í religion said they were impressed by the simple, dignified ceremony. Afterwards Annette's parents served a dinner at their home. All I can remember about the day is how beautiful Annette looked.

For our honeymoon we went to Triberg in the Black Forest and Annette began teaching me how to ski. On our return we moved into an apartment in St Cloud, a suburb of Paris. In the early days of our marriage Annette was puzzled to see me put my underwear under my pillow every night and look into my shoes before I put them on. I felt a little foolish when she asked me about it and I told her that it was because of the scorpions. I no longer sleep on my underwear but I still instinctively check my shoes before I put them on.

I entered Gamlen-Naintré as associate director, second-in-command after Mr Naintré. As I had feared, my work permit was a problem. Mr Naintré applied for one but the labour ministry refused, saying that a Frenchman should be given the position. Remembering my unfortunate experience with Coca-Cola, I wished that the world was ready to accept the Bahá'í principle of one world, one country.

Mr Bensousan, the company lawyer, advised Mr Naintré to reply that he would be glad to hire a Frenchman, if the ministry officials could recommend someone as well qualified as Mr Zahrai. The lawyer explained that bureaucrats refuse applications to shirk the responsibility involved in accepting them. No bureaucrat would want the responsibility of recommending someone for my job. As he expected, I was given my work permit, valid for one year. Every year I had to go through the ordeal of renewing it, never certain that it would be accepted. Eventually I applied for and obtained French nationality.

While I was learning the ropes of my new job, Annette was learning to keep house. Our apartment in St Cloud had a large living room and a view of the River Seine. She enjoyed decorating it and baking cakes and cookies for the firesides that we organized every Wednesday. Now that I no longer travelled so much, I was able to spend some time teaching the Bahá'í Faith. I enjoyed inviting friends and business acquaintances to dinner to show off my beautiful wife. And Annette found a job through an American Bahá'í friend, Colonel John McHenry, who worked with NATO. She became a secretary for the Central European Pipeline Agency in Versailles.

I remember one Sunday morning, a month after our marriage, when Annette woke up at ten o'clock and remembered that I had invited a friend for dinner. She rushed out to a little market near the apartment to do the shopping. When she came back she was bleeding profusely from a big gash in her knee and crying. In her hurry she had slipped on the ice and spilled her groceries. She was crying because she was certain the dinner was going to be a disaster.

'Don't worry', I told her, 'we'll buy a cooked chicken.'

I cleaned and bandaged her knee then went out and bought a roasted chicken. Before our guests arrived I cooked a dish of Persian rice and Annette prepared a tossed salad. Everything went fine but I noticed that after that Annette always did the shopping the day before.

I worked at establishing good relationships with my company's employees. Although I had taken management training courses in Brussels and Tehran, I knew that I lacked experience and that I was both an outsider and a foreigner. I introduced the concept of Bahá'í consultation. The older generation of employees was used to accepting management decisions without question and did not see any need to consult with the lower echelons. But the younger generation was in favour of more democratic methods and gradually I was able to show that consultation worked.

I never forgot the day when, as a young travelling consultant with everything I owned in a suitcase, I had prayed to find a way to settle down and marry. Whenever things got difficult, I managed to find a moment to go and say a brief prayer in the same little office which I considered my prayer corner.

In November 1962 Annette gave birth to Michel Parviz Zahrai. We were able to buy a larger apartment in a nearby building. It had two bedrooms, a large living room and a balcony overlooking the gardens. Annette stopped working to care for our baby. Since we usually communicated in English, Michel spoke English before he spoke French. Annette was used to being very active and at first she felt a bit lonely in St Cloud. So she enrolled in a correspondence course to improve her French and in a sewing course at the local civic centre. She was soon a skilled seamstress and made most of her own clothes. She found that she liked doing things with her hands and later she learned to bind books, frame pictures, do mosaic art and restore chairs.

1963 saw another birth that was more widely remarked. Since the death of Shoghi Effendi, the Hands of the Cause had been working hard to establish the Universal House of Justice and Bahá'ís around the world had been struggling to consolidate the accomplishments of his ministry. We Bahá'ís in France followed events around the world as the Ten Year Crusade bore its fruits. One after another, the countries to which Shoghi Effendi had sent pioneers reported increasing numbers of believers, the establishment of Local Spiritual Assemblies, then Regional and National Spiritual Assemblies. By 1963 there were 56 fully functioning National and Regional Assemblies. They organized national conventions and elected their members, who were delegates to the first international convention which was held in Haifa during the Riḍván festival in April 1963. The convention marked the culmination of Shoghi Effendi's Ten Year Crusade by electing the Universal House of Justice. The nine members came from Jewish, Christian and Muslim backgrounds and lived on four continents. Once the House of Justice was elected, the Hands of the Cause turned over their custodianship of the administration of the Bahá'í Faith to it, while continuing their functions as Hands to serve, propagate and protect the religion.

The following week Annette and I attended the first Bahá'í World Congress at the Royal Albert Hall in London. The newly-elected members of the Universal House of Justice were presented to six thousand participants from around the world. I was delighted to see Enoch Olinga, tall and majestic, give the opening speech.

In August 1964 a second son, Eric, was born to us. By now Annette had become an accomplished hostess but she had no intention of limiting herself to the role of mother and wife. She enrolled at the local university to take a master's degree in English, hiring a Danish au pair to help her with the housework and childcare.

Both of us were active within the Bahá'í community. We attended the 19 Day Feasts and on Wednesdays invited friends who were not Bahá'ís to our apartment to talk about the Faith. The Bahá'í community in St Cloud grew. When George and Diane Starcher, American Bahá'ís, moved into the area, Annette and Diane became close friends. Then Paul and Christine Hakim, brother and sister, brought their enthusiasm and dynamic energy to our small group. Their mother was French and their father, Dr Manuchihr Hakim, was the head of the Bahá'í hospital of Tehran. Soon there were enough Bahá'ís in St Cloud to form a Local Spiritual Assembly.

One of the people I met at Bahá'í meetings in Paris was the early American Bahá'í Mrs Laura Dreyfus-Barney, who had known 'Abdu'l-Bahá. She had gone to 'Akká to meet Him in the early years of the century and at daily interviews had asked Him questions about the Faith. She kept comprehensive notes of their conversations and published them under the title *Some Answered Questions*. She was assisted by her future husband, Hippolyte Dreyfus, the first French Bahá'í. When I met her in Paris she was an elegant old lady, distinguished and lively, still active in teaching the Bahá'í Faith, still eager to participate. She enjoyed sharing her memories of her encounter with 'Abdu'l-Bahá.

Mr Nakhjavani, now a member of the Universal House of Justice, wrote from Haifa asking me to send a written record of everything that Shoghi Effendi had said concerning the Bahá'ís of Egypt. The Egyptian Bahá'ís were being persecuted, the Faith was outlawed and their Centres had been confiscated. Several had been arrested and brought to court as heretics, a criminal charge that could carry sentences of life imprisonment or even the death penalty. With instructions from the Universal House of Justice, I made several trips to Egypt to meet with the Bahá'ís and the Egyptian lawyer who defended them. I also contacted a well-known French lawyer and asked him to go to Egypt as a consultant.

By 1966 my work with Gamlen-Naintré was going well and it seemed a good time to take an extended vacation. I had not seen my mother for 14 years and I wanted to show Annette my homeland. The Shah was organizing a celebration at Persepolis to encourage tourism; it had never before been so easy to obtain entry visas to Iran. In June we flew to Tehran, leaving our two boys in the care of a friend. My brother Aziz and his wife Miriam welcomed us and put us up. Ehsan was then working in Kuwait for a construction company. My mother moved in with Aziz so she could be with us as much as possible.

Aziz was chief executive of the accounts department for one of the biggest companies in Iran, a company owned by Bahá'ís. His son, Fouad, 18, spoke English. Although Annette did not know enough Persian to converse with Miriam and my mother, Razieh found a way to express her affection by sitting next to Annette and caressing her hair. Whenever I was planning on going out, I would ask my mother, 'Khánum, what are you going to do today?' She always smiled and said, 'I'll wait for you to come back.'

Coming from a northern land, Annette was enchanted by the beautiful blue skies of Iran and she would have enjoyed days at the swimming pool but her Persian in-laws were horrified. The women were proud of their pale complexions and preferred to stay inside. One local custom that Annette liked was that of sleeping outside on balconies or on flat roofs when the heat became unbearable. At six o'clock in the morning the vendors coming through the streets, singing their wares, woke her up and she rushed out to buy fruit and pastries. She was fascinated by the oriental way of life and spent hours in the bazaar, watching craftsmen at work and hunting for bargains. A close childhood friend of mine, Djadid Ashraf, accompanied her to the market. Annette soon learned how to haggle with the fruit and vegetable sellers herself but asked for Djadid's help for major purchases. She bought a Persian carpet in the Isfahan style. It had a red and light beige border and was so fine she could pack it in a suitcase. She also bought some gold and turquoise Persian jewellery and a ring.

We visited the magnificent Mosque of Shah Abbas in Isfahan and also went to Persepolis. I was amazed to discover that at Persepolis there was an ancient system of irrigation ditches and canals similar to those that had brought the water to my house when I was a little boy waiting for the *Míráb* to let the water into our reservoir.

We went on pilgrimage to see the house of the Báb in Shiraz. Bahá'í pilgrims had to be extremely discreet to avoid persecution. A small group met early in the morning and had tea together before setting out for the house where the Báb had declared His mission. To my surprise, I recognized the big grin of one of the pilgrims in my group. My cousin Shahab had married a girl from a well-known Bahá'í family and they had moved to Beirut. There Shahab published books about the Bahá'í religion in Arabic and became secretary of the Regional Spiritual Assembly of the Near East. He and I laughed about the days when we had played being postmen in the garden in Qazvin. Our small group of pilgrims walked to the house, careful not to attract attention. All the women, including Annette, wore chadors. When we reached the Báb's house we were greeted by caretakers who offered us tea and allowed us to pray in the room in which the Báb had first declared His mission.

In Tehran we took similar precautions to visit the house of Bahá'u'lláh. Annette told me how impressed she was at the idea that the founder of our Faith had chosen to abandon the luxury of such a home for exile and imprisonment.

Against the advice of some of our friends, we took a

bus trip to the Caspian Sea because Annette was eager to see how ordinary Iranians lived. Once we had left the capital city behind she found that she was an object of curiosity. Provincial villagers rarely saw European women travelling on public transportation and one frightened countrywoman was afraid Annette would put the evil eye on her baby. When the bus stopped for gas, everyone got out and picnicked together.

The trip across the Alborz Mountains to the sea lasted six hours. To make the time go by, Persian music and soft drinks were served in the bus. Annette enjoyed the beaches of the Caspian Sea but afterwards she talked about the bus trip as one of the highlights of her stay in Iran.

While they were together, my mother taught Annette to make pulao, rice cooked with a layer of sliced potatoes in the bottom of the pot: _khurisht_, a stew to serve over the pulao, made with different ingredients but often including onions, celery, parsley and tomatoes and a meat such as chicken, lamb or beef; _ásh_, a kind of vegetable soup thickened with noodles or rice and sometimes including spicy little meatballs. We Persians eat lots of raw vegetables and enjoy salads and fruit. We stop work for tea in the afternoon and have dinner late at night, around nine o'clock.

In Tehran I was able to visit my former partner, Ali Akbar. His business had prospered and Ali had moved to the capital. He received me in the garden of his magnificent home. Tea was served on a beautiful Persian carpet spread on the ground beside a fish pond with a fountain.

His welcome was cordial and we reminisced about the early days in Tabriz when we were two young ambitious men.

Our vacation went quickly, and all too soon we flew back to Paris. After the kind hospitality of the Bahá'ís she had met, Annette found it hard to believe that anyone could wish to harm them.

In May 1968 France was in chaos as the younger generation expressed its dissatisfaction with old systems and values. Annette and I watched the demonstrations on television, convinced that we had answers to many of the problems that were being raised. But Bahá'ís do not march in the streets. We work quietly, unobtrusively, in the belief that one day the world will come to its senses.

As Michel and Eric grew, the apartment in St Cloud began to seem a bit small. One day a brochure came in the mail from a real estate company in nearby La Celle St Cloud. Annette and I talked about it and made an appointment to visit the sales office. We went to have a look at the land on which five new houses were to be built. It was a rainy day and the land was bare and muddy, but there were lots of trees around and we liked the area. We decided that if we could sell our apartment we would buy a house. It was not easy to find a buyer and finance the house but eventually, in spite of numerous delays, we were able to move into a new home in La Celle St Cloud in 1969.

At that time Yvette Ligozat was the only Bahá'í living in La Celle St Cloud. Then Albert Lincoln, a young American Bahá'í, moved to France with his wife Joany and their baby to work for a law firm in Paris. They decided to settle in La Celle St Cloud to strengthen our group. Joany was a musician, so we organized musical evenings through which many people learned about the Bahá'í Faith.

Other American Bahá'ís also settled in La Celle St Cloud along with Bahá'ís from North Africa. Before long there were nine Bahá'ís and we were able to establish an Assembly. The Bahá'ís became an active and highly-respected element in the local community. The Lincolns later went to Africa as pioneers.

Shortly after we moved I received a phone call from my brother Ehsan. My mother was ill.

'How sick is she?' I asked.

'She's not very well. She's in the Bahá'í hospital.'

'Do you think I should come?'

'No, you don't have to worry.'

I told Annette about the conversation and she said at once, 'Ezzat, you should go. If she dies, you will never forgive yourself. And if she doesn't die, okay, you've seen your mother, and you'll know that she's being taken care of.'

I realized that she was right. Within 24 hours I was on a plane to Iran.

When I arrived my mother was suffering so badly from generalized cancer that she didn't even recognize me. The doctors said there was no hope. An operation would alleviate her suffering but it would be only a brief respite. I discussed the matter with my brothers and we agreed to the operation.

After surgery Razieh regained all her mental faculties. She was happy to see me and I spent all my time at her side, saying prayers and talking about my children and my life in Paris. Razieh seemed to enjoy having me with her and while I was talking one day she gently slipped away into the Abhá Kingdom.

I will always be grateful to Annette for her wise, straightforward decision, saying categorically, 'Ezzat, you ought to go.' She didn't stop to think how much the trip would cost. She saw that it was the right thing to do and she made sure that I didn't feel guilty or selfish about it.

Important changes were underway at Gamlen-Naintré. I had been associate director for almost nine years and had travelled to the United States several times with Mr Naintré to meet our American partners. In 1970 Mr Naintré retired and sold his shares in the company to Gamlen. At the same time Gamlen Chemical Company was bought by Sybron Corporation of Rochester, New York. They offered me the presidency of the French division. I was a little concerned about the idea that I, a foreigner, would be in charge of a French company, but I accepted. I have no difficulty remembering the date that I took office. It was April Fool's Day.

In December 1972 Valerie Shirine was born. She was a lovely girl with blond hair and unusual green eyes. At the same time Marion Little, the American pioneer that I had met in Florence, came to Paris. I invited her to dinner and she was delighted to meet Annette and the children. Marion was an elderly woman who had devoted her life to pioneering, going wherever there was a need, telling taxi drivers, hotel bellhops and telephone operators that Bahá'u'lláh, God's Promised One, had come. During dinner Marion suddenly felt chest pains and began repeating a prayer for healing. I called an ambulance but by the time we reached the hospital Marion had passed away. William Danjon, a Bahá'í friend from Andorra, wrote a moving article for the *Bahá'í News* explaining that Marian had gone to the Abhá Kingdom but Valerie had entered the Bahá'í community, a precious reminder of the constant renewal of life.

When Valerie was a year old Annette began work on a master's degree in sociology at Nanterre University. Her thesis was a general introduction to the Bahá'í Faith. Over the years she continued studying, earning another master's degree in English and did doctoral research in sociology. She worked on the Bahá'í teaching committee, the children's committee and Bahá'í summer school programmes. Later she was elected to the National Spiritual Assembly, the governing board of the French Bahá'í community, and I was happy to see that others realized what a special person she was.

Gamlen had developed its business in other European countries – England, Scandinavia, the Netherlands – and in North Africa. Sybron decided to unite the different operations under one management and in 1974 they offered me the post of European Division president. I accepted on condition that the headquarters be in Paris rather than in London, as they had intended. The company continued to expand. Factories were built in Normandy and Holland, manufacturing facilities were installed in Italy and Spain and there were new offices in Hamburg and Oslo. I presided over the entire European and eventually the Middle Eastern operation of Gamlen Chemical Company.

In spite of my professional success, I was having some doubts about the turn my life was taking. I had not left Iran to live in another country with the intention of becoming president of a multinational company. I had made a spiritual decision, dedicating my life to furthering the Bahá'í Cause, but the materialistic rat race of modern life seemed to have caught up with me. Many people of my generation shared similar feelings and some of them tried to escape by giving up their jobs and moving to the country to farm or raise goats. I wrote a long letter to Mr Faizi, explaining that I didn't feel I was doing any major work for the Faith in France and asking for advice. I thought of returning to Africa or going to Reunion, a French island in the Indian Ocean, as a pioneer. Mr Faizi did not reply but a few months later I received a letter from the Universal House of Justice. Mr Faizi had passed my letter on to it for consideration.

The letter said that in the opinion of the House of Justice, it would be best for me and my family to remain near Paris and serve the Cause there. 'Abdu'l-Bahá had stayed longer in Paris than in any other city and had especially loved France. The Guardian had predicted that France would have a brilliant future in the Faith. These words encouraged me to believe that being the divisional president of a multinational company was not incompatible with serving the Cause. I had to admit that pioneering on a remote island would have been difficult for Annette and the children.

Still, I wished I could get away from Paris from time to time. I thought about buying a home in the country and using it for Bahá'í activities. I talked the idea over with Annette and began looking for something that might serve both as a summer home and as a Bahá'í school.

I sent a description of what I wanted to several real estate agents. I remembered a friend from La Celle St Cloud who had moved to Agen in southwest France to open up a real estate agency. I wrote to him and received a letter saying that they had several possibilities listed. I took some time off and went south with Annette, visiting houses on the Cote d'Azur and in the Pyrenees. We saw places that were far too expensive or in need of extensive repairs. When we reached Agen, Mr Fargue showed us an estate which we found rather depressing. We wanted something large enough for a school but with a homey atmosphere.

While we were talking to Mr Fargue, I saw a picture on the real estate agent's desk.

'What about this?' I asked.

'Oh, that's La Blanche. It just came in, I haven't had time to visit it. I don't know what kind of shape it's in.'

'I'd like to see it,' I said.

Annette looked at the picture.

'Yes,' she said. 'That's what we're looking for.'

It took us half an hour to drive to the little village perched among hills above fertile farms and the winding Lot River. The house was just beyond the village, shaded by trees over a hundred years old. The rooms were large and spacious with high ceilings and fireplaces for heat. An elegant stairway led to bedrooms on the first floor.

'This is it,' said Annette.

As usual, she knew what she wanted. A week later I drove down from Paris with my lawyer, made the down payment and signed the sale documents.

As soon as the house was ours, we started organizing classes for Bahá'í children during the holidays. During the day the children studied the history and background of the Bahá'í Faith and prepared activities. Sometimes they went for walks or picnics or put on short humorous plays. Several adults helped with the teaching, the shopping, the cleaning and the cooking. In the evening everyone gathered around the fireplace in the big lounge to sing songs, tell stories and roast chestnuts. If the weather was good we ate outside in the garden and barbecued hot dogs. When the children were in bed, the grown-ups planned the next day's activities. Everyone, children and teachers, had a wonderful time, and later several of them told me that they looked back on the classes in La Blanche as a special part of their lives.

After a few years the summer sessions were so successful that we had up to 32 children and eight adults at a time. The Bahá'í community was outgrowing La Blanche; classes were later organized near Lyon, where the facilities allowed larger groups. But the children who had spent their holidays together in the big old house in the woods, the Veterans of La Blanche, never forgot the fun and the spiritual lessons they had learned. During one of the last sessions a young Egyptian student named Rushdi made an album for Annette. Under each snapshot he wrote a funny comment and we treasured his gift as a souvenir of the wonderful moments we had spent with the Bahá'í children at La Blanche.

I served the Bahá'ís of France for 13 years as an Auxiliary Board Member. On a regional level my functions were similar to those of the Counsellors and Hands of the Cause who worked on a national or continental level to protect and propagate the Faith.

It was unusual in those days to have a foreigner working in a top managerial position in a French company, and my employees frequently had a good laugh over my difficulties with the French language. I worked hard to create a team spirit, building a cooperative relationship between management and labour. I rarely had to impose decisions because I consulted with everyone concerned when a decision had to be made.

When I became president of the European Division, I realized that there would be problems if we did not take into consideration the different cultures involved. I decided from the beginning to have the various nationalities represented on the management committee. I hired a Dutchman as head of personnel and administration, a Scot as financial director, two Frenchmen for marketing and sales, and a Dane for the marine department. In this manner I avoided the hard feelings that could have existed if the board had been all French. I liked to say that my management committee was a miniature European Economic Community.

I also introduced the Bahá'í principles of consultation in the management committee. The pros and cons of issues were thoroughly discussed. I encouraged each participant to share his opinion without worrying that his prestige might suffer if 'his' idea was not accepted. Once an idea is given in Bahá'í consultation it no longer 'belongs' to the person who originated it. The members of the committee also learned to give their full support to whatever agreements came out of the consultation, whether or not they had voted for it. Thus if an action that had been agreed upon failed, it would not be because of a lack of support and the problem could be examined again with no recriminations. Even when I received instructions from the parent company, they were examined in consultation until all the members understood why we were being asked to take action.

This training in consultation paid off when it became necessary to combine two establishments, one located in Clichy and one in another Parisian suburb. Although such displacements are often the subject of labour disputes, through consultation everyone involved was able to express his point of view and solutions were found that allowed the company to make the change to the complete satisfaction of the employees, the unions and the management.

I often had to visit establishments in Europe and I made frequent trips to the United States. When at home I tried to spend as much time as possible with the children and always said their prayers with them at night. But because I was often absent, Annette became the source of authority in our home. When she told the children to do something, they obeyed. I rarely laid down the law, preferring to persuade and consult with them.

Michel was accident prone. As a child he broke both arms twice. When he was only three he proved that he was an undaunted adventurer. His mother had let him play in the park below the apartment while she washed windows. When she looked down, he had disappeared. While she was hunting for him, the police station called. They had picked him up wandering in town and he had given them his name without any trouble. He was very curious and wanted to handle everything new that he encountered. He was always pushing buttons to see what would happen and was an extrovert like Annette.

Eric was quiet and artistic. When he was 15 he painted a bouquet of flowers, a painting his mother still has on display in the living room. She said that Eric took after me because he was thoughtful and well-organized.

Valerie became her mother's best friend. The two of them had a special relationship after the two boys left home for their studies. They played tennis together, went swimming and windsurfing. The children shared Annette's love of outdoor sports. The whole family went skiing together. In addition to her studies, her family duties and Bahá'í activities, Annette found time to join a bridge club in La Celle St Cloud. I admired her never-failing energy and realized that her social activities were also a means of meeting people, making new friends and spreading the message of the Bahá'í Faith.

I received a letter from London one day which gave me

a great deal of pleasure. It was from my niece, Zohreh, Ehsan's daughter, announcing her marriage to Mr Faizi's son, Naysan. I wrote back, telling her how delighted I was to see our families united. Later, the young couple planned to settle in Australia where there was a growing and dynamic Bahá'í community.

In 1978 we went to the Pyrenees for a winter holiday. The boys and their mother were excellent skiers and spent as much time as possible on the slopes, but Valerie was five and just learning to ski. Since I had broken a leg skiing, I avoided the more difficult slopes and enjoyed the opportunity to spend time with Valerie. I took her for walks and at bedtime told her stories about my childhood in Persia, how my family ate sitting on the floor around the *kursí* and slept on the roof during the hot summer season. I told her about seeing the Portuguese fishermen pulling in nets full of sardines. Valerie was amazed – she thought sardines grew in cans. When I had told her all the stories I could think of and she still couldn't go to sleep, I remembered my mother's remedy for insomnia. She used to tell me to repeat nine times Alláh-u-Abhá, the Greatest Name. When Bahá'ís meet, they greet each other by saying Alláh-u-Abhá but they also use the phrase as a prayer. Valerie repeated the words after me several times and began to doze off. I turned out the light and tiptoed out of the room. The next evening when I checked the children's rooms before going to bed, I could hear Valerie's childish voice saying 'Alláh-u-Abhá'. It made me smile to think how thoroughly European my children were, knowing very little about my native country, yet I had passed on to them, almost without knowing it, some of my family traditions.

Wanting to be able to tell my children more about my early Bábí ancestors, I wrote to my cousin, Shahab, in Beirut. Someone had told me that he had investigated our family origins.

My cousin replied with his usual sense of humour, saying, 'Unfortunately, although our forefathers had great opportunities to serve the Bábí Cause, they spent their money and time on gambling and enjoying themselves. And yet they had two Tablets written from Bahá'u'lláh to them in their name. Why should I waste my time investigating the life of people who did little to serve the Cause? I would prefer to pray that our children will do something that will rejoice our forefathers in the next world.'

I laughed at Shahab's answer. I should have known that my cousin was too spiritual and dedicated to spend his time looking into genealogies.

After the signature there was a P.S.

'At the time I'm writing this letter, we can hear shell fire. When I have time, I'll write again.'

As time went on the news from Iran was increasingly worrisome. In 1972 the government decided to impose a special tax on the buildings, lands and cemeteries that belonged to the Bahá'í community. The result of gifts and legacies, the wealth that was being taxed consisted of meeting halls, a hospital, hostels for Bahá'í travellers, orphanages, schools and cemeteries. Many Bahá'ís were ineligible for retirement plans and social security, thus the community had created its own mutual insurance plan to provide pensions and health care for the elderly and the poor. The Bahá'í community as a whole paid the first tax, hoping they would then be left in peace. Their obedience merely convinced the government to ask for more. Unable to pay the second exorbitant demand, the Bahá'ís appealed to the Iranian Supreme Court and the judges decided that the new tax was illegal. Thereupon the Iranian parliament passed a retroactive law which clearly applied only to Bahá'ís.

In 1975, because their religion forbids participating in party politics, the Bahá'ís as a community refused to enrol in the state party, Rastakhiz. This made them even more unpopular with the Shah's government and the state secret police, SAVAK. As tension mounted between the government and the fundamentalist Muslims, SAVAK frequently tried to divert attention from police brutalities by using the Bahá'ís as scapegoats.

Even before Ayatollah Khomeini took power in February 1979 his attitude towards the Bahá'ís was well known. In his book *Islam and Revolution*, he wrote,

> In our own city of Tehran now there are centres of evil propaganda run by the churches, the Zionists, and the Baha'is in order to lead our people astray and make them abandon the ordinances and teachings of Islam. Do we not have a duty to destroy these centres that are damaging to Islam?[2]

In February 1979, while he was still in Paris, Khomeini gave an interview to the American magazine *Seven*

Days. The reporter asked him if the Bahá'ís would be granted religious or political liberties under an Islamic government. He replied, 'They [the Bahá'ís] are a political faction, they are harmful; they will not be accepted'. When the reporter insisted, asking, 'Will they have religious liberty and be allowed to practise their religion?' Khomeini's answer was, 'No!'³

Before the Islamic fundamentalists seized power, there were outbreaks of violence directed against the Bahá'ís. In spite of their refusal to join the Shah's state party, they were accused of collaboration. In January 1978 near Shiraz a mob looking for agents of the Shah's hated secret police lynched a Bahá'í and looted and burned three hundred Bahá'í homes. Other attacks followed, although they were given little coverage by the international press. Worried about what was going on in my homeland, I gleaned as much information as possible from the newspapers and messages from Haifa.

Once a year the Sybron Corporation organized conferences where its division presidents could meet, discuss the annual budget, make plans for the future and get to know each other better. In January 1979 the seminar was to be held in Mexico City. I decided to take Annette with me and stop in Guadeloupe for a week's holiday on the way. I was lying beside the hotel swimming pool when a bellboy said there was a call from Paris for me.

My secretary, Mrs Chevalier, was on the line. She had received an urgent message from Haifa, asking me to get in touch at once. I called back and Ali Nakhjavani, my old friend from African pioneering days, now a member of the Universal House of Justice, said, 'Because of the situation in Iran, the Universal House of Justice has decided to form a small, ad-hoc committee in Paris. If there is any nation that can influence the Khomeini government in favour of the Bahá'ís in Iran, it is France. We want you to chair the committee and to name two French Bahá'ís who might work with you.' I was to cooperate with the French National Spiritual Assembly but to report directly to the Universal House of Justice. I gave the names of Mr Robert Guillo and Mme Jagu-Roche and before I left Guadeloupe I had managed to contact them and set the date of our first committee meeting.

My immediate superior in the Sybron organization was Peter Scott, a naturalized American of Jewish extraction who had lost all of his family in Czechoslovakia during World War II. When I told him that I was working outside of office hours to alleviate the suffering of the Bahá'ís who were being persecuted in Iran, Mr Scott said, 'By all means, go ahead.' Most American companies encouraged their employees to engage in community work and to defend worthy causes, so there was nothing unusual about me using the company telex for committee work. As I told Annette, my American employers looked at the bottom line. As long as the division I was running was making satisfactory profits, they did not ask me how I organized my work. Like many businessmen, I was in the habit of bringing company work home to do during the evenings and holidays, dictating letters and reports into a recorder and sending the cassette to my secretary.

Thus my office became the main link between Paris

and Haifa and the company telex permitted the committee to send and receive messages. Mrs Chevalier and other members of my staff knew about the persecution of Bahá'ís in Iran and were sympathetic. When someone on the management committee saw an article about the Bahá'ís in Iran they cut it out for me. I realized that the Universal House of Justice had shown foresight when they advised me against leaving France. It would have been difficult to find another Bahá'í in Paris with the same resources and access to international communications.

The purpose of the committee was to keep the French press and French authorities informed about what was happening to Bahá'ís in Iran. We received reports from Haifa and sometimes directly from Iranian Bahá'ís that we dispatched to the French press, to the government and to the Bahá'ís of France. Reporters and government officials frequently asked us for confirmation of reports in the international press. When necessary the committee contacted Haifa to furnish the information needed.

One of my colleagues, a former classmate of Jean François-Poncet, the French Minister of Foreign Affairs, wrote to him asking that he intervene on behalf of the Bahá'ís in Iran. Mr François-Poncet replied saying he was concerned with the situation and doing all he could for the Bahá'ís.

The first attacks on Bahá'ís seemed to be the result of spontaneous mob violence. The next step in what appeared to be a long-prepared plan to eliminate the Bahá'ís in Iran was a series of administrative decisions confiscating all property held by Bahá'í organizations. This included a hospital, community centres, retirement homes, schools and cemeteries. Privately-owned Bahá'í enterprises were confiscated and nationalized. Civil servants were dismissed without pay or pensions. Because Bahá'í marriages were not recognized, married women were put in gaol, accused of prostitution. The Bahá'í cemetery in Shiraz was demolished, tombstones overturned and graves defiled.

Bahá'ís were arrested, accused of trumped-up crimes and executed. Dr Samandari of Tabriz, a medical surgeon and university professor, was executed without trial, accused of 'inciting prostitution' because as chairman of the Local Spiritual Assembly he had signed marriage certificates. Soon the Islamic Revolutionary Guards decided that just being a Bahá'í was a crime. In September 1979 Mr Bahar Vodjdani, member of a Local Spiritual Assembly in Kurdistan, was called to a Revolutionary court to testify on behalf of three Kurds accused of plotting against the government. Asked to state his religion, he replied, 'Bahá'í'. He was arrested, tried, sentenced and executed before nightfall.

The sacred shrine of the Báb's home in Shiraz was systematically demolished. In order to protect their community, the Bahá'ís campaigned to be recognized as a religious minority with the same rights as Jews, Christians and Zoroastrians in the Islamic constitution. However, the new constitution did not even mention the largest minority group in Iran which outnumbered the three other minorities combined. With no legal existence, the Bahá'ís could not obtain passports, marry, work in the administration or testify in court. Their children were barred from higher education because they belonged to a religion that the state refused to recognize.

Of course my friends and relatives in Iran were affected. My brother Aziz was fortunate that his children had acquired American citizenship. On reaching retirement age, he had sold his house and moved to the States. He was comfortably settled in Norman, Oklahoma when the revolution broke out.

Ehsan had sent his children to England for their studies. Before the troubles started in 1979 he had bought a house in London and sent his youngest daughter to study in an English university. He and his wife had gone to London for a visit when friends warned them not to return to Iran. Ehsan and his family lost their house and belongings in Tehran but were grateful to have escaped with their lives. He eventually became the head of a liaison office which attended to the needs of uprooted Iranian Bahá'ís.

In a message from Haifa I learned that Djadid Ashraf, my childhood friend who had helped Annette bargain for her Persian carpet in the market of Tehran, had been arrested and executed by the Islamic Revolutionary Guards. The Muslim clergy allowed condemned men to write their testaments before dying. I received a copy of Djadid's will; it was a moving testimonial to his determination to die for his Faith rather than recant. Other familiar names came over the telex. Often when Mrs Chevalier came into my office holding a slip of pink paper, I knew by the expression on her face that it contained bad news. I wondered at the irony of fate. I had often regretted not having gone to university in Tehran. My friends who had taken degrees had become doctors, professors, engineers and lawyers and I had sometimes envied them. Now many of them had disappeared without a trace. Others had fled across the icy, hazardous passes of the mountains of Kurdistan or the deserts of Baluchistan, with all their worldly belongings in a suitcase. It made me realize how foolish it was to envy others, how hopeless it was to try to settle a child's life by making decisions about schools and studies. All parents could do was watch over their children's spiritual growth and pray that they would have the fortitude to meet life's trials. I remembered a prayer, 'O God, my God! Look not upon my hopes and my doings, nay rather look upon Thy will that hath encompassed the heavens and the earth.'[4]

More tragic news reached me, this time from Africa. Idi Amin Dada had outlawed the Bahá'í Faith in Uganda in 1977. When the dictator fell from power in 1979, Enoch Olinga hurried back to Kampala to open the Bahá'í temple, although the capital city was still in the hands of armed bands and after nightfall no one dared go outside. On Sunday, 16 September, Enoch worked with a group of young Bahá'ís cleaning the temple. They ate a picnic lunch and late in the afternoon when the work was finished they played music and danced. Then Enoch, his wife Elizabeth and their younger children, Tahirih, Lennie and Badi, went home. His older children were absent. During the evening a band of armed men burst into their compound and shot and killed the entire family in the house. No one ever learned who the murderers were or why the Hand of the Cause was assassinated. In spite of the continuing disorders in Kampala, hundreds attended the funeral of the Bahá'í pioneer who had done so much for the Faith in Africa.

In August 1980 Annette and I were on holiday with the children in La Blanche when the phone rang early in the morning. Eight members of the National Spiritual Assembly of Iran had been arrested in Tehran. Shortly afterwards Eric Rouleau, a well-known reporter for *Le Monde* who later became the French Ambassador to Turkey, called me to say he was writing an article about the disappearance of the eight Bahá'í leaders and wanted more information. I answered many of his questions and called Haifa for further details. On 29 August a moving article in defence of the long-suffering community of three hundred thousand Iranian Bahá'ís appeared in *Le Monde*. Bahá'í Centres in various parts of France received many calls concerning the events in Iran, and many people first learned of the Bahá'í religion through Eric Rouleau's article.

The Iranian government claimed to know nothing about the arrests and the eight men and women were never heard of again. The Bahá'ís of Iran had foreseen such a possibility and the Assembly was immediately replaced by nine other members.

In September 1980 Mr Hushmand Fatheazam, member of the Universal House of Justice, phoned me. Seven members of the Bahá'í Assembly in Yazd had been arrested, accused of spying for the Israeli government and executed. Because their World Centre was in Haifa, the Bahá'ís were frequently accused of being Israeli spies. To avoid publicity the Islamic authorities obliged the families of the seven martyrs to bury the bodies immediately but two hundred Bahá'ís showed up for their funeral. During the burial Islamic authorities arrested the son and son-in-law of one of the victims. Although Bahá'í communities around the world sent telegrams to the Iranian government protesting the arbitrary executions, no acknowledgement was made.

The National Spiritual Assemblies of nine European countries sent delegates to Strasbourg to ask that the persecution in Iran be put on the agenda. When the Danish National Assembly reported that they had no one free to go at such short notice, Annette represented Denmark. On 19 September the European Parliament passed a resolution unanimously condemning the persecutions and asking the foreign ministries of the European Economic Community to put pressure on the Iranian government.

12

New Departures

*We must gird ourselves for service, kindle love's flame, and
burn away in its heat. We must loose our tongues till we set
the wide world's heart afire . . .*[1]

'Abdu'l-Bahá

I continued trying to help the Bahá'ís of Egypt and
Morocco who were being arrested and persecuted for
their Faith. After my first trip to Egypt I maintained
many links with the community there, and since my
company had agents in Cairo, I was able to carry messages of encouragement to Egyptian Bahá'ís during
business trips. With the Bahá'í administration outlawed
in Egypt, I helped to bring news to the local communities of what was being done outside the country on their
behalf and let the Universal House of Justice know what
was happening in the country. The House of Justice
asked me to find a qualified French lawyer to help defend
those who were in prison. I contacted a well-known
French jurist who accompanied Mrs Dorothy Nelson, an
American jurist and a member of the National Spiritual
Assembly of the United States, when she met with high-
level Egyptian authorities, asking them to intervene on
behalf of the Bahá'ís who were being condemned because
of their religion.

In Morocco I was able to organize trips for members of the Federation of Human Rights to attend the trials of Bahá'ís in Casablanca. I hired a French lawyer to represent the prisoners who had been condemned to death as heretics by a local court. They were eventually pardoned under pressure of international opinion.

In November 1980 I had to fly to England on business despite a bad cold that had been dragging on for some time owing to my weariness. My duties as president of the European Division of Sybron-Gamlen Europe and the time-consuming needs of the ad-hoc committee while tragic events were taking place almost daily in Iran had left me little opportunity to recharge my batteries.

During a business meeting I felt sharp chest pains. At first I hoped they would pass but they became so persistent that after the meeting I called a doctor and asked to be examined. The English doctor said I needed to be hospitalized. I realized my condition was serious but I didn't want to stay in England. I thought I could hold out long enough for the flight home. I called Annette and told her that I wasn't feeling well but I did not say I had seen a doctor.

I remember boarding the plane to Paris but then everything gets confused. When I came to, I was in Gonesse Hospital, some 42 kilometres northeast of my home in La Celle St Cloud. Doctors said I had had a heart attack on the plane. Annette arrived shortly afterwards and I stayed in intensive care for three days. As soon as I could be transferred, they took me to another hospital in Boulogne-Bilancourt, closer to home.

Once I was out of intensive care, I asked Mrs Chevalier to bring me work from the office for there were urgent matters which had to be attended to and telegrams from Haifa. I was still in the hospital when I learned of the passing of my former teacher, Mr Faizi. I thought of his students, a whole generation of young Iranians now scattered around the world, serving the Cause because of his inspiring example. His students had been among the pioneers that had fulfilled Shoghi Effendi's request to open every country and territory in the world to the Bahá'í Faith during the Ten Year Crusade.

Abu'l-Qásim Faizi had not only encouraged young people to serve the Cause, he himself had pioneered to places in difficult circumstances. Other pioneers looked to him as to a father for help and advice. He kept up a voluminous correspondence with former students, friends and other pioneers. After being appointed a Hand of the Cause by Shoghi Effendi, he travelled around the world, working to maintain the unity of the Bahá'í Faith during the difficult period after the passing of the Guardian. Mr Faizi then settled in Haifa and devoted his last years to his own writing and translating *The Priceless Pearl*, a biography of Shoghi Effendi by Rúḥíyyih Khánum, into Persian.

After two weeks I was allowed to leave the hospital for a rest home. Annette came to the rest home to see me but my condition had suddenly grown worse and the doctors had sent me back to intensive care. After another two weeks of hospitalization I was finally allowed to return home. Worrying about business matters and the dangerous situation in Iran made it very difficult to heed the doctors' warnings to take it easy.

In January I was back in my office, trying to make up for lost time. Once again I caught cold and ran a high fever. Annette was worried about my physical condition and scolded me for not listening to the doctors. They insisted on me taking a holiday in the mountains but colleagues from Sybron continued to visit me, bringing work from the office. Annette watched over me, making sure I took my medicine and standing guard when she thought I had too many visitors. But I had to keep up the committee work, for the situation in Iran was getting worse and worse.

Six months after my heart attack Annette developed ulcerative colitis, apparently caused by the stress she had undergone during my illness. She took her medicine and followed the doctor's recommendations as efficiently as she did everything else and soon recovered and returned to her many activities. In July 1980 she had been one of the three representatives that the Bahá'í International Community sent to the Mid-Decade World Conference of the United Nations Decade for Women in Copenhagen at which delegates from all over the world represented both governments and non-governmental organizations. The Bahá'í International Community presented a statement entitled 'Universal Values for the Advancement of Women', which explained, among others things, how Bahá'í women were involved at all levels of the Bahá'í administration.[2]

More tragic news came from Tehran that particularly

saddened the French Bahá'ís. Christine and Paul Hakim, friends of ours and active members of the community in St Cloud, were the children of Professor Manuchihr Hakim, a well-known Iranian physician. He had helped found the medical faculty of the University of Tehran, training over six thousand doctors, and ran the Bahá'í hospital of Tehran, one of the largest and most modern installations in Iran, for 30 years. He had sent his French wife to stay in Paris while he remained in Tehran, working from his home where anyone, of any religion, could come whether or not they had the money to pay for his services. On 12 January 1981 it seems someone called and asked for a consultation after the curfew hours, saying it was an emergency. Professor Hakim was alone when he admitted the mysterious patient. Shortly afterwards the body of the 70-year-old physician was found in his office. He had been shot in the head.

The Bahá'í community of Tehran organized his funeral as a public demonstration of its love and admiration. Thousands followed the funeral procession and accompanied Professor Hakim to his final resting place. When Islamic Revolutionary Guards encircled the cemetery and said that it was mined and must be evacuated immediately, the Bahá'ís replied that they were ready to die and remained until the end of the ceremony.

Between 1978 and 1982, 118 Bahá'ís were killed for the crime of proclaiming their Faith. Those, like Dr Hakim, who were too well-known and popular to be brought to trial, were assassinated. Others, including the members of the National Spiritual Assembly of Iran, were arrested and then disappeared without their families being able to learn what had happened to them. Young girls were kidnapped and their families were told that they had adopted Islam but the parents were not allowed to see their daughters and were unable to learn where they were.

The Universal House of Justice told me to find a highly-qualified French lawyer with an associate to go to Tehran to try to negotiate with the Iranian authorities. Although no one could guarantee the lawyer's safety, he accepted the challenge and flew to Tehran, speaking up for the Bahá'ís who were being dispossessed, put in prison and executed. Gradually, because of international pressure, the persecutions became less flagrant, less visible. Those families that could, sent their young people abroad as students but most remained in Iran, testifying in their daily lives to the firmness of their faith.

In 1982 Michel passed his baccalaureate examination and was admitted to a preparatory school. He planned to go to an American university to continue his studies in development economics. I was very proud of him and encouraged him to continue his education. The following year Eric also passed his baccalaureate exam. Both boys were tall and handsome, with their mother's dynamic energy. Valerie, with her long blond hair and green eyes, seemed to grow more beautiful every day. I felt very grateful for the blessing of a united, loving family.

When it became obvious that the persecutions in Iran were not a temporary phenomenon, the ad-hoc committee was replaced by more permanent structures. The information which the committee had collected was turned over to Jean-Marc Lepain, who wrote a white paper about the persecution of the Bahá'ís in Iran which was distributed to the press, the French government and human rights organizations.

One of the new structures was the liaison office in London headed by Ehsan, which tried to maintain links with Bahá'ís living in Islamic countries. Owing to the Middle East situation, it was easier for representatives to meet in England, Spain or France than in Israel. On one trip to London, I met my cousin Shahab, who was still living in Beirut. Since Shahab had gone to the Persian Gulf as a pioneer we had seen each other only once, on the pilgrimage to the Báb's house in Shiraz. I was delighted to have the chance to spend some time with him in London.

More sad news reached France from Iran as the Iran–Iraq war dragged on. Hearing remarks made by people around me and reading the French press, I realized that most Europeans thought there was little difference between the two countries. As far as they were concerned Indians, Pakistanis, Syrians, Palestinians, Iranians and Iraqis were all the same people and culture. It was difficult to explain to them that, other than Islam, Persians had few things in common with Arabs. Most Iraqis belonged to the Sunni branch of Islam while the Persians were Shi'is. I explained to my friends that Iranians and Iraqis eat different food, use different spices and speak different languages. Although the Arabs had ruled Persia for seven centuries, we Persians had maintained our own culture and were proud of our differences. The war between Iran and Iraq lasted eight years and half a million people died needlessly because of age-old animosities.

On 2 February 1983 I received a telex addressed to the French Bahá'í Assembly saying the Universal House of Justice was installed in its new building on Mount Carmel, fulfilling Shoghi Effendi's wish. I said a prayer of thanksgiving. The world was in desperate need of guidance as it entered a new age. There were signs that the communist regime in Russia was losing its grip, at the same time the populations of western countries were disillusioned with politics and big business capitalism. Around the world there was a growing feeling that neither socialism nor communism nor capitalism had the answers to the problems of mankind. It was fitting that the Universal House of Justice should be established on Mount Carmel. The Guardian had said,

> Then will the banner of the independence of the Faith be unfurled, and His Most Great Law be unveiled and rivers of laws and ordinances stream forth from this snow-white spot with all-conquering power and awe-inspiring majesty . . .[3]

In 1984 Annette was elected to the National Spiritual Assembly of France where she served for five years. We both realized that it was an opportunity to serve but also a great responsibility and that I would have to find more time to help with the children. Later Annette was elected to the administrative board of the French committee of non-governmental organizations which included 82 non-profit-making organizations. The committee coordinated the efforts of the different groups and organized conferences.

In 1989 Annette began working with Christine Samandari Hakim when the Bahá'í Public Information Office opened in Paris. Their role was to create goodwill and friendly relations with the media and to ensure that reports about Bahá'ís appearing in the press were factually correct. On one occasion Annette invited the Albanian Ambassador to dinner so that he could meet some French Bahá'ís. I helped her whenever possible, often feeling like John Kennedy when he said, 'I am the man who accompanied Jacqueline Kennedy to Paris . . .'

In 1984 I was 58 years old and I began to think about an early retirement in order to be free to devote more time to my family and Bahá'í activities. My heart attack had served as a warning. I had given over 20 years of my life to Sybron-Gamlen but my first priorities were Annette, the children and the Bahá'í Cause.

I thought about selling the house in La Celle St Cloud and moving to La Blanche but before making any decision I wrote to the Universal House of Justice. I informed them that I was about to retire and asked if they still felt that I should stay in Paris. I included a copy of their former letter in reply to my request to go pioneering in Africa. Before long an answer came, saying that I could go anywhere I wanted in France but that they hoped I would remain close to the national community.

I discussed the reply with Annette and we felt that it

meant we should keep the house in La Celle St Cloud. La Blanche was almost six hours away by car and living there would necessarily reduce our contacts with the national community. Annette also wanted to keep her many friends and activities in Paris.

Having earned a degree at an American university, Michel volunteered to serve on a development project in Bolivia. Eric was studying at a management training school in Reims. Later he continued his studies in the States. Our house in La Celle St Cloud seemed empty without the two boys.

I retired in January 1985 but I didn't want to be inactive. Since I did not need to work to earn a living, I asked myself what I could do to help the Cause and thought about creating a publishing house in France for the non-Baháʼí market. A young couple in England had created Oneworld, 'Books for Thoughtful People', with admirable courage, determination and some practical business sense. Why couldn't I do something similar in France where very few Baháʼí books were available? I began investigating the publishing business.

For years Annette and I had talked about visiting our friends, Joany and Albert Lincoln, in Africa. They were then living in Douala, Cameroon. Now that I was retired we decided that it was time to make the trip. We planned it for the summer so that Valerie could come with us. On 6 June we boarded a Swissair plane in Geneva and flew to Douala.

After the air-conditioned airplane cabin, the humid heat of the tropical city hit us like a blow in the face. A

Persian couple, Mr and Mrs Bushrui, who had been pioneers in Douala for many years, were waiting for us at the end of the customs inspection line. While they drove us to the Lincolns' home in a residential neighbourhood, we had glimpses of beautifully-kept homes and luxuriant gardens behind high walls. African cooks in white uniforms slouched against the gates, having a quick cigarette during a break.

As soon as the car drove in the driveway Al and Joany Lincoln rushed out to embrace us. Hanging behind was Joshua, a tall 16-year-old. When we had last seen him he had been a baby. Two other children, Daniel and Jessica, came up and shook hands. They had been born in Bangui, in the Central African Republic, where the family had pioneered before moving to Douala. Al had given up an excellent job with an American law firm to go to Africa but he did not regret his decision. In Douala he earned what appeared to be a good salary but the cost of living was very high and there was so much criminality in the city that Europeans found it necessary to hire day and night watchmen to protect their homes.

The next day Annette, Valerie and I set out to visit Dr and Mrs Samandari in the city of Buea, in what was formerly British Cameroon. Joany took us to a bush taxi station and warned us to be careful of pickpockets. I managed to avoid several attempts to jostle me by being watchful. We got into a very decrepit station wagon that was going to Buea and waited for the driver to start his engine. In pidgin English he explained that he was waiting for other passengers. A large woman with a baby asked to join us. She had several parcels which it took a great deal of time to install on the roof but the driver still wasn't ready to leave. Two young men in suits and ties got in but the driver continued to nap in the front seat. Only when he had ten passengers crammed in elbow to elbow did he wake up and start the ignition.

Once we got beyond the vast shanty towns that surrounded Douala we drove through well-tended palm plantations and the road started to climb the slopes of Mount Cameroon, although we could not see the volcanic mountain because of the low clouds. We were told that a few years before there had been an eruption. The country was green and beautiful. I thought I would make a few notes for my journal while we rode but my pen had disappeared from my inner pocket. I remembered Joany's warning about pickpockets but it's possible I had dropped it somewhere.

Buea was a lovely city high on the mountain, famous for its tea plantations and rose gardens planted by the British. Because of the high altitude the climate was cooler than in Douala. When the other passengers got out of the taxi, the driver asked me where we wanted to go. I told him that we had come to visit 'the white doctor'. The driver knew immediately who I meant and drove us to Mehdi Samandari's house, where we were greeted with joyful shouts of 'Alláh-u-Abhá!'

I had first met Mehdi Samandari and his wife Ursula at the Intercontinental Conference in Kampala in 1953. She was an English horticulturist and they had met while he was studying in England. Like many other young pioneers at the conference, they had dedicated their lives to service to the Cause. They went first to Somalia and later came to Cameroon to continue the work begun by Enoch Olinga. Dr Samandari was 74 and I was too polite to ask Ursula her age. Yet they were both energetic and joyful, content to spend what remained of their lives on earth in a small bush town in conditions that were far from luxurious. Although their house was small and did not have the conveniences that most expatriate Europeans enjoyed, it was clean and arranged in a charming style that reminded me of Isobel Sabri's home in Dar-es-Salaam. Ursula gave us a tour of the garden, showing us plants that she had brought from Nigeria, Kenya and Zaire. The rich, volcanic earth had produced a magnificent array of flowers.

Ursula had kept her sense of humour. She told us about a trip she had made in a bush taxi. She had been squeezed up against a polite young man who wondered what she was doing in Cameroon. She explained that she loved the people and the country and hoped that she would be able to stay there until she died. At the end of the journey the young man shook her hand and said that he hoped she would have a very nice funeral!

Two young Iranian girls were living with the Samandaris. Fari and Farah Aqdasi had been nurses in Iran but they had lost their jobs when the Bahá'í hospital was seized and their families had sent them out of the country. They were looking for work but the Cameroonian government discouraged giving contracts to foreigners unless they were highly qualified. The girls had prepared a delicious Persian meal with rice, meat and fresh fish. There were mangos and pineapples for dessert. After lunch, visitors dropped in, two young Cameroonian women who had become Bahá'ís. One of them had named her son Mehdi, after Dr Samandari.

Late in the afternoon we took another taxi, just as decrepit and crammed as the previous one, back to Douala. On the way it started to rain and Annette was impressed by her first African deluge. Sheets of water fell across the windscreen, blinding us, but the driver seemed to have memorized the road and when he stopped we discovered we were back in the station in Douala. We then realized that we didn't know how to give directions to the Lincolns' home but a fellow passenger, a young African girl, volunteered to help us. With her assistance we managed to find the residential sector near the airport and the street we were looking for. Wherever we went in Cameroon we never failed to find people who were friendly and helpful.

While we were staying with the Lincolns, we were invited to a dinner party by the manager of the Bank of Boston in Cameroon. It was held in a beautiful villa with a large terrace overlooking a swimming pool. The meal was served buffet style and tables were set up in the garden so that the guests could enjoy the cool night air. They were mostly expatriates and local dignitaries. One man that I was introduced to was a former cabinet minister. Afterwards I discussed with Al the importance of maintaining contacts with Cameroonian officials so that they were familiar with the Bahá'í Faith and its principles, avoiding misunderstandings that could result in persecution.

A few days later we set out for a small town on the ocean south of Douala. Kribi was known for its white sand beaches. Many Europeans went there for Christmas and Easter holidays but the rest of the year it was deserted. Once again we travelled by bush taxi. The first part of the trip went smoothly but after the city of Edea the road was unpaved, just a wide laterite track through the jungle. Another tropical storm burst on us and the red laterite dirt turned into slick, treacherous mud. The driver went slowly and kept his car on the road. I told him that I appreciated his caution and the driver replied, 'I've got a wife and three children. I don't want anything to happen to me.'

Five hours later we reached our goal. In the pouring rain our only glimpse of Kribi's famous beaches were rows of leaning coconut trees, their fronds buffeted by the strong winds. We had been told we could rent rooms at Annette Bar but discovered it was just a hut on the beach with some chairs and a table sitting outside in the rain. We then went to a run-down, straggling building called Strand Hotel, run by an elderly German woman. It was more expensive but slightly cleaner and there was a hot water shower, so we took a room there. The restaurant was closed, so we walked through the African quarter to Chez Amélie where we had fresh fish roasted on a grill and plantain French fries. Annette and Valerie were nervous about walking through the dark streets at night, especially since we passed several crowded bars with loud music and bright lights, but the people we met were friendly and helpful and afterwards we laughed about our fears.

The next day the sun was shining, the sky was immense and blue and the beach in front of the hotel was glorious. Annette and Valerie put on their bathing suits and dived in immediately after breakfast. I lay on the beach, reading and writing in my journal. Valerie came out and teased me until I joined them and I discovered that the water was warm and relaxing.

The following day we visited Albert Mandy, a Cameroonian Bahá'í who was in charge of the port facilities. He had accepted the Faith after reading *Thief in the Night* by William Sears and practised his religion conscientiously. I had a long consultation with him about how to make the Local Assembly more active and responsible. Later I met with the local Bahá'ís, introducing myself and answering their questions about the Faith and its activities around the world. A man called Ntonga offered to accompany me to a village on the palm tree plantation where there were a few Bahá'ís.

Another man named Daniel impressed me as an intelligent young man who was sincerely dedicated to the Cause. He was a schoolteacher and on vacation, so we spent the next few days together. Daniel had many questions and I enjoyed our long conversations. I was impressed by the knowledge of Bahá'í history and the sacred scriptures that Daniel, Ntonga and Mandy had. They were obviously well-educated people who had thoughtfully studied their new religion and could quote from the writings of Bahá'u'lláh and 'Abdu'l-Bahá as well as some who had been brought up in Bahá'í families. I remembered the firesides I had held under baobab trees in Mombasa and admired the excellent work that had been done by Bahá'í pioneers since then.

After a week in Kribi, we returned to Douala and prepared to visit the capital city, Yaoundé. I had some kind of intestinal bug and was running a high fever, so we decided to fly in comfort rather than take the train, which was said to be an adventure. In Yaoundé we were met by a member of the Cameroonian National Spiritual Assembly and informed that we were to pay our respects to the provincial governor the next day. I went to see a doctor and took the antibiotics that he prescribed. My fever dropped and the meeting with the governor went well. I said a prayer of thanksgiving, for antibiotics also came from God.

We stayed with Iraj Yeganeh and his wife Naz. They were Persian pioneers who had been living in Mogadishu in 1953. They had two children who were studying in France. Their peaceful home was the centre of many Bahá'í activities and friends dropped in all the time. They introduced us to the Bahá'í community in Yaoundé and Annette and I gave short talks about our activities in France and our impressions of the work being done in Cameroon.

After Yaoundé we went north to Garoua on the edge of the Sahara Desert. Fortunately it was the rainy season and the savannah was green with fresh grass. There we visited a small village of mud huts where the headman was a Bahá'í. There had been an Assembly in the village but many had left to look for work in the larger towns and there were no longer nine adults to form the Assembly. While we sat and talked with Joseph, the headman, anyone who was curious about the foreign visitors came and sat down with us, as was the custom in Africa. We were soon surrounded by a crowd of men, women and small children, sitting outside in Joseph's walled court-yard. When it grew dark someone brought a kerosene lamp and we continued our conversation. We said prayers and I looked up at the bright stars that seemed so close I could reach out and grab them. I could imagine 'Abdu'l-Bahá sitting with us, His arms around the little children, giving them His blessing.

In Garoua we met a Persian pioneer, Reza Songorabadi, who lived alone in a little house in the African quarter. In Iran he had worked for the Pepsi-Cola Company as a mechanic for many years before deciding to go to Africa as a pioneer. He went on pilgrimage to Haifa, then came to Africa and presented himself at the Pepsi-Cola bot-tling plant in Garoua where he was hired immediately. He could have had a large house and a company car but he preferred to live like the Africans he worked with. He was a familiar sight in the streets of Garoua, where he was affectionately known as 'the Christian who goes on foot'. Not having studied foreign languages in school, he spoke a mixture of pidgin English and broken French, which everyone seemed to understand.

Before coming to Cameroon Reza had been in Gabon where the Iranian embassy had confiscated his passport. He had been given a temporary resident card by the Cameroonian government but on a train trip to Ngaoundéré he had lost his bag with all his identification papers. Someone suggested that he report the loss to the police. Unfortunately, the officers who questioned him decided that he was a terrorist and threw him into prison. They found a picture of 'Abdu'l-Bahá on him which confirmed their suspicions because of a photograph of Ayatollah Khomeini that had appeared in *Newsweek* magazine. Unable to convince them that he had nothing to do with the Islamic fundamentalists, Reza went on hunger strike. After several days his fellow prisoners convinced him that it was useless and coaxed him into eating some soup and a papaya. But his stomach was too weak and he began vomiting repeatedly until the police decided to send him to hospital. Reza found himself in a ward reserved for dying patients.

After several days he was able to establish his identity and the police released him. He was still convalescing and not yet strong enough to go back to work. His story reminded me of my experience in Mozambique. Reza thought that he would leave Garoua soon. He was starting to think about marrying and raising a family.

We continued our trip, admiring the magnificent scenery and picturesque sites, visiting with Bahá'ís wherever we could. In a small mud hut with a conical thatched roof we were welcomed with cries of 'Alláh-u-Abhá' and saw the Persian calligraphy of the Greatest Name framed on the wall. Here, in an isolated region in the very heart of Africa, Bahá'u'lláh was known, loved and honoured.

Wherever we went we were impressed by the vitality, spirituality and willingness to serve of the friends we met. The Africans received us with open hearts and ready hospitality.

When we returned to France, I couldn't help remembering my early struggles to establish a foothold for my Faith in Africa. Our trip had allowed me to see that my prayers had been answered. All three of us looked back on our vacation in Cameroon as a spiritual experience and a lesson on the universality of our Faith.

In 1986 I received tragic news from Beirut. On the 20th of June two civilians had come to my cousin Shahab's home, saying they were government officials. They told him that it was imperative that he accompany them to their office. Shahab went with them and never returned. Such disappearances were not unusual in Beirut at the time. No ransom was ever asked for and the local government appeared to know nothing about the officials who had taken him away. His family finally came to the reluctant conclusion that he had been killed. His wife and children were able to go to Canada where they had friends who could take them in. I mourned the cheerful playmate who had joined in our games in the garden in Qazvin.

My plans for a publishing house progressed and in June 1987 I was ready to open shop. All that was needed in order to register my company was a name. Looking for inspiration, I leafed through my copy of *Gleanings* at random and the book fell open to a page containing a text in which Bahá'u'lláh wrote about the future of Iran, saying that one day Tehran would become the admiration of the world. The divine Messenger had referred to the city of Tehran as the City of Ṭá, the name of the Persian letter 'T'. At first I thought of calling my company simply 'T', but when I went to register the name I learned that it had already been used by a Chinese company. 'Ta' had also been used, so I thought of Ta Corporation. But before I filled in the registration form, it dawned on me that Tacor was the name of the village where Baháʼuʼlláh had been raised as a child. The family mansion, a Baháʼí shrine, had recently been destroyed by the Islamic fundamentalist government. I liked the idea of replacing the physical building that the fundamentalists had demolished with something immaterial, a publishing company that was basically a means of transmitting dreams and ideas. So I called my publishing house TACOR.

On a trip to the United States I went to Princeton University to attend a conference by Ervin Laszlo, one of the original signers of the report by the Club of Rome concerning overpopulation, pollution and other problems in urgent need of attention if the human race were to survive the 21st century. Although Laszlo was not a Baháʼí, many of his ideas were very close to Baháʼí concepts. Throughout his lecture I found myself nodding in agreement. Laszlo said:

> ... (mankind's) truly decisive limits are inner, not outer
> ... Living on the threshold of a new age, we squabble
> among ourselves to acquire or retain the privileges of
> bygone times . . . We contemplate changing almost

anything on this earth except ourselves . . . We have reached the threshold of a global society, impelled by our physical and informational powers and technologies. Let us not hesitate to develop the vision and will to achieve this new, adult society.[4]

I went up after the talk and introduced myself to Mr Laszlo, and suggested that I would be interested in publishing his books in France. We soon came to an agreement and signed a contract. As soon as I returned to Paris, I arranged for the translation of *The Inner Limits of Mankind* into French.

Several years before I had met Erik Blumenthal, a Bahá'í psychologist who was a disciple of Adler. He had published several books about interpersonal relations in German. Although they were addressed to the general public, Blumenthal's books were based on Bahá'í principles of mutual respect and tolerance. I had no difficulty obtaining his permission to publish his books in French. With Annette as my only staff member, I negotiated with printers and distributors, determined to produce attractive books at a reasonable price.

Even while the first books were coming off the press, I was working on another, more ambitious project. There were several books presenting the Bahá'í Faith written by Bahá'ís but I thought that non-Bahá'ís interested in the ideals and concepts of the Faith would like to read a more objective introduction written by a non-Bahá'í investigator. Through a French publishing house I contacted a reporter, Colette Gouvion, who had never before heard of the

Baháʼís, and asked her to undertake the project. I offered her access to all the historical documents she would need and promised the cooperation of any Baháʼís she wanted to interview. Later I arranged for her to go to Haifa and interview Baháʼís from many different countries who were working there as volunteers. She became interested in the project but stipulated that she would be absolutely free to draw her own conclusions, that no form of censure would be used during her investigation or afterwards. She asked me to promise that the book would be published exactly as she wrote it, whatever her final conclusions. I told her that those were exactly the conditions I intended to propose.

Mrs Gouvion and her son, Philippe Jouvion, spent a year researching and writing *Les Jardiniers de Dieu*. Published in association with Berg International, a non-Baháʼí French publishing firm, the book was TACOR's first 'success', selling over three thousand copies in a country where there are fewer than fifteen hundred Baháʼís. The English translation, *The Gardeners of God*, was subsidized by the French Ministry of Culture and published by Oneworld in England. A Baháʼí organization founded by the Samji family in Brussels contributed funds to have it translated into Russian. It was also translated and published in Hungarian, Dutch, Spanish, Romanian, Persian and Arabic.

In April 1988 Annette and I flew to Bolivia to attend Michel's marriage to a lovely Bolivian girl named Margarita. Six months later we attended Eric's wedding in the United States. His bride, Margaret, was a young American student. The Zahrai family, like the Baháʼí religion, had its origins in Persia and now stretched around the world.

In July 1990 Ervin Laszlo had been asked by UNESCO to prepare a book on the diversity of world cultures. He invited me to attend a meeting with writers, philosophers and scientists from around the world. During the coffee break I started up a conversation with a Chinese university professor who was interested in the books published by TACOR. When I mentioned *The Gardeners of God*, the professor nodded.

'I know quite a few Bahá'ís. There are Bahá'ís in Beijing and I know them quite well.'

I was surprised and cautious, for I knew that being a Bahá'í in Communist China was extremely difficult.

'How have you come to know about the Bahá'í Faith?'

'I have many friends in Beijing who are Bahá'ís. Do you know Mrs Rabbani?'

'Yes. How have you come to know her?'

'She came to our house when she visited Beijing. My wife and I were honoured to offer hospitality to her.'

I was puzzled. 'Do you often meet Bahá'ís?'

'Oh, yes. Regularly.'

'How often?' I asked.

'Every 19 days.'

I smiled and gripped his hand. 'Then you are probably a Bahá'í yourself!'

'Yes, I am. Many Bahá'í meetings take place in our house. I am the one who took the Bahá'í books to the Chinese authorities to acquaint them with Bahá'í principles. However, we must be careful.'

'I am a Bahá'í too,' I said. 'I am very pleased to meet you.'

The Chinese professor was so excited he stood up and bowed several times.

'Bahá'u'lláh has put you in my way, here in this vast city. The friends recommended that I should look up the Bahá'ís in France but I did not know how to go about it. Now here you are, sitting right in front of me.'

I invited my new friend home where he met Annette and Valerie. The following day we went to the National Bahá'í Centre and met Christine Samandari Hakim, who gave him some recently published documents to take back to China. I offered him a copy of *The Gardeners of God*.

The next day when we said goodbye, the professor embraced me and said, 'Two days ago we were strangers and now we are like two brothers.'

He invited Annette and me to visit him in China, promising to be our guide.

In 1992 I learned of the passing of Hassan Sabri's wife, Isobel, in a London hospital. The Sabris had been living in Haifa, working at the World Centre. The prayers of the Universal House of Justice and Bahá'í friends around the world had accompanied Isobel in her last illness. She was buried in the same cemetery as the beloved Guardian. Among those present at the funeral was an African friend from Tanzania, who said a prayer in Swahili. I remembered the young woman who had welcomed me to Africa and shown me her charming little house on the hill above Dar-es-Salaam. I said a prayer, certain that her spirit was rejoicing in the Abhá Kingdom.

I also received a letter from Ali, my former business partner in Tabriz. He had left Iran and moved to Sydney, Australia. His company had become very important, with offices in Houston, Sydney and Tehran, but Ali Akbar still remembered with pleasure 'the good old days' when he had convinced a young bank clerk to give up a secure position to help him start his enterprise. I read his letter on the terrace of La Blanche and remembered the mixed emotions I had had on leaving Iran, excited about going to an unknown country to serve the Cause but not really certain that I was doing the right thing.

I now seem to spend a lot of time looking back at that young Iranian pioneer who had set out to participate in Shoghi Effendi's world-embracing Ten Year Plan.

At a Bahá'í summer school in Luxembourg where I had gone to speak about business ethics, an elderly gentleman came up to me and said, 'I really came here for you. I remember when you were chairman of Young Expo in Brussels.'

I stared at him. 'How do you remember that?'

'Because I'm as young as you are. I was associated with the Luxembourg pavilion.'

I told him about other friends from Young Expo. I had kept in touch with several members of the executive committee, particularly with the Czech delegate who occasionally came to France and had hosted Annette and me in Prague. I had lost touch with the American, Mitch Smith, but had recently heard from him through a strange coincidence. Mitch had become dean of a Texan university and had worked on a committee which organized a reception for foreign students. While talking to an Iranian engineer who lived in Texas, he mentioned that he had had a good friend from Iran during the Brussels Expo. He got out an old picture and the Iranian, who was a Bahá'í from Qazvin and knew my family well, recognized me and gave Mitch my address.

Our friends in La Celle St Cloud, George and Diane Starcher, had moved to Chambéry, near Grenoble, but we kept in touch and frequently visited each other. George had graduated from Harvard Business School and managed a major American consulting firm in France and Italy for many years. He and I had common interests since we were both familiar with high-level business management and convinced that the Bahá'í Faith had much to offer to those seeking ethical solutions to modern dilemmas. We decided to invite some Bahá'í business friends to a discussion group on the application of spiritual principles to economic problems. The talks were held in Chamonix, France. We were surprised at the enthusiastic response to our sessions and on a long hike into the mountains above Chamonix discussed the possibility of continuing the adventure. Within a year we officially created and registered the European Bahá'í Business Forum as a non-profit organization. Today EBBF has more than 500 members in over 60 countries. Open to all those with a legitimate interest in business, whether Bahá'í or not, it sponsors seminars, two international conferences annually, over two hundred other events every year and a website, publishes scholarly articles and offers career counselling to young professionals. It has held workshops at forums of non-governmental agencies participating in United Nations world summits. It has been especially active in Eastern Europe where the EBBF conference on business ethics in Sofia, Bulgaria was a yearly event. Among the core values which EBBF promotes are ethical business practices, the social responsibility of business, sustainable development, the partnership of men and women in all fields of endeavour, and non-adversarial decision-making through consultation. George and I both had business experience, multicultural backgrounds and concern for spiritual values that were valuable in setting up and developing the organization. Over the years I found myself giving more and more of my time to EBBF but when I saw the eager reception of our discussions, particularly in formerly communist countries, I felt it was time well spent. George and I were delighted to help set up university courses on 'Emerging Values for a Global Economy' in the Czech Republic.

I was invited to attend a ceremony in Haifa in honour of the Knights of Bahá'u'lláh. On 29 May 1992, the gardens of Mount Carmel were in flower. The sun was shining and birds sang in the trees and men and women from every corner of the world gathered before the steps and the majestic white pillars of the seat of the Universal House of Justice. The young pioneers who had set out almost 40 years before in reply to Shoghi Effendi's call for a World Crusade returned with grey hair and wrinkled faces. They wore badges on which were marked the names of the 131 countries, territories and islands that they had opened, proclaiming Bahá'u'lláh's name for the first time under distant skies.

A scroll inscribed with the names of all the Knights of Bahá'u'lláh was put on display, then sealed in a special cylinder and placed in a vault just under the threshold of the tomb of Bahá'u'lláh in order to preserve for all time the memory of the Bahá'í community's gratitude for their service.

My friend Ali Nakhjavani opened the ceremony. After a prayer, Rúḥíyyih <u>Kh</u>ánum came to the speaker's podium. Her crown of auburn braids had strands of silver but she was as erect and elegant as she had been when I had first met her in 1953. She spoke in a relaxed, conversational tone with a spritely twinkle in her eye, like an older sister teasing her younger siblings.

> Friends, it's a very wonderful occasion for us to be here today. When you think of the beginnings and then you think of what we're celebrating here today, the Knights of Bahá'u'lláh who conquered the whole planet.'

She paused and looked out at us and I realized that there was something challenging in her attitude.

> When you leave Haifa and go back to your own countries . . . Don't say how lovely everything was and how beautiful the flowers were and the shrines and how marvellous it is to have this wonderful House of Justice, and all of these things. When the Knights of

Bahá'u'lláh leave Haifa they shouldn't go out and tell everybody what a lovely time it was.'

She smiled and shrugged her shoulders.

That's not the thing to go out and tell them. Go out and tell them there's an awful lot of work to be done and that they should get cracking on it. I think that's the message that the Knights of Bahá'u'lláh are going to carry away from the Holy Land.

She paused and let her message sink in.

I'm sure all of the people here, from whatever country they come, realize that we've turned a corner. Doors are open that were never open before. The name of the Faith is known as never before. A whole new vista of service is open.

She smiled and the twinkle in her eye grew brighter.

And I would like to say one thing to the elderly Knights of Bahá'u'lláh. There's no reason why you can't serve, whatever age you are. Don't think one knighthood is enough. Go out and add laurels to your wreath. Don't sit down and bask in being a Knight of Bahá'u'lláh. Get up and see if you can't do something more to add to it.[5]

* * *

We sat on the terrace of La Blanche, listening to the crickets in the night. As he finished his long story, Ezzat said, 'I have many reasons to be grateful. But I feel very deeply that the greatest reward I have had was Annette. I fell in love with Annette from the first instant I saw her: her education, her good manners, her intelligence, her open, liberal mind, her interest in my country, in my beliefs. She charmed me. She was lovely and I admired the way she gave the Bahá'í Faith the same serious, open-minded application she gave to her university courses. When she became the only Bahá'í in her family, she confronted their disapproval with serenity and emerged victorious, teaching them to respect her decision and her new religion. She has been an outstanding mother, always available, ready to help, ready to listen, giving up a career so that she could raise our children. Since my work often took me away from home on business trips around the world, she felt it was important that the children find her at home. I tell the children that Annette is the soul of our home. When I went on pilgrimage to Haifa, I had prayed that I would be able to found a united family. With Annette my prayers were answered. Sometimes we get upset, like any couple. But we have never had a quarrel that we did not settle the same day. I thank God for His great bounty.'

The moon was shining on the terrace of La Blanche, tracing the silhouette of Ezzat's head with silver. He spoke quietly.

'I had gone to Haifa in the complacent expectation of being honoured for past achievements. I'm grateful to Rúḥíyyih Khánum for reminding me that the Bahá'í Faith

has no sinecures. She gave to the Knights of Bahá'u'lláh something far more precious than an honorary title. She gave us a challenge to continue serving the Cause, winning new victories, surpassing anything done in the past.'

Thus the sturdy white-headed Knight sitting in the twilight shrugged off the nostalgia of the past and looked forward, into the 21st century.

Bibliography

'Abdu'l-Bahá. *Paris Talks*. London: Bahá'í Publishing Trust, 1967.

— *Selections from the Writings of 'Abdu'l-Bahá*. Haifa: Bahá'í World Centre, 1978.

Amatu'l-Bahá Rúḥíyyih Khánum. Speech to the Knights of Bahá'u'lláh. Haifa, 27 May 1992.

Bahá'í International Community. 'Universal Values for the Advancement of Women'. http://www.bic.org/statements/universal-values-advancement-women.

Bahá'í Prayers: A Selection of Prayers revealed by Bahá'u'lláh, the Báb and 'Abdu'l-Bahá. Wilmette, IL: Bahá'í Publishing Trust, 2002.

The Bahá'í World. vol. 14. Haifa: The Universal House of Justice, 1974.

Bahá'í World Faith. Wilmette, IL: Bahá'í Publishing Trust, 2nd ed. 1976.

Bahá'u'lláh. *Gleanings from the Writings of Bahá'u'lláh*. Wilmette, IL: Bahá'í Publishing Trust, 1983.

— *The Kitáb-i-Aqdas*. Haifa: Bahá'í World Centre, 1992.

— *Kitáb-i-Íqán*. Wilmette, IL: Bahá'í Publishing Trust, 1989.

— *Prayers and Meditations*. Wilmette, IL: Bahá'í Publishing Trust, 1987.

Balyuzi, H. M. *The Báb: The Herald of the Day of Days*. Oxford: George Ronald, 1973.

Gouvion, Colette and Philippe Jouvion. *The Gardeners of God: An Encounter with Five Million Bahá'ís*. Translated by Judith Logsdon-Dubois. Oxford: Oneworld, 1993.

— *Les Jardiniers de Dieu: A la rencontre de cinq millions de Bahá'ís*. Paris: Berg International and TACOR International, 1989.

Hatcher, William S. and J. Douglas Martin. *The Bahá'í Faith: The Emerging Global Religion*. San Francisco: Harper & Row, 1984.

International Bahá'í Council. Letter in the possession of Ezzat Zahrai.

Islam and Revolution: Writings and Declarations of Imam Khomeini. Translated and Annotated by Hamid Algar. Berkeley, CA: Mizan Press, 1981.

Laszlo, Ervin. *The Inner Limits of Mankind: Heretical Reflections on Today's Values, Culture and Politics*. London: Oneworld, 1989.

Lights of Guidance: A Bahá'í Reference File. Compiled by Helen Hornby. New Delhi: Bahá'í Publishing Trust, 5th ed. 1997.

Man of the Trees: The Selected Writings of Richard St. Barbe Baker. Edited by Karen Gridley. Willits, CA: Ecology Action, 1989.

Momen, Moojan. *The Bábí and Bahá'í Religions, 1844–1944. Some Contemporary Western Accounts*. Oxford: George Ronald, 1981.

— 'Shoghi Effendi'. *Encyclopaedia Iranica*. www.iranicanonline .org/articles/shoghi-effendi.

Nash, Geoffrey. *Iran's Secret Pogrom*. Sudbury, Suffolk: Neville Spearman Limited, 1982.

Seven Days. 23 February 1979.

Shoghi Effendi. Letter to the Bahá'ís of Persia, 27 November 1929. Translated in *Bahá'í World*, vol. 14, p. 438.

— *Messages to the Bahá'í World*. Wilmette, IL: Bahá'í Publishing Trust, 1971.

References

Chapter 1: Childhood

1. 'Abdu'l-Bahá, *Selections*, p. 136.
2. ibid. p. 135.
3. ibid. p. 147.
4. ibid. p. 112.

Chapter 3: Tehran and Tabriz

1. ibid. p. 147.
2. Balyuzi, *The Báb*, p. 157.
3. Hatcher and Martin, *Bahá'í Faith: Emerging Global Religion*, p. 146.

Chapter 4: Departure

1. Bahá'u'lláh, *Gleanings*, p. 43.
2. Bahá'u'lláh, *Prayers and Meditations*, p. 94.
3. 'Abdu'l-Bahá, quoted in a letter written on behalf of Shoghi Effendi to the National Spiritual Assembly of the British Isles, 11 February 1925, in *Lights of Guidance*, p. 88.
4. Bahá'u'lláh, *Prayers and Meditations*, p. 320.
5. Bahá'u'lláh, *Gleanings*, p. 250.

Chapter 5: Kenya

1. 'Abdu'l-Bahá, *Selections*, p. 299.
2. Bahá'u'lláh, *Gleanings*, p. 277.
3. *Man of the Trees*, p. 15.
4. 29 February 1952.
5. Bahá'u'lláh, in *Bahá'í Prayers*, pp. 309–10.
6. Bahá'u'lláh, *Gleanings*, p. 250.

Chapter 6: Wandering

1. 'Abdu'l-Bahá, *Paris Talks*, p. 178.

2. Bahá'u'lláh, in *Bahá'í Prayers*, pp. 310–11.
3. 'Abdu'l-Bahá, in *Bahá'í Prayers*, p. 61.
4. From a cablegram of Shoghi Effendi, 19 August 1953, in Shoghi Effendi, *Messages to the Bahá'í World*, p. 50.
5. ibid. p. 51.
6. Amatu'l-Bahá Rúḥíyyih Khánum, in a speech to the Knights of Bahá'u'lláh, Haifa, 27 May 1992.

Chapter 7: Mombasa

1. Bahá'u'lláh, *Gleanings*, p. 129.
2. Bahá'u'lláh, quoted by 'Abdu'l-Bahá in Shoghi Effendi, *Messages to the Bahá'í World*, p. 136.

Chapter 8: Teaching

1. Letter of the International Bahá'í Council. In the possession of Ezzat Zahrai.
2. ibid.
3. 'Abdu'l-Bahá, *Paris Talks*, p. 100.
4. Bahá'u'lláh, *Kitáb-i-Aqdas*, Questions and Answers, p. 105.
5. 'Abdu'l-Bahá, *Paris Talks*, p. 52.

Chapter 9: Haifa

1. Bahá'u'lláh, *Gleanings*, p. 15.
2. 'Abdu'l-Bahá, in *Bahá'í World Faith*, p. 416.
3. Hatcher and Martin, *Bahá'í Faith: The Emerging Global Religion*, p. 42.

Chapter 10: Brussels

1. 'Abdu'l-Bahá, *Selections*, p. 117.
2. From a letter of Shoghi Effendi, October 1957, in Shoghi Effendi, *Messages to the Bahá'í World*, p. 127.
3. Bahá'u'lláh, *Gleanings*, p. 81.

Chapter 11: Paris

1. Bahá'u'lláh, *Kitáb-i-Íqán*, p. 227.
2. Khomeini, *Islam and Revolution*, p. 129.
3. Interview with Khomeini in *Seven Days*, 23 February 1979, quoted in Nash, *Iran's Secret Pogrom*, p. 77.
4. Bahá'u'lláh, *Prayers and Meditations*, p. 318.

Chapter 12: New Departures

1. 'Abdu'l-Bahá, *Selections*, p. 267.
2. See http://www.bic.org/statements/universal-values-advancement-women.
3. From a letter of Shoghi Effendi to the Bahá'ís of Persia, 27 November 1929, translated in *Bahá'í World*, vol. 14, p. 438.
4. Laszlo, *The Inner Limits of Mankind*.
5. Amatu'l-Bahá Rúḥíyyih Khánum, in a speech to the Knights of Bahá'u'lláh, Haifa, 27 May 1992.